DE STIJL AND
DUTCH MODERNISM

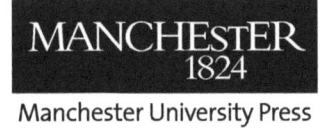

Manchester University Press

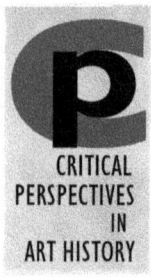

CRITICAL
PERSPECTIVES
IN
ART HISTORY

SERIES EDITORS
Tim Barringer, Marsha Meskimmon
and Shearer West

EDITORIAL CONSULTANTS
Nicola Bown, John House, John Onians,
Marcia Pointon, Alan Wallach and Evelyn Welch

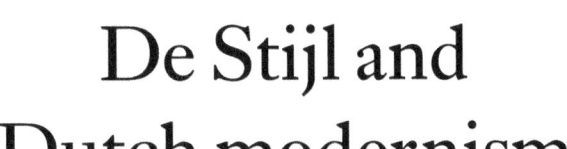

De Stijl and
Dutch modernism

MICHAEL WHITE

Manchester University Press

Published by Manchester University Press
Oxford Road, Manchester M13 9PL
www.manchesteruniversitypress.co.uk

British Library Cataloguing-in-Publication Data
A catalogue record for this book is available from the British Library

Library of Congress Cataloging-in-Publication Data applied for

ISBN 978 0 7190 6162 2 *paperback*

First published 2003

Typeset in Ehrhardt by
D R Bungay Associates, Burghfield, Berks

This book is dedicated to my Opa,
Jan de Klerk, the most modern man I have ever known

Contents

List of illustrations

Plates

Figures

Acknowledgements

This book was written between 2001 and 2002 but is the result of research initiated at least a decade before. During this time I have received assistance from a number of people whom I would like to take this opportunity to thank. They include Dawn Ades, Jane Beckett, Carel Blotkamp, Marco Entrop, Sjarel Ex, Christopher Green, Alfred Marks, Jaap Oosterhof, Evert van Straaten and Marcia Zaaijer. I am also very grateful to Jan Derwig, Frans Postma and Werner Schmalenbach for their help in supplying photographic material for the book. I would also like to thank my colleagues in the Department of History of Art at the University of York for the supportive and intellectually stimulating environment they have provided for me over recent years. In particular, I would like to mention David Peters Corbett who has always been on hand to offer sound advice and guidance.

Finally, many thanks to my wife Renni for her help with the picture research and for taking photographs for the book. I am extremely grateful for the way she got involved with the project and managed to look interested while being dragged around the housing estates of Rotterdam when she would much rather have been lazing in a café beside a canal. I could not have written this without her.

Preface

The journal De Stijl (The Style) was first published in the Netherlands in November 1917. Over the course of the following year, it contained articles and illustrations by a regular group of contributors: the painters Piet Mondrian, Vilmos Huszár, Bart van der Leck and Theo van Doesburg (who was also its editor): the architects J. J. P. Oud, Jan Wils and Robert van 't Hoff: the sculptor Georges Vantongerloo, and a poet by the name of Anthony Kok. In November 1918 a *Manifesto of De Stijl* appeared in the journal, translated into four languages and accompanied by the names of seven 'collaborators'. Of the original contributors just named, Van der Leck had already decided to withdraw his participation while Oud was reticent about the tone of the manifesto and declined to feature as a signatory. From this point until 1928, when the journal ceased appearing on a regular basis, lies a fractious history of exclusions, withdrawals and internal disputes whereby, excepting Van Doesburg himself, none of those named above would maintain their participation until the end, although many who had severed their links would return to feature in the tenth anniversary edition of the journal in 1927 and the final memorial edition published after Van Doesburg's death in 1931. Over the years, Van Doesburg recruited additional collaborators to fill the gaps, such as the painters Friedrich Vordemberge-Gildewart and Cesar Domela, the set designer Frederick Kiesler and the architect/furniture maker Gerrit Rietveld. The case of the latter is particularly interesting in that his furniture is now synonymous with De Stijl, despite the fact that some items, such as the form (if not the colour) of his famous *Red/Blue Chair*, predate his involvement.

To make up for this untidy background, a number of myths have been spun around De Stijl, some at the moment of the journal's appearance, others accruing later. The very first is brought into effect by the way we are forced to name it; from the publication of the manifesto on, De Stijl has been seen as more than a journal. Its readership was intended to understand that behind the name there existed a coherent body of theory, a stable set of participants and a collection of exemplary objects which represented its aspirations. In recent years a number of new histories of De Stijl have attempted to unpick this particular myth, the phantom image of an artistic movement, by distinguishing the journal itself from the rhetoric of some of its contributors. In such accounts the reader is obliged to consider De Stijl (the movement created by modernist historiography) differently to *De Stijl* (the journal), and even on occasions *De stijl* (the title of the journal according to Dutch orthography).[1] Careful consideration is then given to the place of these alternative headings in specific narratives such as the history of modernism, the interaction between the international avant-gardes during the interwar period and, finally, the emergence of a specific Dutch avant-garde.

The new historiography of De Stijl was a necessary counter to the representation of De Stijl as an international artistic phenomenon fully formed from the moment of its inception. It often comes as a surprise to students of modernism to discover that the De Stijl collaborators had very little personal contact with each other. They were geographically dispersed and often as much involved in local associations as in De Stijl. There was only ever one De Stijl exhibition, held in 1923 at Léonce Rosenberg's *Galerie de l'Effort Moderne* in Paris. This presented De Stijl as primarily concerned with architecture. Mondrian was not represented in it at all (despite the fact that Rosenberg was his dealer at the time). In fact no paintings were exhibited, only architectural drawings, models and photographs. How strange, then, that a mere thirteen years later Alfred Barr could describe De Stijl, in the catalogue of the Museum of Modern Art exhibition *Cubism and Abstract Art*, as 'one of the longest lived and most influential groups of modern *artists*' [my italics].[2] For Barr it was Mondrian's abstract painting which was at the forefront of De Stijl activity. The chronology of De Stijl he provided began not with the publication of the journal or the manifesto but with Mondrian's paintings of 1910, the point where he moved from a neo-impressionist to cubist idiom. Barr's narrative runs to 1932, when De Stijl gives way to Abstraction-Création, after Van Doesburg's death. De Stijl, in this account, had a twenty-two-year lifespan.

Barr's version of De Stijl became deeply imbedded in twentieth-century art history following the Second World War. A 1951 De Stijl exhibition at the Museum of Modern Art and the Stedelijk Museum restated the position adopted in 1936. This was shortly followed by Hans Jaffé's monograph, *De Stijl: The Dutch Contribution to Modern Art*, published in 1956. Mondrian's abstract painting was clearly placed as the foundation of De Stijl which was then presented as a coherent entity. In Jaffé's words, 'a common attitude of mind exists both to the world in general and to art, and this attitude finds its visual expression in the work of the De Stijl artists and then, almost immediately, its definition in the pages of De Stijl'.[3] Painting, and the theorisation of abstract painting, are presented here as the core De Stijl activities, sidelining architecture and design.

The monolithic view of De Stijl began to break down in the 1980s. Archival sources became more freely available to researchers, most significantly the Van Doesburg Archive. Monographs appeared on lesser known figures, such as Vilmos Huszár. The Schröder House in Utrecht was restored to its original state. All these events exposed precisely the lack of a 'common attitude' in De Stijl and the need for a more pluralistic account of its enterprise. I will mention here just three of the publications which brought about the reorientation of its history. Carel Blotkamp's *De Stijl: The Formative Years 1917–1922*, first published in Dutch in 1982 and then in English translation in 1987, broke De Stijl down into a series of biographies. The product of a multi-author research project, the book fragments De Stijl into a sequence of individual stories which intersect but do not add up to just one De Stijl. From Barr's twenty-two-year history, we are left with only five years in which Blotkamp sees any substantial collaboration. A different tack was taken by Nancy Troy in *The De Stijl Environment*, published in 1983. Here she placed the emphasis not purely on painting but the attempts to place painting within three-dimensional space. It is the fraught relations between artists and architects which forms the narrative of her book, exploring collaboration and its breakdown. Finally, an exhibition generated by the Walker Arts Center in 1981, *De Stijl: Visions of Utopia 1917–1931*, accompanied by a scholarly catalogue, connected De Stijl to political events, urban planning, transformations in interior design – a whole panoply of contexts previously excluded by Barr and Jaffé.

The success of the new historiography of De Stijl has led to the point where one hesitates to use the name at all. Paul Overy has commented, in true postmodern fashion, of the remaking of De Stijl with each publication, so that 'there is no "real" De Stijl which can be uncovered, if only we could go back to the primal (or primary) source'.[4] Indeed the more primary material that has entered the public realm in recent years the further we seem to get from a 'real' De Stijl. Yet to my mind this anxiety concerning the manufacturing of a history has unfortunately created an artificial distance between the production and reception of De Stijl. As I will discuss in greater detail in the final chapter of the book, well before Alfred Barr integrated it into his chart of the succession of modernist movements, De Stijl was clearly connected to an institutional framework in the Netherlands which accorded it a similar position. In fact, rather than being later absorbed by the Museum of Modern Art, I argue that De Stijl was generated by the emergence of such institutions in the first place.

In this book I will therefore be returning to the most catholic definition of De Stijl, using it unitalicised to mean the journal, the practitioners associated with the journal and the idea of a movement. Whether or not it was ever the desire of Wils or Huszár, say, to be associated with a very narrowly defined programme, the manner in which Van Doesburg presented De Stijl both in the Netherlands and abroad inevitably led to such a perception. Of course, by means of this strategy Van Doesburg was able to promote himself from humble editor to erstwhile leader of a group, which proved a useful entrée when making international contacts in the early 1920s. In addition, the fact that Dutch language articles always featured prominently in the journal, even after Mondrian and Van Doesburg had based themselves in Paris, does not necessarily mean that straightforward divergences existed between a local and international agenda; it was always Van Doesburg's aim that De Stijl should represent the Netherlands to the rest of Europe and there existed a powerful need to demonstrate to both a foreign and native audience how it dominated the discourse of Dutch modernism, even if this was far from being the actual situation.

My re-engagement with the rather unfashionable notion of the modernist movement does not mean that I try to disassociate the idea of De Stijl either from the history of its internal arguments or its contexts. My aim is quite different: to consider how this idea came into being and its peculiar connection to contemporary circumstances. To do so I will move back and forth between different chronological moments, and between the various geographical locations in which the idea of De Stijl was produced, giving priority but not exclusive attention to the Netherlands. This is by no means a comprehensive history of De Stijl but a highly selective reinterpretation. It has become very apparent over recent years that a simple chronology which would give a picture of De Stijl in its formative and developed stages, moving seamlessly from Leiden to Paris and ultimately New York, is virtually impossible to produce now, even if it were ever desirable.

Notes

1 See in this regard Jane Beckett, 'Discoursing on Dutch Modernism', *Oxford Art Journal* 6: 2 (1983), pp. 67–79; Nancy Troy, *The De Stijl Environment* (Cambridge MA and London: MIT, 1983), pp. 2–7, Carel Blotkamp (ed.), *De Stijl: The Formative Years, 1917–1922* (Cambridge MA and London: MIT, 1986), pp. viii–xi; Paul Overy, *De Stijl* (London: Thames and Hudson, 1991), pp. 7–17.

2 Alfred H. Barr Jr., *Cubism and Abstract Art* (New York: Museum of Modern Art, 1936), p. 141.

3 Hans Jaffé, *De Stijl* (London: Thames and Hudson, 1970), p. 11.

4 Overy, *De Stijl*, p. 17.

List of abbreviations

CMU Centraal Museum Utrecht
NAI Netherlands Architecture Institute
RKD Rijksbureau voor Kunsthistorische Documentatie

Introduction:
who's afraid of red, yellow and blue?

De Stijl has a place in many histories: the development of abstract art, the interwar avant-gardes, international style architecture, modern design, modernism in the Netherlands. This book will touch on just about all of these but give most emphasis to the roots of De Stijl in its country of origin and the impact it had on its host nation. This does not mean that I discount either the international influence of De Stijl or the striking internationalist outlook expressed in the journal. Rather, I want to demonstrate how the vocabulary of De Stijl was drawn from clearly identifiable local discourses and that, for all its dissemination into the general histories of modernist painting and architecture, De Stijl was connected to very distinct modernising projects in the Netherlands. This will not be a social history of De Stijl, though. For example, a key discussion in this book will be the continuity De Stijl expressed with the tradition of *gemeenschapkunst* (community art) which had, since the 1890s tried to create a new audience for modernism by using monumental art forms such as wall painting and stained glass.[1] The key concepts which feature in De Stijl rhetoric, those of monumentality and collective activity, were both inherited from a previous generation and the language used by De Stijl, both visual and theoretical, constantly drew the connections, such as the editorial in the very first issue of the journal which described De Stijl as a *geestelijke gemeenschap* (spiritual community). Yet it is clear that the community imagined in De Stijl never existed. However, the vocabulary of collective enterprise can be found even in private discussions, such as the following letter drafted by Gerrit Rietveld in the spring of 1926 to a certain Mr Van Meurs, editor of a journal called *Bouwen* (Building):

> Dear Mr. Van Meurs, thank you for sending me 'Bouwen'. It is a wonderful journal. I also found some photos in it of the Paris exhibition [*Exposition Internationale des Art Décoratifs*] that I had not seen anywhere before.
>
> Constructivism – I do not know who was the first to use this word to describe an art movement but I find some merit in it. Whenever, for example, I want to connect 3 strips together, I look for a joint to place the strips purposefully in mutual relation to each other and dependent on the join. I grant that the connection is the most significant feature, rather than postulating a sort of art form, and I look for a join which is the least disruptive or, in other words, is the most cooperative.

The word constructivism does not explain the join but (in the example of the 3 strips) the mutual placement of the lines makes a sort of formation possible through the way they are brought into relation with each other. I do not mean that these activities occur separate from each other – the development of the join entails possibilities of construction and vice versa.

Further I can tell you that all that I strive for, especially in the interior, is not a composition which appears complete in itself but all that is necessary for it to appear as a moving background to life.

The direct collaboration of the commission giver, Tr. Schräder made this even more possible.

Best wishes
Yours sincerely

Rietveld arch.[2]

The end of the letter reveals that Rietveld is responding here to comments made about the Schröder house of 1924 (Figure 39) which Van Meurs attempted to place under the heading of Constructivism. He wanted to position Rietveld (and by extension De Stijl) in connection to that trend prevalent in several European countries which sought to bring the worlds of fine art and industrial production closer together. As is apparent from his reply, Rietveld was sympathetic to the idea that he might be part of some grand international effort (although he expresses ignorance of its origins). However, the rather abstruse way in which he described his own practice is peppered with idiom. There is no trace of the concern for materials one might find at the Bauhaus, nor any of the political agenda which dominated in Russian Constructivism. All emphasis is placed on a sequence of terms loaded with meaning in Dutch but quite vague when translated. Thus Rietveld discusses in detail a wood joint and repeats over and over again the importance of *verbinding* (joining) to him. The fixing he describes is his now famous crossing joint where elements extend past the point of junction (Figure 1); it features in the *Red/Blue Chair* as well as many other contemporary items of Rietveld furniture. This novel fixing allowed each structural element to preserve a separate visual identity while clearly expressing its dependency on its neighbours. The word *verbinding* carries connotations both of conjunction and union, as well as communication and combination (especially of colours). Rietveld continues to elucidate his wish to find a means to bring separate parts into mutual relation and extends the logic of construction to personal relationships in the form of the *samenwerking* (collaboration) of Truus Schröder. The notion of *samenwerking* was a central concern of De Stijl from the outset, expressed in the first *Manifesto of De Stijl* as a necessary resistance to individualism. Rietveld describes how the principles of combination and collaboration can be made visible in manufactured objects (be they paintings, buildings or items of furniture) by expressing collective interdependence. In the example he gives of joining together three pieces of wood, Rietveld describes how a composition can be made which results in *beelding*, a term central to De Stijl theory but one that is virtually

untranslatable. It has connotations of
structure making, image creation or
forming. The way that Rietveld uses
the word *beelding* in his letter suggests
that the visual qualities of construction
were as significant to him as materials
or processes of production, and were
thought to provide direct analogies to
social interaction.

Rietveld's vocabulary corresponds
closely to the definition of the 'De Stijl
idea' provided by Yve-Alain Bois who
has identified its two basic principles as
elementarisation and *integration*.
According to Bois' argument, De Stijl
activity was defined by the proposition
that each collaborator, be he painter,
architect or sculptor, should effect the
reduction of his practice to its irreduc-
ible core and once this process had been
completed, the distinct fields could be

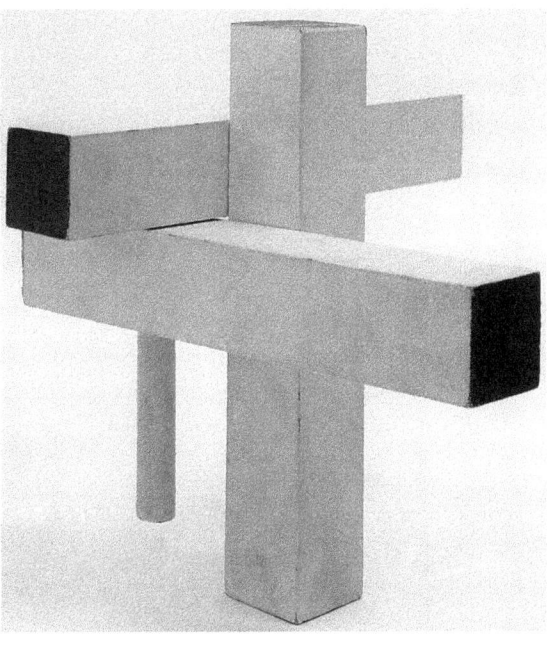

1 Model of 'Rietveld Joint', 1958

united into 'a syntactically indivisible, nonhierarchical whole'.[3] The two principles
of *elementarisation* and *integration* account for, respectively, the consistent promotion in De Stijl of abstract art and the interaction between painters and architects
which its most notable product. While I sympathise with the great clarity of Bois'
summary of De Stijl, my correction to it in this book will be to provide a historical
dimension he chooses to ignore. *Elementarisation* and *integration* may well be two
persistent components of De Stijl theory but Bois covertly introduces a temporal
priority to their relation which overlooks the background from which De Stijl
emerged. *Integration*, as he terms it, had been an aspiration of Dutch modernism for
over two decades before De Stijl began its promotion of a radical abstraction. What
Bois described as *elementarisation* was in fact a process of untangling or *dis*integrating
practices which had become very closely associated. Having set out to show continuity with *gemeenschapkunst*, the second conclusion that will be drawn in this book is
that the utopian impulse in De Stijl was fuelled by a destructive and sometimes nihilistic urge. The collaborative strategy, which has been taken naively at times to imply
that De Stijl projected an image of a harmonious social order, produced well–docu-
mented antagonisms. These were not, in my view, the unfortunate breakdown in
practice of a good idea in theory but the necessary outcome of De Stijl's challenge to
gemeenschapkunst and thereby to the existence of a *gemeenschap* (community) that it
suggested.

The appearance of the concept of *integration* in De Stijl must therefore be carefully reconsidered. In the first manifesto it is couched in very vague terminology

and expressed as the end of 'individual domination in every area' and the demand for a new 'balance between the universal and the individual'. In the dying days of the First World War this could be interpreted in a variety of ways. It was a suitably broad demand to accommodate the hopes of those such as Wils and Van 't Hoff to align De Stijl with left-wing politics alongside the philosophical ruminations of Mondrian and Van Doesburg. The latter two saw politics as a rather lowly field in comparison to the arts and for them the 'universal' had more esoteric resonance. In both cases, though, integration is proposed as a reorientation of a modernist pursuit of the essential towards a greatly expanded audience. The discussion of the integration of individuals (and the practices they represented) in De Stijl was a displacement of concerns for the integration of the arts with a common culture. Thus nearly all of the collaborators would try their hand at projects aimed at a large public, be it social housing, advertising or mass market furnishings. This point leads to my third reappraisal of De Stijl, a reconsideration of the theoretical division which has been placed between modernism and the avant-garde.

For several years a dominant conceptual framework for understanding the visual arts of the early twentieth century has distinguished, in crude terms, between modernism, represented as a desire to separate art from life, and the avant-garde, characterised as a wish to reunify art with praxis. Abstract art, interpreted as the inevitable outcome of a process of formal purification, has been aligned with modernism. It is seen to distance itself from mass culture by becoming remote and shrouding itself in esoteric theory. On the other side of the dichotomy are placed the constructivists, dadaists and surrealists who engaged with the new media of their day, were politically active and undermined the institutional definition of art which modernism had accepted. An obvious problem awaits the historian of De Stijl which has a foot in both the history of abstraction and constructivism. Bois' model of *elementarisation* and *integration* negotiates the divide by introducing the temporal priority mentioned above; the desire of the avant-garde to reintegrate art and life cannot come about without the previous separation of art from life. This dynamic is clearly explained in Peter Bürger's *Theory of the Avant-Garde*, from which much of the contemporary discussion of the avant-garde is derived. According to Bürger, the wish to reintegrate art and life shares the modernist rejection of the world as it is. The avant-garde attempts to 'organize a new life praxis from a basis in art. In this respect also, Aestheticism turns out to have been the necessary precondition of the avant-gardiste intent.'[4] However, the two most problematic aspects of Bürger's theory are his denial that modernism has a praxis and the historicist model of the passage from modernism to avant-garde he devises. I will take these points in turn.

Bürger describes modernism as the apogee of bourgeois art on the basis that its production and reception both occur at the level of the individual rather than collective. The distance modernism asserts from life guarantees a parallel distance from effective intervention in the social realm. Art becomes a specialist sphere of interest with its own institutions and definition. Aesthetic pleasure can be disconnected from any other interest. My difficulty with this description is connected to what Bürger himself outlines as the 'problem of the autonomy of art'. There is a disjuncture between the relative autonomy accorded to the aesthetic in modern culture, a phenomenon produced out of a set of historical circumstances (division of labour in industrial society, patterns of consumption, creation of public and private spheres), and the assertion of absolute autonomy made by modernist artists. The latter is, according to Bürger, a distorted (i.e. ideological) understanding of the former. What Bürger declines to consider any further are the connections between this distorted understanding and a praxis. An ideological position can, by definition, only occur at a collective rather than individual level. The first chapter of this book attempts to show how the move into abstraction by De Stijl artists, accompanied by the emergence of a modernist vocabulary in contemporary architecture, was not merely the taking of the autonomy of art as the content of art, as Bürger would have it. Rather, abstraction was seen as an appropriate means to address, among other things, the new spatial relations of modern life, the place of the human figure in the industrial landscape and the new modes of consumption of visual imagery. The subsequent chapters place these concerns within definite fields of praxis such as urban planning, advertising, interior and exhibition design.

Bürger's reluctance to address modernism from the point of view of praxis is the direct result of his historicist model of the avant-garde as the heir to the concept of autonomy. Without a notion of absolute autonomy there could be no avant-garde reconciliation of art and life, in his terms. As mentioned above, Bürger makes modernist aestheticism the precondition of avant-garde activity. The praxis imagined by the avant-garde is not the praxis of life as it is, but a praxis remade from a basis in art. The avant-garde has to fulfil the dual task of negating modernist autonomy while preserving it as the guarantee of critical distance. However, because absolute autonomy can be considered to be an ideological construction, the avant-garde negates and preserves a false perception of reality. This leads Bürger to conclude that the avant-garde is inevitably doomed to fail. We may contend that it fails a project that it never actually had. Bürger bemoans that in the place of the avant-garde we find pulp fiction and commodity aesthetics which reconcile art and life in a way that obliterates the critical consciousness he seeks in the avant-garde. However, he never pauses to reflect on the interaction of the avant-garde with these forms in their infancy, such the development of modern advertising.

If we wish to continue to use the term avant-garde in the sense which Bürger does, as a form of art that is radically engaged, then it is clear that it cannot be placed after and in opposition to modernism. Instead, the avant-garde exists somehow within modernism. I would strongly hesitate to call all of De Stijl activity avant-garde when clearly it was not. Indeed this book can be understood as the attempt to discover which aspects of De Stijl did have critical potential against the background of a general modernist discourse. These moments will not be found solely in painting or in architecture or in design. Also, it is clear to me that the version of modernism (and its

Janus face of the avant-garde) which De Stijl stands for appeared in the Dutch context precisely at the moment when certain 'high' and 'low' hierarchies began to break down. *Gemeenschapkunst*, which I described earlier as the first attempt in the Netherlands to forge a common culture from modernist aesthetics, had kept such hierarchies carefully in place. In De Stijl they are far more uncertain than has previously been appreciated.

The three arguments I have outlined above, the continuity with *gemeenschapkunst*, the nihilistic aspects of De Stijl utopianism and the redefinition of the avant-garde, are not separated in the chapters which follow but are constantly interwoven. The first chapter is the most restricted chronologically and examines the discourse of abstraction in the formative moments of De Stijl. The subsequent chapters are more thematic and consider in turn the fields of urban planning, advertising, interior design and forms of display, where De Stijl collaborators were most active and where the interaction between abstraction and mass culture was most keenly felt. In each instance, the reader will find commentaries reaching back into the late nineteenth and early twentieth centuries which provide a background to later De Stijl concerns. In the case of advertising, for example, I describe how the involvement of artists such as Van Doesburg, Van der Leck or Huszár in the production of commercial art was nothing new in itself but closely corresponded to the poster work produced by Jan Toorop and others in the 1890s. Toorop was heavily involved with *gemeenschapkunst* and saw advertising as a means to disseminate fine art to a mass audience. However, his enlightened standpoint had become rather sullied by the end of the First World War when advertising was closely associated with propaganda and acquired negative connotations. Abstraction in advertising was proposed as an economical and effective remedy, drawing on recent theories of psycho-physical response to colour and shape. While supposedly creating an 'art for the people', to use Huszár's expression, the ethical position of *gemeenschapkunst* was sharply undermined at the same time as the borders between fine art and mass production were blurred.

When I describe a general modernist discourse in the Netherlands, I could summarise this as an obsession with the idea of style, a phenomenon by no means particular to De Stijl. The emergence of *gemeenschapkunst* in the last decade of the nineteenth century was directly connected to contemporary concerns regarding the lack of a modern style. Not only did artists produce wall painting, stained glass and monumental sculpture in order to place their work directly in the built environment but they also tried very seriously to forge stylistic unity between architecture and the visual arts. It had also been in the context of *gemeenschapkunst* that the first discussions were held concerning the ability of artists to represent collective 'ideas' rather than the visible world. Although the key representatives of this tendency, artists such as Antoon Derkinderen and Richard Roland Holst, worked predominantly in a representational mode, great emphasis was laid on their ability to produce symbolic content rather than naturalistic accuracy. In order to comprehend the intellectual background to De Stijl then, it is crucial to understand that the pursuit of essential qualities and the promotion of collective activity were well established in the discourse of Dutch modernism. What distinguishes De Stijl from this heritage is the nihilistic way in which it reformulated the vocabulary of *gemeenschapkunst*. For example, point six of the manifesto, which addressed abstraction, did so by calling for 'all who believe in the reformation of art and culture to annihilate these obstacles of development as they have annihilated in the new plastic art (by abolishing natural form) that which prevents the clear expression of art'. Other parts of the manifesto described the process of destruction initiated by the war and placed De Stijl as part of this inevitable force of dissolution. It is this quality that makes it distinct from its forerunners and other contemporaries, as we shall see, and also comprises an important ingredient of its utopianism.

The name itself, De Stijl, can help us in the quest to reconfigure the aspirations which brought about its existence. Van Doesburg originally planned to call the journal The Straight Line, which would have neatly summarised its visual aesthetic and the view of historical progress he promoted in it. The change to De Stijl orientated the journal from fine art more towards architecture and design, reflecting the intense debate in those fields around the concept of style. The leading light in this discourse was the most influential modern architect in the Netherlands, Hendrik Petrus Berlage. In a series of publications, from the last decade of the nineteenth to the first quarter of the twentieth century, he relentlessly pounded away at the deficiencies of contemporary architecture and design, calling for a return to basic principles. Berlage also saw the regeneration of style as indelibly tied to social change. In his view capitalism was unable to foster great architecture and the achievement of a great modern style to equal that of antiquity or the middle ages would only come with the emancipation of the working classes. Some of the original founders of De Stijl were extremely close to Berlage, such as Wils who worked in his architectural office for many years, and Oud who was a close personal friend. Van der Leck worked alongside Berlage on commissions for the shipping and mining company Müller & Co. Indeed Van Doesburg had hoped to recruit Berlage to De Stijl but without success. Nevertheless many aspects of his theories reappeared in Van Doesburg's own writing, though frequently with the political angle removed.

Berlage's most celebrated achievement was the building of the Amsterdam Stock Exchange which opened in 1903, a sublime paradox for a such a committed socialist. Nevertheless the architectural and artistic programme of the building was the crowning moment of *gemeenschapkunst*, featuring the collaboration of three painters (Antoon Derkinderen, Richard Roland Holst and Jan Toorop), two sculptors (Lambertus Zijl and Joseph Mendes da Costa) and a poet (Albert Verwey). The sobriety of Berlage's architecture was mollified by the elaborate decorative scheme which featured stained glass, wall painting, tile painting, inscription, free standing and relief sculpture. Verwey's verses established the narrative structure for the building which celebrated the commercial enterprise of the city of

Amsterdam while simultaneously evoking the potential of modern economic wealth to produce a classless society. The following stanza, inscribed in the passageway between the trading halls of the Stock and Commodities Exchanges, provides a flavour of the themes adopted:

> The deeds of many make one man's burden slight
> Thousandfold freight is carried in one load,
> Thousands become one, though neither truck nor boat
> Was used to carry them, still their weight was light.[5]

The tone of Verwey's poetry was matched by representations of industrial and agricultural labour produced by Toorop and Roland Holst which further celebrated the commercial productivity of the city while intimating a political agenda. Toorop's tile paintings in the foyer, for example, depicted the emancipation of women made possible through industrial development. The combination of painting, sculpture and poetry was intended to produce a non-hierarchical model of collective endeavour. Yet the Stock Exchange project was unable to completely resolve the problem of the relation between architecture, fine art and decoration. Was the building the frame for the art it contained? Were these objects merely dressing for what was otherwise a largely unornamented structure? Was it Berlage who had final control over the content of the building? Did not the individual styles of the artists involved contradict the aim of the project to determine one truly modern style?

From an architectural point of view, Berlage had some answers to these questions. He was very much responsible for promoting the ideas of Gottfried Semper in the Netherlands; Berlage's 1904 book, *Over stijl in bouw- en meubelkunst* (Concerning Style in Architecture and Furniture Design) was entirely based on Gottfried Semper's classic *Der Stil* (The Style) of the 1860s. Although much simplified and abbreviated, Berlage retained Semper's key theses concerning the origins of style and the proper application of ornament in architecture. According to Semper, ornament appeared with the first social structures and was derived from the first technologies of weaving. The two significant conclusions he made from these observations were, firstly that decorative motifs could be traced back to the manipulation of certain materials and secondly, more controversially, ornamentation preceded building. In Semper's view, the hanging of textiles to indicate the outside and inside of social space was anterior to the construction of permanent physical structures. Architecture as art therefore preceded architecture as building. He marketed *Der Stil* as a practical handbook for architects and designers because he identified for them certain *Grundformen* (basic types) of decoration and also explained how they were integral to a building rather than additions to it. At the centre of *Der Stil* lies Semper's *Prinzip der Bekleidung* (Principle of Clothing) whereby he described architecture as the clothing of space. Berlage's promotion of Semper was a crucial source of the anti-functionalist agenda of De Stijl and its concern for spatial design above questions of construction.

From the point of view of painting or sculpture the problem of style remained unresolved by the Stock Exchange project. Meanwhile, the concept of style had become key to the work of art historians who were busily engaged in dividing up museum collections into period or national styles, and using individual stylistic traits to make attributions. Their work gave credence to the idea that art had its own distinct history and fuelled even more the desire of contemporary artists to produce a 'modern' style now seen as the climax of a two thousand-year lineage from antiquity to the present. Van Doesburg's 1922 lecture *Der Wille zum Stil* (The Will to Style) explicitly drew on such style theory to justify the pre-eminence of abstract art as the true heir to the tradition of Western art.[6] By bringing style to the forefront, he made a clear demarcation between fine art and the rest of human activity, and in so doing made precisely the distinction between modernism and mass culture that I deny lies at the heart of De Stijl.

The contradiction between Van Doesburg's use of style theory to promote aesthetic autonomy and the ambition to synthesise stylistic forms throughout all levels of culture can be resolved by thinking through the main arguments of this book. Firstly, we should reconsider how De Stijl assimilated the notion of integration from *gemeenschapkunst* which was most clearly expressed in the attempt to interplay painting and architecture, the use of monumental art forms such as stained glass and the production of certain mass market imagery. The search for a common style had introduced the problem of the free-floating nature of style in modern culture, which was linked to the notion of the autonomy of art. I argue that De Stijl was less the site in which the theory of autonomy was created than where it was tested – tested by pushing it to its limits and often undermining it.[7] It is in this activity that we glimpse the avant-garde interior of De Stijl. Here I rely on the distinctions drawn by Karl Mannheim between utopian and ideological consciousness.[8] The are many problems with Mannheim's theory but his attempt to distinguish the two is a crucial antidote to the orthodox Marxist denigration of all utopias as merely concealed ideologies. For example, Mannheim contrasts the static nature of ideologies, which are intended to preserve the status quo, to the dynamism of utopias, which desire change. Ideologies serve to maintain power, utopias to gain power. Most controversially, Mannheim suggests that ideologies are always unrealisable whereas utopias aim at realisation. In my view, this description of utopianism characterises aspects of De Stijl very closely, given its appearance during a period of dramatic change in the Netherlands and challenge to certain established institutions. Whether or not the vision of the world expressed in De Stijl was ever realised, it did make way for others that were, such as I explore in my discussion of urban planning.

I have borrowed the title of this introduction from a series of paintings made by Barnett Newman in the 1960s. Newman used the title to lay down a gauntlet to the tradition of abstract art represented by Mondrian. Red, yellow and blue in geometric arrangement had become by this time the instantly recognisable badge of De Stijl. Newman tried to show that these elements could be reused without the need merely to repeat a previous model. Moreover, he suggested that De Stijl could be consigned to the history books as part of the succession of styles in painting, one which his own practice had superceded. This book argues against the logic of Newman's act and recovers De Stijl as movement with great cultural force not restricted to such a narrowly defined field. It shows how its utopianism can be read as dynamic rather than conservative and how abstraction played an unexpected role in shaping the Netherlands in the interwar period.

Notes

1 The term *gemeenschapkunst* was first used by Jan Veth in 1891 to describe a series of wall paintings made by Antoon Derkinderen in the town hall of 's-Hertogenbosch. Derkinderen was deeply involved in the Roman Catholic revival of the period and the term *gemeenschap* had specific implications for him of resistance to secularisation and Liberal politics. By the turn of the century *gemeenschapkunst* was replaced by the less inflammatory term *monumentale kunst* (monumental art) although the key concepts behind it were retained. For the sake of clarity I will use the former term throughout the book.

2 'Zeer Geachte Heer Van Meurs, dank voor de zending van "Bouwen", 't is een keurig blad. Ik vond er ook fotos van de Par.tent. die ik nog nergens zag. Constructivisme – ik weet niet wie dit woord het eerst is gaan gebruiken om een kunst richting aan te duiden, maar ik vind er wel iets goeds in. Wanneer ik b.v. 3 regels met elkaar wil verbinden kan ik een houtverbinding zoeken en de regels plaatsen naar aanleiding of afhankelijk van die verbinding onderling plaatsen. Ik zou dan de verbinding als voornaamste laten gelden in belangstelling met een soort kunstvorm voorop te stellen en dan een verbinding zoeken die het minst stoort of misschien hoogstens meedoet. Het woord constructivisme duidt niet op de verbinding, maar op (in 't geval van de 3 regels) de onderlinge plaatsing van die regels wat een soort beelding mogelijk maakt, door de wijze waar door ze met elkaar in verband gebracht worden – dan eerst volgt de eigenlijke verbinding. Ik bedoel niet dat deze handeling afgescheiden van elkaar gescheiden – de ontwikkelingen van de verbinding brengt mogelijkheden van constructie's mede en omgekeerd. Verder kan ik U nog zeggen, dat vooral binnen niet gestreeft is naar een compositie, die altijd in zich zelf volledig verschijnt, maar alles wat noodig is als bewegelijke achtergrond van het leven te doen verschijnen. De directe samenwerking met de opdrachtgeefste Tr.Schräder maakte dit nog meer mogelijk. Met vr. groet. Hoogachtend. Rietveld arch.' Letter from Gerrit Rietveld to Mr de Meurs undated, Rietveld Schröder Archive, Centraal Museum Utrecht.

3 Yve-Alain Bois, 'The De Stijl Idea', in *Painting as Model* (Cambridge MA and London: MIT, 1990), p. 103.

4 Peter Bürger, *Theory of the Avant-Garde* (Minneapolis: University of Minnesota Press, 1984), p. 49.

5 'De daad van velen is elke enkeling licht/De duizendvoudge vracht in-eens gedragen,/ Maakt van duizend die in schuit noch wagen/Vervoerders vonden van hun licht gewicht.' Albert Verwey inscription in Beurs van Berlage, Amsterdam, 1903.

6 Theo van Doesburg, 'Der Wille zum Stil' *De Stijl* 5/1 (1922), pp. 23–32; 5/3, pp. 33–41. Certain concepts featured in the lecture concerning the historical

development of art had earlier been outline in Van Doesburg's book *Klassiek Barok Modern* (Antwerp: De Sikkel, 1920). Both of these texts contain much style theory derived from Alois Reigl and Heinrich Wölfflin.

7 If we follow Nancy Troy's argument, we can see how the concept of autonomy is not a constant in De Stijl but transforms across time. The breakdown of collaboration she charts could be read as a gradual hardening of the autonomy principle, a historical development which runs exactly opposite to that proposed by Bürger. See Nancy Troy, *The De Stijl Environment* (Cambridge MA and London, 1983), in particular pp. 72–121.

8 Karl Mannheim, *Ideology and Utopia: An Introduction to the Sociology of Knowledge* (San Diego, New York, London: Harcourt Brace, 1985).

1

Abstraction and utopia

If there was one single feature that distinguished De Stijl from other competing versions of modernism in the Netherlands it was the consistent promotion of geometric abstract art.[1] The claim was repeatedly made in the journal by different contributors that painting was reaching a point of self-purification ahead of all other practices and was the model to be followed, particularly by architecture.[2] Only once architecture had gone through a similar process of reduction to its essential nature could it be reintegrated with painting to produce a properly modern monumental form, and a similar process was also predicted for sculpture and literature. Emphasis on the flatness of the picture plane, autonomy of colour, banishment of literary subject matter – all traits seen today as typical of modernism – were thought to herald a collective style. This style would then bind the arts together and, by association, represent the cultural achievement of a unified society.

As I outlined in the Introduction, it is simple to take the claims made for the autonomy of art in De Stijl and transfer them to the actual paintings to become their sole content. This was a dominant art historical approach to De Stijl for many decades and assisted in its assimilation into a history of modernism understood as progressive technical reflexivity. The parallel to the assertion of autonomy was an account of the interest of painters such as Mondrian in esoteric philosophy. This did little to unravel the construction of the concept of autonomy, and in fact served to reinforce the distance between abstraction and its historical context. It is only in the last two decades that a serious challenge has been made to this historiographical model. For example, Mark Cheetham's 1991 book *The Rhetoric of Purity* associates Mondrian's pursuit of perfected form and unstinting faith in rational progress with the technocratic, instrumentalist and even fascistic tendencies in modernism.[3] The concept of autonomy is read in this example as a side effect of bourgeios society's relentless drive towards modernisation. Unlike Peter Bürger, Cheetham does not see autonomy as either possible or desirable, but as thoroughly ideological. However, the desperate weakness in his account of Mondrian's painting is that he, exactly as the modernist art historians before him, takes Mondrian's own writings as the primary source for understanding abstraction without once questioning how they were produced or even who the audience for them might have been.

This chapter has one very clear purpose, to investigate the crucial moment of the formation of De Stijl, which coincided with the appearance of geometric abstract painting. As will become apparent in this discussion, to my finding, the issue of the purification of painting was often only a secondary concern in De Stijl despite the rhetoric frequently present in the journal. In fact a large proportion of the objects made by De Stijl collaborators were still obviously figurative. More crucial than autonomy was the notion of monumentality, defined through the proper relation between painting and architecture. Later on in the chapter I begin to explore the interaction between painters and architects to elaborate this point. However, attention to the persistence of the figure in De Stijl production opens out to a series of new considerations: the attempt to comment on the effects of industrialisation on the body, a redefinition of the relation between spectator and object, attention to contemporary patterns of consumption. The role of abstraction was by no means solely to affirm a bourgeois subjectivity by providing an exclusive form of aesthetic enjoyment. This point can be made very clearly by beginning with a highly problematic painting which had a great influence on all the artists connected with the journal.

In December 1916 Hélène Kröller-Müller took receipt of a large three panel painting recently finished by Bart van der Leck (Plate 2). Over the previous two years he had been employed by her family company, Müller & Co., to produce graphic works, interior colour schemes and stained glass for a variety of company projects. He had resigned his post in early 1916 frustrated by the limits it imposed on his creativity. One final commission in late 1916, to collaborate with the architect H. P. Berlage on the redecoration of a room in the Kröller's house, had ended in bitter dispute. Fortunately, Kröller-Müller decided to maintain her patronage and Van der Leck was transferred to a private contract, negotiated by her artistic advisor, the critic and collector H. P. Bremmer. The arrangement provided Van der Leck with a monthly salary in return for his paintings. The first paintings to pass to her through this contract, *De Storm* (The Storm) and *Havenarbeid* (Dock Work), depicted scenes of seafaring and labour closely connected to the business affairs of Müller & Co., a shipping and mining company. The triptych followed this pattern and was originally conceived of by the artist as *Ertsmijn met Mijnwerkers* (Ore Mine with Mineworkers). It became commonly known as *Mijntriptiek* (Mine Triptych) although at the time of its completion and submission to Kröller-Müller it was titled by Van der Leck simply as *Compositie 1916 no. 4* (Composition 1916 no. 4). All of these titles motivate a reading of the painting in a particular direction which has a bearing on the outlook of De Stijl. I will take them in turn and consider their implications.

As has been thoroughly described elsewhere, the subject of the painting was derived from a series of studies made by Van der Leck on his journey to North Africa and Spain in 1914–15 to view the mines owned by Müller & Co.[4] The main activity of the company was mining iron ore which was then shipped via Rotterdam down the Rhine to Germany's industrial belt in the Ruhr. The sketches were first used by Van der Leck to produce a large stained-glass window, *Het Mijnbedrijf* (The Mining Business) (Figure 2), installed in the company headquarters in The Hague in 1916. The window represented the many facets of the mining business, from

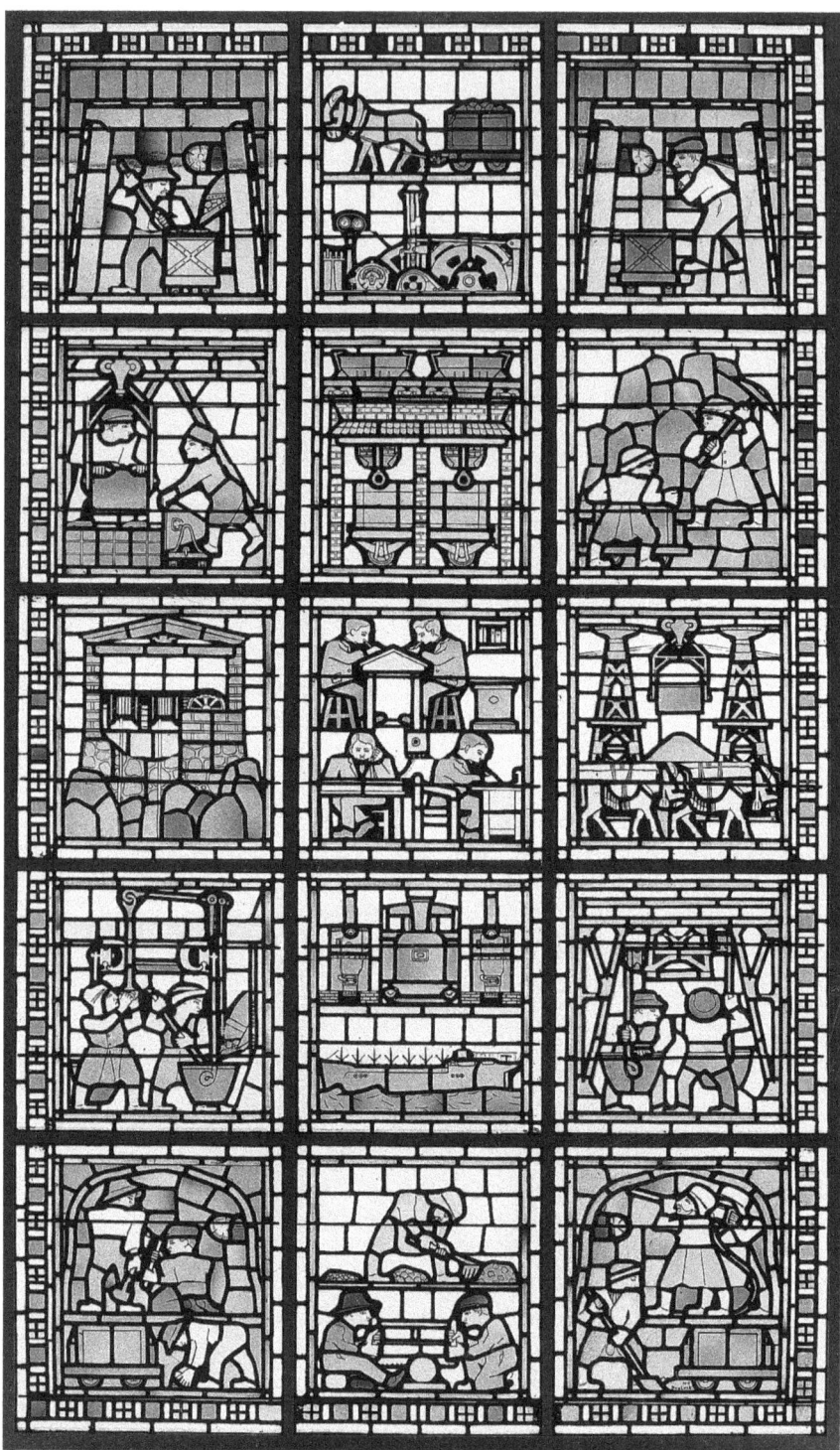

2 Bart van der Leck, *The Mining Business*, 1914–16

work underground to shipping and, in the very centre, the clerical activity that co-ordinated the whole enterprise. Van der Leck integrated many interesting juxtapositions into the composition, between manual and intellectual work, mechanical and natural forms, beasts of burden and modern means of transportation such as trains and steam ships. He tried very carefully not to give an explicit vertical hierarchy to the composition with bosses at the top and workers underneath, although the mining theme would have lent itself very easily to such a scheme. Instead he placed an office scene at the centre of the window, representing the communications hub of the company. Van der Leck also avoided constructing a linear narrative that would take us from the depths of the mine to a finished product. Instead he emphasised the teamwork of the company over and above the disparities between workers and owners. The mining subject allowed him to contrast scenes above and below ground by interspersing clear and painted backgrounds, admitting more or less light. While still essentially figurative, *The Mining Business* was much simplified to a narrow set of colours and the figures were depicted in Van der Leck's characteristic flattened quasi-Egyptian manner.

Reading the subsequent painting with the title *Ore Mine with Mineworkers,* we can see how it might have been derived from the earlier conception of the window. The large central panel with a predominant white background appears to have been derived from an image of the mine entrance. The two side panels, with black backgrounds, represent individual miners working underground. The contrast between light inside and dark outer panels can be seen already present in the window at the top and bottom. Van der Leck also used a technique of painting the white and black backgrounds on top of the colours which had the effect of suspending them in the pictorial field, much like a stained-glass window.[5]

Van der Leck had his early training in a stained-glass workshop during the 1890s and was fully aware of the technical possibilities of the medium. He followed his craft education with fine art training at the Rijksacademie in Amsterdam and on leaving this institution in 1904 began to make paintings of street scenes and working-class life following the model of local artists such as George Breitner and Isaac Israels. The Müller & Co. commission gave him the first opportunity to bring together the two sides of his interest: the depiction of social reality and the monumental arts. These two themes can readily account for some of the features of *Ore Mine with Mineworkers*, notably its rigid structure, which mimics stained glass, and the choice of subject matter. However, the triptych avoids depicting mining as dirty or dangerous; the entrance to the mine is radiant and the two large miners flanking the central panel are stood upright rather than bent under their tasks. Yet their transformation into almost robotic figures should not be overlooked. Commenting on another of Van der Leck's paintings in 1918, Bremmer noted that it depicted people as 'puppets without a will of their own, driven by an invisible force', a judgment to which the artist reacted with approval.[6] The geometric mode Van der Leck adopted marked both the modernity of the subject and also the potential of industrial labour to dehumanise.

One factor that the above account cannot do true justice to is Van der Leck's use of a triptych format for the painting, combining rather incongruously a secular subject with a religious format. In its transformation from *Ore Mine with Mineworkers* to *Mine Triptych*, a different mood takes over the painting, which has been described by Carel Blotkamp in these terms:

> The thought forces itself that Van der Leck associated the difficult circumstances of the miners with the pre-eminent example of human suffering, the passion of Christ. The mine entrance, towards which attention is drawn, is defined by a T-form cross composed of a black horizontal and a yellow vertical stripe. The mine can be interpreted as a modern version of the place of crucifixion, the hill of Calvary, subject of countless triptychs especially in the fifteenth and sixteenth centuries.[7]

In support of this interpretation Blotkamp has drawn attention to a likely source for Van der Leck in Constantin Meunier's triptych *The Mine* of c.1900.[8] In the latter work, the three panels represented miners on their way to work (centre panel), miners entering the lift to take them down to work (left panel) and miners emerging from the same lift at the end of the day (right panel). To enforce the connection that Meunier wished to draw with religious painting he titled these panels *Calvary*, *Descent* and *Return* respectively. Blotkamp connects this obvious reference to the Crucifixion and Resurrection to the heroic depiction of Belgian peasants and workers begun by Van Gogh in the late nineteenth century.[9] He reads the motif across to Van der Leck's triptych and, as quoted above, describes not only the centre panel as Calvary but the miners either side as saints or donors according to the traditional format.

While I agree with Blotkamp's identification of Meunier as a source for Van der Leck, what interests me about it is the conceptual shift made by Van der Leck from ore mining in North Africa to coal mining in Belgium. There is no hint of a religious narrative in his preparatory work nor even in the stained-glass window, where it might have been expected. The change may not seem significant but when contemporary circumstances are considered it begins to become rather more important. At the time he made the painting Belgian coal fields were under German occupation and the coal supply to the Netherlands in crisis. Before the First World War two-thirds of coal consumed in the Netherlands came from Belgium and Germany. The war resulted in Germany becoming the sole exporter of coal to a country unable to produce enough supply from its own fields in Limburg. As A. J. Barnouw put it: 'Suspension of those supplies was the Damocles sword with which Germany threatened to cut off Holland's frail economic existence.'[10] Van der Leck's confusion of his original commission with the sentimental depiction of Belgian miners demonstrates that the move into abstraction has a far larger dimension than the process of reduction to essentials that has previously been used to describe it. Here we could describe the process of painting as not so much one of reduction rather than cancellation, obliteration or masking. Unable to represent miners in their actual circumstances, he replaced them with an idealised notion of mining as sacrifice.

As has already been mentioned, *Mine Triptych* was one of the first of Van der Leck's works to pass into the private collection of Kröller-Müller, from whom he was receiving a salary. His income was therefore being derived from a mining business but, unlike coal mining, not one in crisis. Müller & Co. was in fact making very good profits indeed. The director of the company was Anton Kröller, who had married Hélène Müller, the owner's daughter, in 1888. Kröller had been closely involved with the establishment of the *Nederlandsche Overzee Trustmaatschappij* (Netherlands Overseas Trust), a private organisation set up in 1914 to administer foreign trade relations during the war. In order to maintain neutrality, the Dutch government was forced to relinquish this role and the Netherlands Overseas Trust took over the management of all imports and exports. In turn the trust was obliged to guarantee that the goods it transported did not advantage either of the warring parties. Müller & Co., which had the largest commercial fleet in the Netherlands, profited greatly from the arrangement as other Dutch businesses were forced to use its ships. Kröller-Müller was then able to turn some of the profits to the advantage of artists like Van der Leck, while expanding her already significant private collection.

The transformation of the subject matter of Van der Leck's painting from mining as labour to mining as sacrifice is, in my view, partly derived from the artist's self-consciousness about his financial dependency. This is partly born out in Kröller-Müller's adverse reaction to the work.[11] She had profound difficulty in ascertaining the starting point for the composition and asked Van der Leck to send his preparatory studies to her. It was totally unrecognisable to her as a representation of her family business in the way that the stained-glass window had been. Two months earlier she criticised Van der Leck for letting himself be too greatly influenced by Mondrian without achieving the same sense of mood or mystical feeling she saw in the latter. Van der Leck vociferously defended himself against this charge and in a letter to Kröller-Müller in October 1916 stated his aim: 'No illusion, no mood, no fascination, but a monumental clarity is what I have in mind.'[12] He chose his words carefully here, particularly dismissing *stemming* (mood), which had been a term prevalent in art criticism in the Netherlands since the late nineteenth century, used often in support of impressionist painting. Instead Van der Leck connected himself to the tradition of monumental art, the *gemeenschapkunst* I described in the Introduction. It is with this in mind that I will mention another potential source for *Mine Triptych* – the murals produced by Richard Roland Holst for the Stock Exchange in Amsterdam in 1903.

Much of the subject matter of the decorative programme of Berlage's Stock Exchange building was highly ambitious and socially committed. It was intended to remind the brokers who worked in it that the stocks and commodities in which they dealt were not mere abstractions but connected to the lives and labour of real people. Thus Richard Roland Holst painted two large murals depicting Industry (Figure 3) and Trade in the main staircase in the south-west corner of the building, which led from the main entrance to the Chamber of Commerce. The two subjects

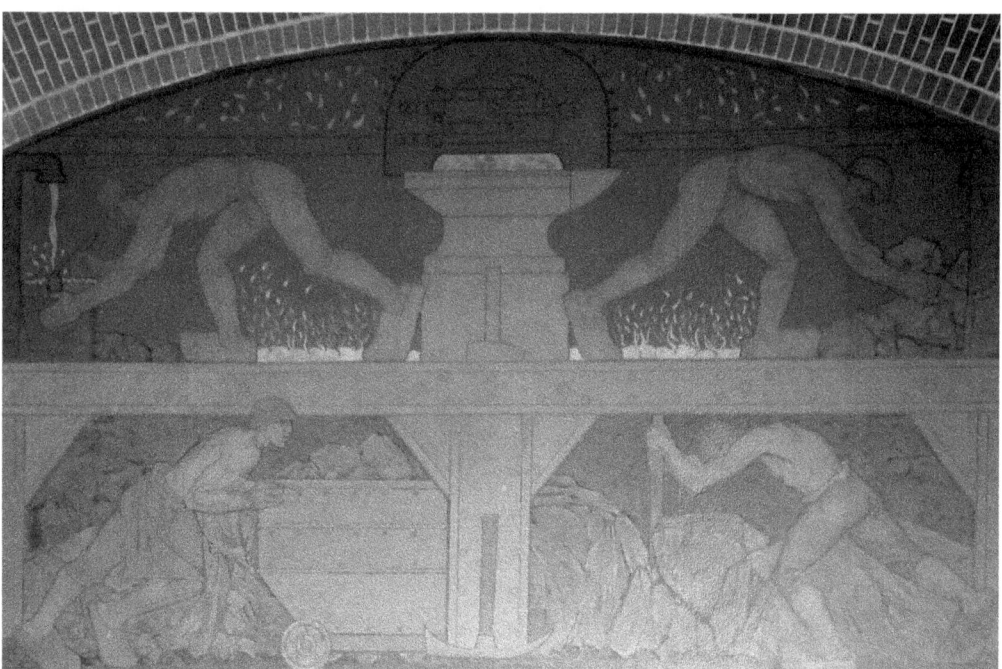

3 Richard Roland Holst, *Industry*, 1903

are represented by paired figures of miners, steel workers and stevedores engaged in heavy labour. Rather than find tame allegories, Roland Holst emphasised that the modern economy of the Netherlands rested on physical work and he depicted his figures bending, straining and lifting. There is some degree of artifice to the composition, however. Each panel is horizontally bisected, with two figures above and below (thus two steel workers above two miners and two pairs of dock workers above and below the deck of a ship). The paired figures face outwards at the top and inwards at the bottom so that their dynamic poses create strong diagonal axes, both compositions mirroring each other exactly in this regard. For some critics these murals were the high point of the entire Stock Exchange project as they managed to bring about the perfect union of painting and architecture. In equal numbers though, other critics found the geometry of the composition too contrived and overly subservient to the system of proportion Berlage used in the building based on the so-called Egyptian triangle.[13]

As mentioned above, Van der Leck had finally quit his job with Müller & Co. after disagreement with Berlage over the decoration of a room in the Kröller family residence. His return to easel painting in 1916 involved a reconsideration of the relation between fine art and architecture which he began to theorise as in opposition to each other. I would offer an interpretation of *Mine Triptych* as Van der Leck's correction to Roland Holst's Stock Exchange murals. This would account for the powerful diagonals he used which were not present in his paintings to this date. Unlike Roland Holst, Van der Leck did not subsume all of the angles to one specific compositional order. There are numerous slight variences which give the *Mine Triptych* a sense of boundless space. Similarly, if one concentrates hard enough it is possible to see that the miners in the side panels face outwards (unlike donor portraits) and also appear to be twisting in space. If modernist painting is often read as asserting flatness, Van der Leck is demonstrating the opposite here. He is repudiating the flatness of Roland Holst's murals and replacing it with spatiality. As Van der Leck subsequently stated in the first issue of De Stijl, painting was essentially 'open' in contrast to the 'closed' nature of architecture.[14]

The connections between *Mine Triptych* and *gemeenschapkunst* can be further elucidated by reference to Van der Leck's movements at the time. During his years in the employ of Müller & Co. Van der Leck lived in The Hague, close to the company's head office. Following his resignation he moved with his family to Laren, a small village between Amsterdam and Utrecht which had been a favoured location for artists since the end of the previous century. Moreover Laren, and the neighbouring village of Blaricum where the Van der Lecks would permanently settle in 1919, were home to numerous 'alternative' communites: anarchist, communist, vegetarian, pacifist. These activities, immortalised by the poet Adriaan Roland Holst in his book *Bezielde Dorpen* (Inspired Villages), have led to comparisons with the colonies of Ascona in Switzerland and Worpswede in Germany, given their similar combination of political radicalism, modernist cultural activity and what we now term 'new age' living.[15] This was not Van der Leck's first experience of the area though. He had lived in Laren for a short period in 1907, attracted there by the presence of Antoon Derkinderen, the originator of the notion of *gemeenschapkunst* and then director of the Rijksacademie. At the turn of the century Derkinderen had attempted, with limited success, to establish a workshop in Laren along medieval lines based on the apprentice, journeyman and master system. It seems that Van der Leck wished to join Derkinderen's venture but unfortunately arrived too late when the workshop was on the point of folding. Later, when commissioned to produce the stained-glass window for the Müller & Co. office, Van der Leck once again turned to Derkinderen for help and hoped to revive the Laren workshop where Derkinderen had designed his large stained-glass window for the Stock Exchange building, but again without success. Laren was very much connected in Van der Leck's mind with the tradition of monumental art. Richard Roland Holst was also still a resident there, for example. However, rather than establish contact with such artists, Van der Leck encountered a painter with very different ideas, namely Piet Mondrian.

It is Mondrian's influence that provides the third title of *Mine Triptych*, and that by which it should be properly known, *Composition 1916 no. 4*, which removes virtually all chance for the unsuspecting viewer to recognise the subject from which it was originally derived. Van der Leck felt able to give this non-descriptive title by following Mondrian's example; the latter had been using titles such as *Painting* or *Composition* since 1913. The three paintings which precede *Composition 1916 no. 4*

all share a similar mode of production; Van der Leck selected a standard genre subject (a portrait, a women with cows and a harvesting scene, respectively) and put it
through a process of selection, erasure and reduction until it became virtually
indistinguishable. He called this manner of working *doorbeelding*, a difficult word to
translate but which approximates to something like 'decomposition'. As with its
companion pieces, *Composition 1916 no. 4* may have been announcing the future
condition of art as autonomous but it was doing so through a peculiar demonstra-
tion of the dissolution of the tradition of naturalist painting. The way that the
forms hover between abstraction and figuration is crucial for the meaning of the
painting. This provides another explanation for the use of the triptych form. It is
thoroughly referential to the history of painting while placing that very history
under erasure.

As I stated above, it was my intention to start this chapter with a discussion of
Mine Triptych precisely because of its complex history, to demonstrate how much
was bound up in the emergence of abstraction at the outset of De Stijl. We have
already seen how necessary is recourse to the history of monumental art in the
Netherlands to explain how modernist painting was seen to be in competition with
architecture. It has also become very apparent that Van der Leck used abstraction not
as a means of registering purification but to indicate, at least in the case of the *Mine
Triptych*, the dehumanising effects of modern labour. In contrast to the salvationist
interpretation offered by Blotkamp, I have read religious format of the painting as an
uncomfortable reference to the war context (which certainly made Kröller-Müller
suspicious of the painting). Finally we have seen how Van der Leck conceived his
own working practice in negative terms such as destruction and decomposition.
With all these issues in mind I will now move on to examine a range of responses to
Van der Leck and consider the early moments of De Stijl in this regard.

After a year or so during which he barely finished a single painting, Mondrian's for-
tunes were lifted at the beginning of 1917 when he, like Van der Leck, began to
receive a monthly salary. The source of his income was Bremmer, who also began
buying Mondrian's paintings for Kröller-Müller. This arrangement allowed
Mondrian to initiate some new works which would be exhibited at the Stedelijk
Museum in Amsterdam in May 1917 at the *Hollandsche Kunstenaarskring* (Dutch
Artists' Circle) exhibition. He submitted three paintings to the exhibition,
Composition in Line (1916–17), *Composition in Colour A* (1917) and *Composition in
Colour B* (1917), and hung them so that the largest of the three, *Composition in Line*,
was in the centre, slightly raised with the coloured pair flanking it symmetrically
(Figure 4). While the paintings do not seem to have been made with a triptych form
in mind, this arrangement did produce a solution to showing the three together.
Once again Blotkamp has been the most alert to the significance of this event and has
connected Mondrian's 1917 display to his one and only authentic triptych of 1911,
Evolution (Figure 5).[16] According to Blotkamp's argument, Mondrian was drawing a
conceptual continuity between his most abstract work to date and his earlier, most

4 Installation photograph,
Hollandsche Kunstenaarskring, 1917

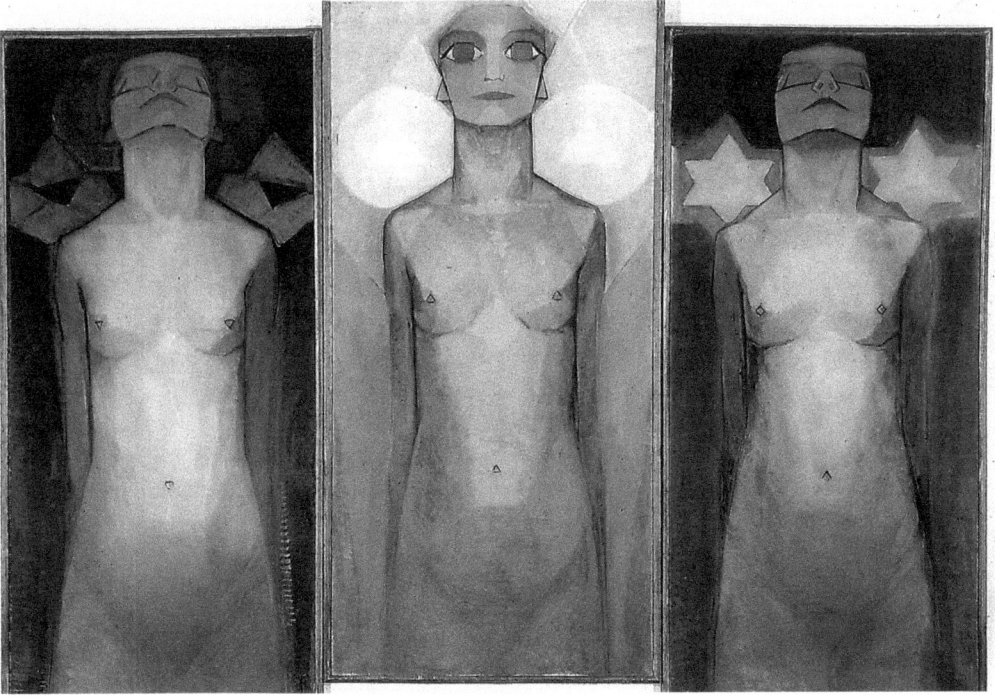

explicit, attempt to cast theosophical
doctrine in symbolic form. Blotkamp
goes so far as to contrast the material
source of the two coloured compositions, perhaps still based on the motif
of a tree that the artist had been engaged
with for some time, against the 'ethe-
real and spiritual qualities of the centre
panel, painted in black and white'.[17]

There is an enormous gap between
the compositions exhibited in 1917 and *Evolution*, both technical and theoretical.
For, by 1917, Mondrian saw himself on the verge of dispensing totally with subject matter. His one completed painting of 1916, *Composition*, is the final work in
a series dating back to 1913 based upon architectural features, beginning with the
cityscape of Paris and then church facades on his return to the Netherlands in
1914. *Composition in Line* seems related instead to the *Pier and Ocean* series of
1914–15, a sequence of black and white images all featuring 'plus' and 'minus'

5 Piet Mondrian, *Evolution*, 1911

hatchings. Unlike these earlier works, *Composition in Line* avoided the sense of
recession still apparent in the earlier paintings derived from interplay between
the perspectival thrust of the pier against the diffusive nature of the ocean, their
naturalistic starting point. What all three of the paintings exhibited in 1917
retain from their immediate predecessors is a certain 'edge consciousness'. They
contain, like many cubist works, an internal oval frame, not always explicitly
demarcated, but which prevents the composition interacting too much with the
edge of the canvas. This has previously been described in certain formalist
accounts as the prevention of pure painterly space being destroyed by its
encounter with the literal space which surrounds it. In addition, the 1917 exhibition was notable not only for the adoption of the triptych form but also for two
other features that characterise Mondrian's subsequent practise. Firstly all three
paintings had recessed frames, i.e. the picture plane stood out in front of the
frame which retained its purpose of forming a border but could no longer be read
as a window. Once again modernist theory has an explanation for this phenomenon, describing it as the assertion of the autonomy of the object whereby the
viewer can no longer ignore the flatness of the picture plane by imagining the
painting to be a deep space behind the edge of the frame. The second new feature of the 1917 works is the texture of the paint surfaces themselves. From this
point on Mondrian began to apply paint to the canvas in horizontal and vertical
strokes so that perpendicular relationships were not only represented by lines
and planes but embedded in the very paintwork.[18] All of these elements would
suggest that Mondrian was both literally and metaphorically framing his painting
with the rhetoric of autonomy.

During his enforced sojourn in the Netherlands Mondrian had focused his
greatest attention on producing a lengthy written account of his conception of
abstraction. He originally conceived this text, *De Nieuwe Beelding in de schilderkunst*
(The New Plastic in Painting), as a book, but it was to become a series of articles in
the very first issues of De Stijl. *The New Plastic in Painting* is a fascinating text not
least because it names an as yet unrealised product. What we think of as the first
properly Neo-plastic paintings were not made until after Mondrian returned to Paris
in 1919. The war years, which he spent in the Netherlands, were difficult for him,
personally and professionally, but they are the crucial ones of transition and the subject of much scholarship.[19] Not only was Mondrian between cubism and abstraction,
he was also between two sets of ideas: the theosophical explanation of natural phe-
nomena and the fully fledged theory of Neo-plasticism. By the later 1920s he was to
extend this theory from being specifically about painting to incorporate all realms of
human life. It is my opinion that Mondrian developed the theory of Neo-plasticism
to challenge and overcome theosophy while also seeking to address the new audi-
ences he came into contact with. This can be highlighted by further discussion of the
triptych exhibited by Mondrian in the Stedelijk Museum in 1917.

One clear explanation for Mondrian's use of the triptych format in 1917 is
simply as a response to Van der Leck. Mondrian produced a visual commentary on

Composition 1916 no.4 and suggested that Van der Leck had no need to retain any reference to the mine and the miners. This correlates with Mondrian's hope to use a photograph of his paintings at the exhibition to accompany the first installment of *The New Plastic in Painting* in the first issue of De Stijl. Here his article would be competing with a reproduction of another recent Van der Leck painting, *Composition no.5*, and the latter's article *De plaats van het moderne schilderijen in de architectuur* (The Place of Modern Painting in Architecture).[20] As it turned out Mondrian could not use the photograph due to difficulties with attaining a clear reproduction. It is worth considering, though, how it could have been read alongside his text, which is his first clear formulation of a theory of abstraction, typified by the following extract:

> Painting is capable of consistent intensifying and interiorizing of its plastic means without overstepping their limits. The new plastic in painting remains pure painting: the plastic means remain form and colour – in their greatest interiorization; straight line and plane colour remain the pure means of painting.[21]

The other prominent feature of Mondrian's text is repeated reference to duality, be it in traditional philosophical terms such as mind and body, or artistic ones such as colour and form. The theory of Neo-plasticism states that painting, above any other form of human activity, has the ability to reconcile these dualities. Already present in the very first instalment of *The New Plastic in Painting* is Mondrian's idea that painting can overcome the tragedy of modern life by surmounting the opposition of subject and object. In his view, the 'new man' would develop from the 'new vision' promoted by abstract art, the composition of which bridged both the variable (subjective, individual) and invariable (objective, universal). Such thinking is extremely difficult to read across to a triptych format where we are obliged then to read the two compositions in colour, A & B, in opposition to each other and then resolved into *Composition in Line*. This is clearly not the case. Whatever Blotkamp is able to read into the hanging concerning the material and the spiritual, the scheme does not add up visually because the larger central painting was not placed in such a relationship to the pair which flanked it.

The emphasis I am giving here to the visual success of Mondrian's hanging experiment is derived from his own constant accentuation in *The New Plastic in Painting* of the ability of painting to make the situation of modern man visible in a way that nothing else was able to. Moreover, he understood this process of visualisation as distinct from one of symbolisation.[22] The criticisms drawn by *Evolution* at the time of its exhibition in 1911 were predominantly based around its attempt to give symbolic form to theoretical content with one writer going as far as to mock it as a representation of the 'Theosophical Graces'.[23] Just as telling was the review in a national newspaper which commented that 'its intention could be put into words far more precisely'.[24] That Mondrian never repeated the mode of representation he had adopted for *Evolution* says enough about his dissatisfaction with its achievements. The return to the triptych form in 1917 must mean that he felt that he had solved the problems *Evolution* had thrown up and devised a means of visualisation that functioned in a non-symbolic fashion. I would suggest therefore that we reconsider the second aspect of the 1917 hang which referred back to *Evolution*, namely raising the central painting above those on either side. In the earlier work this arrangement distinguished the central image as the climactic moment. All the panels were of a similar format, represented identically sized figures and could otherwise have been mistakenly read in a sequence left to right. As I mentioned above, I do not find the literal reading of *Compositions in Colour A & B* as material to *Compostion in Line* as spiritual at all convincing. However, the height to which the latter was raised above the others is exceptional. From the installation photograph it is possible to estimate the height the three paintings were hung based on their known dimensions. The bottom edge of *Composition in Line* would have been about 1.6 metres from the floor, an average eye line that runs through the centre of the two smaller paintings on either side. As Els Hoek has cleverly argued this gives the spectator an upward-gazing attitude towards the central painting which mimics that of the central figure in *Evolution*.[25]

Evolution had attempted to represent a female figure arriving at spiritual illumination. Reading the three panels in sequence, left, right and centre, her head is represented tilting slowly upwards and her eyes are rising from the material world towards some form of higher knowledge. Transferring this role from painting to spectator is a clever reversal which not only implies a different way of approaching art but an altered relationship between object and viewing subject. It should be noted that Mondrian's discovery of the role of the spectator occurred at the same time that he was assimilating the ideas of the 'christosophist' Mathieu Schoenmaekers, whom he had met in 1915. As I described earlier, Laren, where Mondrian lived from 1914–19, was the centre in the Netherlands for 'alternative' thinkers. Schoenmakers had joined Mondrian at regular soirées held by a farmer's wife who brought together artists, writers, musicians and intellectuals.[26] When Van Doesburg visited Mondrian in Laren for the first time in February 1916, he wrote later to Anthony Kok that:

> I have the impression that v. Domselaer [a composer] and Mondriaan are in the grip of Dr. Schoenmaekers' ideas. He has just published a book on 'Plastic Mathematics.' Schoenmaekers' basis is mathematics. He regards mathematics as the only purity; the only pure measurement of our emotions. That is why, according to him, a work of art must always have a mathematical foundation.[27]

The book that Van Doesburg referred to was the recently published *Beginselen der Beeldende Wiskunde* (Principles of Plastic Mathematics). Mondrian drew much of the vocabulary of Neo-plasticism from this source, beginning with the term *nieuwe beelding* itself. Also to be found in the text is extensive reference to dualisms such as internal and external, representation and expression, horizontal and vertical which predominate in Mondrian's early writings. Schoenmaekers termed himself a 'christosophist' to indicate his peculiar mixture of Christianity and theosophy. A former Catholic priest, he declared his thought to be 'thoroughly catholic and at the same time thoroughly anti-church and especially anti-Roman. . . . I am more catholic than the Roman church, more catholic than the Pope.'[28] Schoenmaekers has been repeatedly mentioned in previous literature as a source for Mondrian, but what has seemed to go amiss in these discussions is the real substance of his theory. The central thesis of *Principles of Plastic Mathematics* is that thought cannot exist independent of perception. Taking mathematics as his key example, Schoenmaekers describes how abstract ideas need to be visualised in order to be truly understood. At a very early stage in the book Schoenmaekers rejects the idea of meditation. In his view we cannot become totally present to ourselves but always need an object of contemplation.[29] By the end of the book he proposes his catholic mathematics as an antidote to the protestant over-emphasis on inwardness.[30]

We can quickly appreciate the significance of Schoenmaekers' ideas for the emergence of Neo-plasticism. The gaze of the central figure of *Evolution* had been totally without focus. Turning away from visible reality, the figure is depicted achieving a state of inner self-awareness. The *Pier and Ocean* series had adopted this gaze and represented it as the view from a fixed point out into the undifferentiated, in this case the pulsing waves of the sea. The arrival of abstraction involved a reversal; the view towards nowhere became the view *from* nowhere. If the raising of the centre painting at the *Hollandsche Kunstenaarskring* exhibition gave the spectator a position to adopt, it came with the realisation that the viewing subject no longer determined this position from his subjectivity but was moved at the behest of the object. While it may be contested that fixed-point perspective had similarly constructed an ideal viewing position, the notion of perspectival projection had previously permitted the spectator the fantasy of being its origin.

The second significant aspect of Mondrian's encounter with Schoenmaekers is the latter's interest in the relation between writing and the visual. As has become clear, during his time in the Netherlands during the First World War, Mondrian gave more and more attention to the written word and had originally conceived *The New Plastic in Painting* as a book.[31] Schoenmaekers tackled this situation directly in *The Principles of Plastic Mathematics* where he commented that:

> How is it that many modern fine artists come to talk and write about their work? – A new insight into relative objectivity is growing strongly in present day humanity. This new insight must first be stated in words which can broadly explain the natural circumstances. Then our culture will perceive anew the relativising of it in fine particularities of life. And then a new fine art will expose its observation . . . without words.[32]

For Schoenmaekers, abstraction was just the art form that would express the modern situation without any need for further development or explanation, and his interest in visualisation is the key to the emergence of Neo-plasticism. The notion that a visual event does not need any representational content was Mondrian's big discovery in 1917. His attempts to put his ideas into writing from

1915 onwards demonstrated the gap between theory and practice, but also his difficulty freeing himself from an audience still stuck in a symbolist discourse. Thus
when he read the introductory sections of *The New Plastic in Painting* to the local
lodge of the Theosophical Society in Laren at the beginning of 1917, it was greeted
with incomprehension. By the end of the year Mondrian had also severed his links
with Schoenmaekers. His agreement to publish *The New Plastic in Painting* in De
Stijl, rather than as the book he originally intended, shows that he thought he had
found a sympathetic readership who would comprehend the eradication of symbolism that he was performing at the time. Certainly many parallels can be drawn
with Van der Leck and the process of 'decomposition' he was engaged in. As
Mondrian stated in the final issue of De Stijl, he readily responded to Van der
Leck's 'exactness', that is to say his unsentimental, anti-mystical approach, despite
rejecting the figurative residue in the latter's paintings. Significantly though, we
have seen how Mondrian's concern to locate the spectator maintained a connection
between abstraction and the human figure; abstraction as opposition to figuration
was not Mondrian's concern in 1917, nor was is that which gave De Stijl its critical
impetus. This point can be best expressed by reference to a rather unusual painting
he completed in 1918, a self portrait commissioned by a major patron and close
friend, Salomon Slijper (Figure 6).

Slijper, an Amsterdam estate agent, had met Mondrian in 1915 after seeing some
of his paintings exhibited in Laren. The two struck up an instant rapport and by
the end of 1917, when Slijper moved into a property in Blaricum, they were in
regular contact. While Slijper seems to have been almost exclusively interested in
Mondrian's pre-cubist naturalistic paintings, and often commissioned copies of
the older works from him, he began to collect all kinds of paintings from the artist.
The *Self Portrait* that Mondrian made for him cleverly integrates the old and the
new by placing a rather conventional depiction of the artist in front of one of his
latest, abstract, paintings. While this painting within the painting does not appear
to correspond directly to any particular known work of the time, its general size
and format is kin to the series of *Compositions with Colour Planes* initiated in 1917.
Mondrian posed himself in the foreground wearing a dark suit. Correspondence
between Mondrian and Slijper around this time frequently makes mention of a
suit, and it seems that Mondrian gave the painting to Slijper in exchange for it.[33]
Both men were keen dancers and Mondrian was especially concerned to have a
decent outfit to wear to the regular outdoor dances held at the Hotel Hamdorff in
Laren during the summer. At these events he performed his 'geometric' dance style
in front of his fellow artists, friends and locals.[34] Maaike Middelkoop recalled:
'Dancing was a very serious occupation for him. He danced bolt upright, with his
head slanted upwards and made "stylised" steps.'[35]

In the self portrait Mondrian is less dynamically posed but there are some compositional tricks which link together his figure with the geometry of the background
painting. On the left-hand side, the bottom edge of the internal painting is ambigu-
ously represented as either framed or resting on a shelf (or perhaps an easel). The

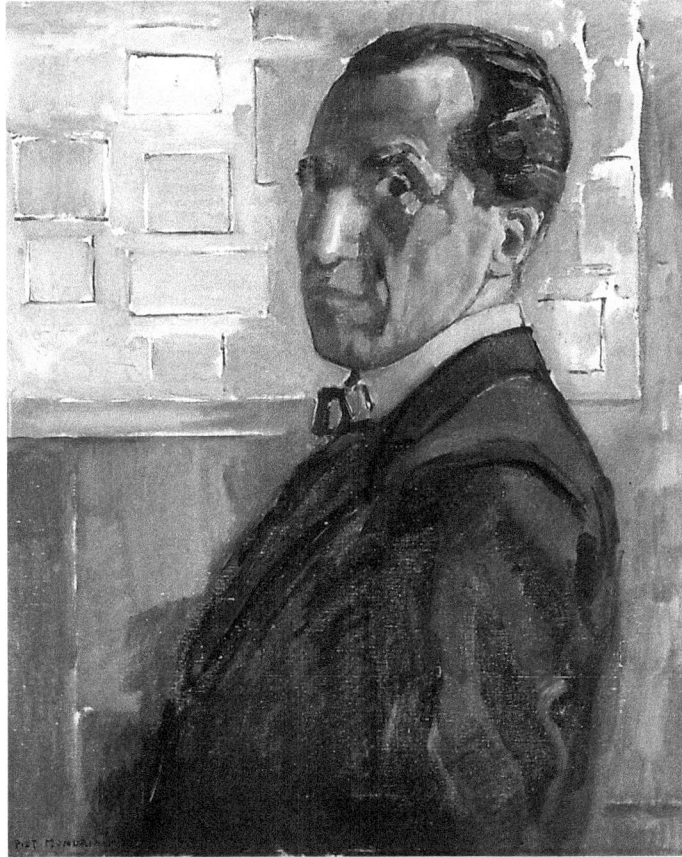

6 Piet Mondrian,
Self Portrait, 1918

line formed here, which exactly bisects the canvas on the horizontal axis, meets the figure of Mondrian at the level of his collar into which the frame/shelf runs. This line has the effect of separating his head from his body. The juncture of internal frame and bow tie also occurs at the very centre of the canvas. Above it we are shown Mondrian's face against the backdrop of his abstraction, an effect which could be read as enforcing the old symbolist distinction between mind and body. Indeed the dark suit tends to negate the body, as it does in much seventeenth-century painting. Yet, as Mondrian's head turns to engage us, we are lead to consider the right-hand side of the canvas where such dualities are far less clear. The frame which so clearly divides up space on the left-hand side disappears, the upper and lower portions of the canvas interact with each other and the tones are carried over from one area to the other. The art object is represented dissolving into the environment. As it does so, it demands a new type of embodied spectator and undermines old certainties.

Once again I have argued against an understanding of abstraction as the pursuit of essence. Even in the case of Mondrian, it is clear that the modernist rhetoric of autonomy was being accompanied by something very different. He used the model provided by Van der Leck to pick apart the symbolist vocabulary he had inherited and produced a mode of visualisation clearly distinguishable from the attitudes of inwardness, meditation and self-sufficiency he had tried to give form to in the *Evolution* triptych. As much as he appeared to be closing painting down to a limited set of intrinsic elements, he was in fact opening it out and formulating a new mode of spectatorship.[36] If desired, we could call these two aspects modernism and avant-garde. In whatever way we choose to term them though, clearly one does not necessarily precede the other.

As a final comment, I would like to draw attention to a source for the *Hollandsche Kunstenaarskring* triptychal arrangement that has so far gone unnoticed. While Mondrian's three paintings hung in their unusual arrangement in the Stedelijk Museum, not far away could be found a very similar installation in the living room of Johanna van Gogh-Bonger, widow of Theo van Gogh. Three of the orchard paintings Vincent van Gogh had made as decoration for his brother Theo's apartment in 1888 were hanging there. Van Gogh-Bonger displayed these works as a triptych, true to Vincent's wishes. Following a drawing he made in a letter, the vertical format *Peach Trees in Blossom* was placed between the horizontal pair *The Pink Orchard* and *The White Orchard*. While it is unknown if Mondrian ever saw the inside of Van Gogh-Bonger's home, he would have had every chance to read the edition of Van Gogh's letters which she published in 1914, where this configuration is described. Given that the pair *Composition in Colour A* and *Composition in Colour B* were more than likely based on the image of a blossoming apple tree, the comparison becomes even more convincing. The final context this reference gives us for the emergence of Neo-plasticism, therefore, is the decoration of the private interior. The triptych, for all its religious connotations, was relocated in a domestic setting, forging a connection between exhibition space and the home which I explore more fully in later chapters. This might well explain some comments Mondrian made to Van Doesburg shortly after the *Hollandsche Kunstenaarskring* exhibition opened. Responding to some observations about the colours of his paintings, Mondrian wrote:

> As to the blue, you are right too, though the light in Suasso [Stedelijk Museum] seems to change the colour values. In my – too small – studio the effect was different. It is much of a technical question: I feel that my work should be made on location and in connection to a location. I also regard my work as the new decorative art, in which the pictorial melts together with decorative.[37]

Mondrian's description of Neo-plasticism, in its nascent form, as a type of installation art, is undoubtedly connected to the discourse of monumental art which predominated in Dutch modernism. As with Van der Leck's concept of 'decomposition' we are given yet another description of the dissolution of easel painting, here described as melting into decoration. While Mondrian did not immediately follow through his idea of site-specific painting, Van Doesburg and Huszár were directly exploring   how   abstract   art   could   be   placed   within   an   architectural context. I shall now turn to the early attempts to locate abstract painting within three dimensional space to explore how the application of colour served to expose unexpected figural concerns within modernist architecture.

Between Christmas and New Year's Eve 1916 Van Doesburg accompanied Huszár on a visit to the Kröller-Müller collection in The Hague where they were able to see her latest purchases, such as Mondrian's *Composition 10 in Black and White* of 1915 (which Van Doesburg had extensively described in a review when it was first exhibited) and Van Doesburg's own *Composition 1 (Still life)* of 1916. The reason for their visit and the work that most excited them was, however, Van der Leck's *Mine Triptych*. In the following year both Van Doesburg and Huszár would make frequent use of Van der Leck's notion of 'decomposition' and investigate the possibilities for a new monumental art based on the opposition between painting and architecture that he had also formulated. More than any of the other artists involved with De Stijl, Van Doesburg and Huszár collaborated with the architects Oud, Wils and Van 't Hoff on a wide range of projects contributing anything from colour designs for interiors to stained glass, tiling, mosaic and furniture. To take one example, a stained-glass window designed by Van Doesburg for a house built by Wils in 1917, we can quickly see how Van der Leck's example was closely followed.

The window in question, titled *Stained-Glass Composition IV* (Plate 1), was installed in the stairwell of the De Lange house in Alkmaar. The frame into which it was placed was three metres high and vertically divided into three separate panes, adding yet another triptych to my narrative. This gave Van Doesburg the perfect opportunity to utilise Van der Leck's *The Mining Business* and *Mine Triptych* as his model, although it is far more difficult in this case to deduce a naturalistic basis for his composition. A contemporary sketchbook shows that Van Doesburg was making numerous figure studies of urban types falling broadly into two categories: workers (mainly dockers and bargees) and entertainers (musicians and dancers). A previous stained-glass window of comparable design, installed in Oud's Villa Allegonda in Katwijk in 1917, appears to have been based on the motif of a young girl knitting on a dockside. *Stained-Glass Composition IV* is slightly different in that it is comprised of two units of different proportions and configuration. Whether these might have been originally conceived as a musician and a dancer, or represented work and play, is not deducible. Having adopted these units, Van Doesburg reflected or rotated them to create what appears to be a random composition but one that is actually derived from a sequence of highly contrived symmetries. Significantly, the predominant axis used for both reflection and rotation is a horizontal line which exactly bisects the window. As in Van der Leck's *The Mining Business*, Van Doesburg restricted vertical movement (which would have been architecturally logical given the staircase location) by giving the centre compositional priority. Moreover, while there is also a degree of reflection across the vertical axis, the central window does not correspond to it and disguises it. The effect produced was, as Van Doesburg mentioned in his correspondence, to release the colour planes from the structure of the window so that they seemed to float in space.[38] As in Van der Leck's paintings, this effect relied on a background, be it white, black or transparent, creating a sense of boundlessness around the sharply delineated foreground colours.

In his stained-glass work of 1917 Van Doesburg repeatedly explored ways of reducing a motif to a few basic lines and planes. He experimented with ways of combining the structural framework of a window with his compositional strategies to test the relation between pictorial space and the surrounding architecture. As the year progressed, so the motifs Van Doesburg adopted became more and more dynamic: from the girl by the harbour to skaters and dancers. As we have seen, in *Stained-Glass Composition IV* rotation and reflection take priority over reduction as the prime determinants of the composition. By the end of the year Van Doesburg had designed a second window for the Villa Allegonda, *Stained-Glass Composition V*. As Oud commented in an article on Van Doesburg's stained-glass work, qualities of rhythm had replaced all other concerns and had overcome 'the *set* harmonic element'.[39] When promoting his diagonally composed *elementarist* paintings in later years, Van Doesburg introduced a concept of dissonance into his art theory, using this musical analogy to describe how abstract art could be seen as anti-naturalistic. Dissonance was already present at this early stage, however, where Van der Leck's 'decomposition' was adapted to an anti-harmonic, disruptive aesthetic. As I now want to describe, the gradual eradication of the figure from Van Doesburg's compositions, or its fragmentation into abstract rhythms and counter-rhythms, was connected to the reformulation of architectural space currently engaged in by the architects associated with De Stijl, a point that can be made by reference to at least one more triptychal composition.

The triptych in question was placed directly in an architectural project, the building known as *De Vonk* (The Spark) (Figure 7), designed by Oud in 1917 in the small coastal town of Noordwijkerhout. The building functioned as a holiday home for the *Leiden Volkshuis*, an organisation concerned for the welfare of factory workers.[40] In 1917 funds were raised for the construction of a house on the coast, six miles west of Leiden, where young women could find respite from the daily grind of their working lives. The director of the *Volkshuis*, Emilie Knappert, knew Berlage through her involvement with the Dutch socialist movement and originally approached him with the commission. Unable to take on the project himself, Berlage recommended Oud who began working on the building during the summer of 1917. Following the model of monumental art established by Berlage, Oud enlisted Van Doesburg to collaborate and asked the artist to design colour solutions for the floors, doors, corridors and stairwell in the interior of the building. For the first time, Van Doesburg also had the opportunity to create something for the exterior of the building and devised a scheme of three glazed brick mosaics which were placed at the entrance. He set his three panels above the doorway and to the left and right hand sides, taking an almost identical structure to Mondrian's experimental triptych at the *Hollandsche Kunstenaarkring*.

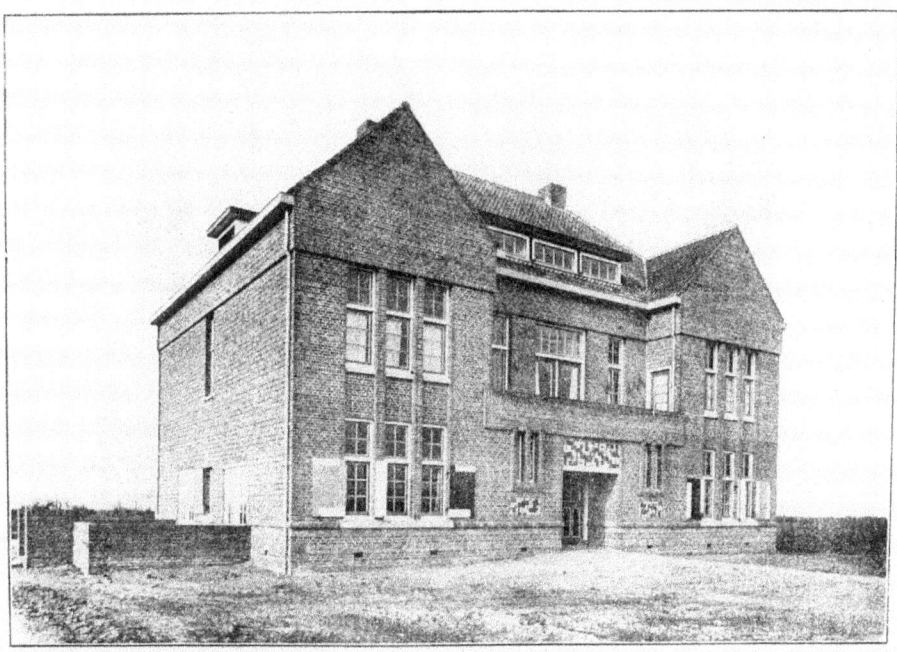

BIJLAGE II VAN „DE STIJL" TWEEDE JAARGANG N° 2. VACANTIEHUIS TE NOORDWIJKERHOUT
ARCHITECT: J. J. P. OUD. (ZIE OOK BIJLAGE I EN BESCHRIJVING IN HET VORIGE NUMMER.

7 J. J. P. Oud, *De Vonk*, Noordwijkerhout, 1917–19

While *De Vonk* enjoys a privileged status as the first example of the extensive collaboration that was to be the hallmark of De Stijl, it has often been criticised for the conservative nature of its architecture, the two most notably backward looking aspects being its rigid symmetry and use of traditional pitched roof. Oud's plans show how he developed the building around a central staircase that was, according to Jane Beckett, 'the pivot of the whole plan . . . both formally and conceptually'.[41] Featuring built-in benches, the staircase was conceived as a transitional area between the privacy of the upstairs bedrooms and the communal activities of the ground floor. Residents could sit on the benches and engage in individual pursuits such as reading or sewing without being either separated from the rest of the occupants or disturbed by them. By separating the walls of the staircase from the independent walls of the passageways that flank it, Oud had attempted to create a free-flowing space that broke up the traditional load and support structure of the building, with light from the stairwell passing through to illuminate otherwise dark corners. The exterior decoration also followed a recognisable model; coloured brick had been used extensively in Dutch architecture for exterior decorative detail and the tympanum was a favoured spot. Just as in the interior, though, distinct modifications to this unexceptional medium presage the direction De Stijl was to take.

Where traditional brick decoration tended to be arranged in an easily recognisable pattern, or series of patterns, Van Doesburg's innovation was to make his
designs appear completely random. The size of the bricks he used was in ratio to
those used in the main structure but the orientations, while always orthogonal, do
not seem at first sight at all predictable. To date the most accepted explanation of
this feature has been Van Doesburg's desire to counteract the symmetry of Oud's
facade. As with Van der Leck's rejection of the role of decorator, Van Doesburg
was hereby refusing the role of art as architectural ornament. His colour designs
are not supplementary to the structure but in conflict with it. While this is an
acceptable interpretation of the *De Vonk* designs, of more interest are the later
deductions of concealed symmetries within the panels. Using reflection and rotation, Van Doesburg managed to conceal order subliminally within disorder. As
Allan Doig notes, this is not totally out of keeping with the building:

> [T]he ground plan is strongly axial, but allows controlled variation on either side of
> the axis in response to function. The abstract compositions above and on either side
> of the main entrance emphasise the axial structure, recognise the variation within the
> symmetry, and respond to the material by accepting the implied grid of brick con-
> struction as the geometric determinant of the composition.[42]

As such, Van Doesburg's panels are a good preparation for what to expect in the
interior of the building.

Beckett further suggests that Van Doesburg's panels play a symbolic role, in
that the largest and most significant one above the doorway is placed below the
balcony of the director's office. The side panels come much lower down (about
half the height of the doorway) and produce a clear hierarchical structure. Given
the role of the staircase as signifier of the educational aspirations of the *Volkshuis*,
the invitation to raise one's gaze upon entry is also not out of keeping with the
plan. Yet to recall the earlier discussion of Mondrian's triptych and the new
demands it made of the spectator, what we are faced with in *De Vonk* is in fact the
disintegration of the symbolic and the pictorial. In Mondrian's installation, the
placement of the central painting well above a normal sight level was to transfer
the upward (but now focused) gaze of the enlightened figure of the *Evolution* triptych to the gallery visitor. As we saw, Mondrian's discovery of the role of the spectator parallelled his theorisation of the demise of the painting as window on the
wall. Modernism, understood as the assertion of the object status of painting, was
seen as developing a new type of visual experience where the new subject and
object relations created by modernity were brought into play. Transposed into
architectural terms, the relation between spectator and space is deconstructed in a
similar fashion.

De Vonk is characterised by the contrast between an extremely inflexible symmetrical plan and a central space (the stairwell) that promoted intermingling,
mixed used, confusion of private and public. On its own, the facade did little to
suggest these ambitions. The glazed brick panels suggest how the facade had to be

rethought if a truly modern architecture was to develop. For the triangular placement of the panels is in fact carefully planned to correspond exactly to the diagonals created by the pitched roof and their proportions are tied firmly to the size of
the windows. In my view it is asking a lot of them that they be read as undermining the symmetry of the facade, especially given that the smaller pair reflect
each other exactly (as did the colours Van Doesburg painted the window shutters).
Rather, by relating the glazed brick decoration so closely to the constructive elements of the architecture, Van Doesburg called into question the proper relation
between the two. If architecture, as Oud was intimating in the design of the
hallway in *De Vonk*, should emphasise spatial rather than planar elements, then
the status of the wall (and its decoration) had to alter. The coloured bricks, with
their irregular orientations, show how a wall can be read not as load and support
but simply as a textured surface. As I mentioned in the Introduction, Berlage had
promoted the ideas of Gottfried Semper in the Netherlands and what we see
appearing in the formative stages of De Stijl is closely related to the German
architect's *Prinzip der Bekleidung* (Principle of Clothing). Semper had argued that
the first human habitations were created by hanging textiles. Interior and exterior
space were registered not by stability of construction but by pattern. By placing
decoration prior to building Semper sought to recover architecture as an art and
promote it as 'the clothing of space'. The use of colour in architecture promoted
by De Stijl consistently opposed the idea of mere decoration. Rather, colour was
seen to be a significant constructive element that permitted space to become visible.[43]

In the interior of *De Vonk* Van Doesburg designed a tiled floor which covered
the intermediary spaces of the hallway on the ground and first floor, and also
devised colour schemes for the doors. As Oud later recalled:

> Here it may be the first time that the doors in a room were in actuality painted dif-
> ferent colours to one another in order to create a spatial colour composition. Moreover,
> a dissolving activity should begin thereby, in contrast to the restrictions that belong to
> the nature of architecture. The rigidity of construction could become cancelled out
> for the eye by means of the dissolving effect of this way of painting.[44]

In this commentary Oud transfers Van der Leck's idea of 'decomposition' in
painting to the encounter of painting and architecture in which construction
undergoes the process of 'dissolution'. He also adopts Van der Leck's view of
painting and architecture as oppositional. Oud's expression that painting cancels
out construction 'for the eye' suggests a form of illusion or disguise. According to
Semper's principle of clothing, art plays the same role in architecture as textiles do
on the human body. It can both reveal and conceal, draw attention to certain points
and mask others. Once again we see how abstraction maintained a concern for the
figure, in this case the idea of architecture as body and painting as clothing. The
connections between architecture as space and the human figure were made far
more explicitly by Jan Wils.

While *De Vonk* can be seen as the prelude to the De Stijl environment, it remained anchored in an Arts and Crafts tradition which, as Beckett has pointed out, gave emphasis to the hallway as a site for decoration.[45] The transitional area from outside to inside is the most carefully managed space in many late nineteenth-century buildings and can often be read in terms of a barrier between the chaotic modern world and the refuge of the individual subject. Oud's concentration on the staircase at *De Vonk* showed his interest in opening up space within an otherwise unremarkable block-like construction, but for some this did not go far enough. In 1918, when work on *De Vonk* was nearing completion, Jan Wils published a long article in a new journal, *Levende Kunst* (Living Art), entitled *De Hall in het Woonhuis* (The Hallway in the Home) which elucidated the connections between the decorated entrance space and the Arts and Crafts tradition. The article specifically mentions Norman Shaw and Charles Voysey in this context and also discusses Herman Muthesius's mediation of this tradition into continental Europe through his 1903 book *Das englische Haus* (The English House). However, the article concludes that this is a tradition which has run dry and should no longer be continued. It had been overtaken by Frank Lloyd Wright's organic architecture, whose flowing spaces made the extravagant hall redundant. Such grand reception areas were not only wasteful of space, Wils argued, but also encouraged the division of the ground plan into separate rooms. Given the attention Oud and Van Doesburg were devoting to the entrance of *De Vonk* it is understandable that Wils would wish to publish this article outside of De Stijl.

The following issue of *Levende Kunst* carried another article by Wils on *De Nieuwe Bouwkunst: bij het werk van Frank Lloyd Wright* (On the New Architecture: about the work of Frank Lloyd Wright). This, Wils' first major statement about the American architect, contained illustrations of the Unity Temple, Larkin Office and Oak Park Studio among others, as well as translating sections of Wright's 1914 text *In the Cause of Architecture*. It combined simple exposition of Wright's techniques with impassioned rhetoric about its capabilities for social integration and utopian transformation:

> It is the painters such as Picasso and Mondrian, the sculptors such as Archipenko and Brancusi, architects as Olbrich and Behrens in Germany, Berlage and van 't Hoff here, Sullivan and Wright in America, who, with all the individual differences in their work, reveal the new time which has come, the new time for the new man! Therefore we rejoice . . . and only one wish animates us: to build together with all our powers towards that young building of beauty in the new society.[46]

It is uncertain precisely how Wils came into contact with the other De Stijl collaborators. Between 1914 and 1916 he worked as a draughtsman in Berlage's architectural office in The Hague, while the latter was in the employ of Müller & Co. He could easily have met both Oud and Van der Leck via this position. As a member of the *Haagsche Kunstkring* (Hague Artists' Circle) he was also likely to have encountered Huszár. In January of 1917 he exhibited with the *Leidsche Kunstclub De Sphinx*

(Leiden Art Club, The Sphinx), a group set up by Van Doesburg and Oud in the spring of the previous year. Over the following years Wils worked extensively first with Van Doesburg and then Huszár on a range of commissions.

At the time he wrote the article quoted above, Wils was engaged in the renovation of a café-restaurant, *De Dubbele Sleutel* (The Double Key) in Woerden, midway between Leiden and Utrecht (Figure 8). Although he had to work around an existing ground plan, Wils did his best to apply Wrightian ideals concerning the organic arrangement of spaces and their expression on the exterior of the building. Van Doesburg was also called upon to supply the colour schemes for both interior and exterior which he once again conceived of as 'destructive', although on this occasion there was no dominant axis to contend with. In fact Wils ensured that the building projected in rather unexpected ways.

From the front and the side, *De Dubbele Sleutel* created a certain pyramid effect, as the building had a central core rising to three storeys. However, the café enjoyed an advantageous corner location and seen from this angle the most imposing line is that created by an exceptionally large chimney breast which rose along the side wall and extended far beyond the roof line. Offset from the centre, this dramatic vertical held the structure in place visually, while a sequence of horizontals shifted outwards away from it, culminating in the projecting garages to the rear and left. As the chimney sinks into the ground floor, its relation to the surrounding space becomes more difficult to read. This is because the space it met there was the part of the building Wils tried to keep as open as possible, namely the seating area of the café. In fact the hearth hardly projected into this area at all, an effect enhanced by the bay on the right-hand corner which gave the room an L shape. On the other side, windows opened out onto a terrace so that the hearth must have looked almost like a free standing object suspended between the interior and exterior of the building. On the opposite wall was a serving counter, the colouring of which Van Doesburg paid great attention to. Disregarding normal considerations for soiling on a surface against which people would often lean or brush, Van Doesburg painted a large white horizontal band on it, bordered by narrower strips of orange, green and blue. The vertical framework of the counter and the counter surface itself were painted black. As in *De Vonk*, the composition actually seems as much derived from the nature of the architecture as in opposition to it; painting articulated space rather than eradicated construction. The white band on the counter front created a strong horizontal line which mimicked those on the exterior while also emphasising the recession behind the counter.

Wils and Van Doesburg also designed special furniture for the café (which does not seem to have been used) where similar structural/anti-structural effects were attempted. The chairs, for example, were based on a simple cubic shape and made using flat planks of wood. The legs of the chairs were rotated so that on each side one leg was visible in profile and one face on. The effect was made more complex by reversing this orientation above and below the leg supports. Not only was verticality severely challenged by a series of powerful horizontal shapes but even more

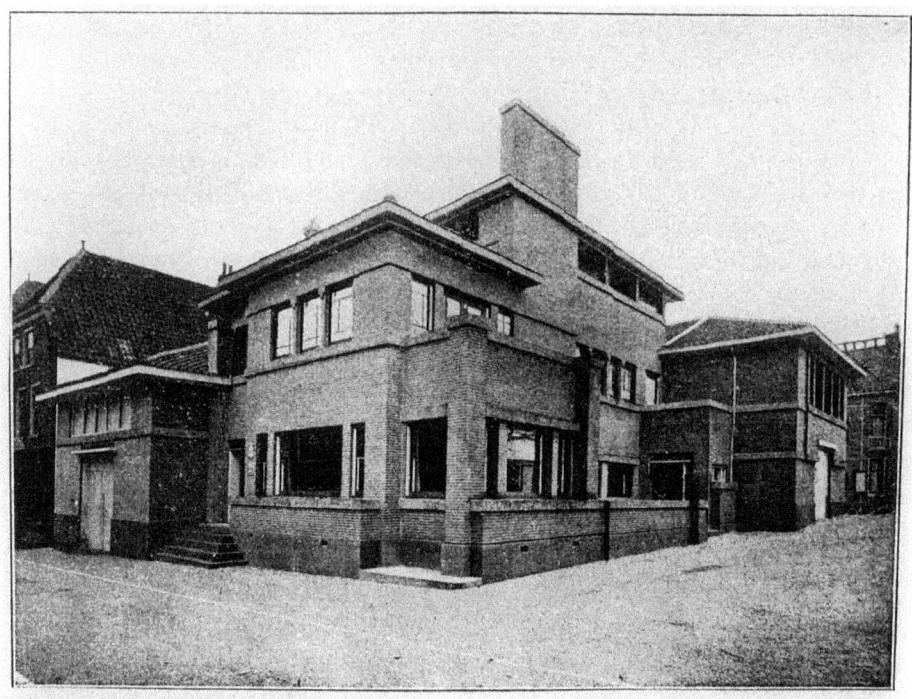

BIJLAGE X VAN „DE STIJL" TWEEDE JAARGANG No. 5, HOTEL: „DE DUBBELE
SLEUTEL' WOERDEN, ARCHITECT JAN WILS.

8 Jan Wils, *De Dubbele Sleutel*, Woerden, 1918

novel was the transformation of a traditionally symmetrical object into an asymmetrical one. In the case of something like a chair, which by implication suggests
the attitude of a body, asymmetry is quite disturbing. Wils was well aware of these
concerns and described them in a fascinating (and underrated) article in De Stijl
titled *Symmetrie en Kultuur* (Symmetry and Culture), where he accounted for the
passage towards asymmetry with an almost Darwinist view of evolutionary development from basic life forms to the human.

   In *Symmetry and Culture*, Wils dismissed any kind of Ruskinian 'return to
nature' and described the history of cultural forms as the passage from simplicity
to complexity, from the symmetrical to the asymmetric. In Wils' schema the Greek
temple is likened to a plant stage and the Gothic cathedral to higher animals. Only
modern architecture has the potential to be fully human and, like the machines
which are the ultimate products of modernity, be least concerned with symmetry.
Man, according to Wils, is the least symmetrical animal, therefore his environment
should reflect this. We may contend that the human figure is bilaterally symmetrical and therefore we have a preference for structures which are balanced across
the vertical axis. However, Wils is describing not a figural characteristic but a

relationship to space – the human being distinguishes left from right in a way that animals do not. Bilateral symmetry may be of comfort to the static body but in movement this symmetry is completely destroyed.

Just as the theory of the autonomy of painting asserts certain intrinsic aspects of the medium such as the picture plane, primary colour, significant form and so forth, so a similar set of terms grew up in connection to architecture: emphasis on volume, eradication of ornament, propriety of materials. As with the rhetoric of abstraction in De Stijl, so the modernist architectural discourse held within it an avant-garde moment. The asymmetric, mobile architecture Wils dreamed of took architecture away from the production of perfected, isolated objects and moved it towards the production of space.

I began this chapter by considering a series of triptychs in which issues such as symmetry and balance had some significance. From Van der Leck through to Wils, these qualities were repeatedly undermined. Asymmetry, decomposition and dissolution constantly occur as key terms for understanding the contemporary relevance of the objects produced in the formative moments of De Stijl. Similarly it has become strikingly apparent that the emergence of abstraction which was so heavily promoted in De Stijl did not by any means dispense with reference to the figure. Van der Leck's process of starting with a recognisable motif and then systematically eradicating it was the most influential practice at the time. The total absence of figuration in Mondrian's paintings was supplemented by a revised role for the spectator. When placed in an architectural setting, abstraction encouraged an anthropomorphic view of architectural space as bodily form. Some of these points can be summarised by considering in conclusion to this chapter the activities of Vilmos Huszár, whose central role in the formulation of De Stijl is still being recovered.[47]

As a Hungarian of Jewish origin, Huszár is an unlikely representative of what has so often been mistakenly seen as a Calvinistic idiom. He had been resident in the Netherlands since 1906 and was well embedded in the artistic life of The Hague by the time he met Van Doesburg in 1916. He knew the influential critic Bremmer very well and was an active member of the *Haagsche Kunstkring*. He was enrolled in this organisation under the architecture and applied arts section, no doubt because of the long standing interest he had in stained glass. Van Doesburg was highly influenced by Huszár in his stained-glass work of 1917 and 1918.

I have already mentioned the visit Van Doesburg and Huszár paid together to the Kröller-Müller collection in 1916 to see Van der Leck's *Mine Triptych*, and its significance for Van Doesburg's subsequent compositional practice. Huszár was also encouraged to begin working in a similar way to Van der Leck with the decomposition of the human form evidenced by such paintings as *Compositie II (De Schaatsenrijders)* (Composition II (The Skaters)) of February 1917. Like Van der Leck, Huszár chose a familiar genre scene from the history of Dutch painting and put it through a process of dissolution. By the summer of that year Huszár was at

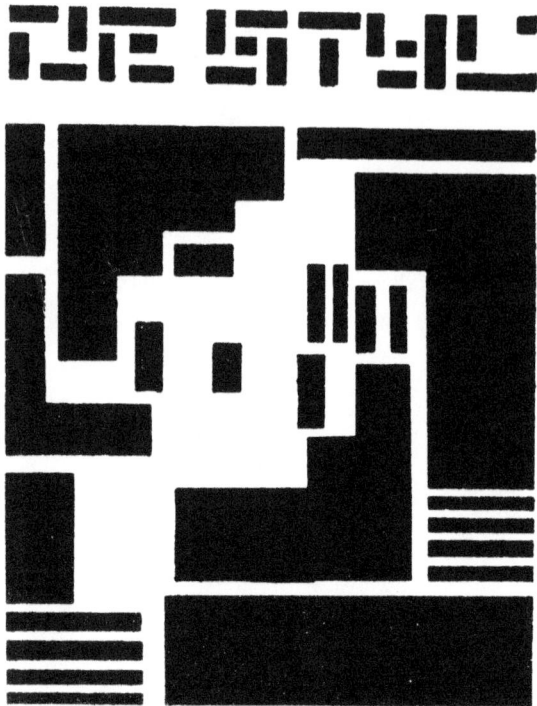

MAANDBLAD VOOR DE MO-
DERNE BEELDENDE VAKKEN
REDACTIE THEO VAN DOES-
BURG MET MEDEWERKING
VAN VOORNAME BINNEN- EN
BUITENLANDSCHE KUNSTE-
NAARS. UITGAVE X. HARMS
TIEPEN TE DELFT IN 1917.

9 Cover of De Stijl, 1917

work on two intriguing projects. The first was for a logo for De Stijl, the second a strange mechanical shadow puppet. In both designs important questions about figure and ground relationships are worked out but also the definition of a modern visual aesthetic is developed.

When De Stijl was published in November 1917, the front cover carried the title and a small vignette (Figure 9). The letters which make up the words De Stijl were formed from brick-like blocks reminiscent of Van Doesburg's *De Vonk* designs and the vignette was a simple, one-colour woodcut. For many years authorship of the typography was ascribed to Van Doesburg but it seems just as likely now that Huszár conceived the entire look. The vignette itself is intriguing for the manner in which it juggles figuration and abstraction. Sjarel Ex comments that: 'No contour of a figure or an object is recognizable; the interaction between the planes and the interstitial space appears to dominate.'[48] But it is clear to me that there are two figures present in the image. The logo is closely related to a drawing and painting Huszár made in the same year of a head in profile. In an identical manner, Huszár creates one profile from the semi ziggurat in the top left, which forms the shape of the head and hairline. Three small blocks below it form and ear, eye and mouth. The mouth is shared by the second profile which looks upwards from the lower right. The four stripes in bottom left, lower right and top right are all identical to the abbreviated form used by Huszár to represent hands in comparable works of the time. The intertwining of the two profiles can possibly be read as the reconciliation of art and architecture taking place in the realm of abstraction. At the same time we are faced with the literalised rendition of a multiple viewpoint.

In the summer of 1917, at the same time as he was working on the De Stijl logo, Huszár initiated a project of much greater complexity. A letter from Van Doesburg to Anthony Kok announces that 'he [Huszár] has invented something totally new, moving painting'.[49] It seems that some futurist-inspired experiments Huszár had been engaged in since the beginning of the year had taken a novel, theatrical form. He had begun the construction of a shadow puppet which could be mechanically controlled to produce a limited variety of poses (Figure 10). The first public performance of the *Mechanische Dansfiguur* (Mechanical Dancing Figure) came in 1920, and later, during the Dada tour of the Netherlands in 1923, it was shown to packed halls all over the country. A brief description of it appeared at this time in Kurt Schwitters' journal *Merz*:

> This mechanical dancing figure appears on a white screen as a shadow. The planes on the figure are transparent, green and red. Movement is directed from behind, below the stage, by means of keys (of which there are ten) connected to the figure by strings. Each movement is determined in a right angle and nothing is accidental. The head can also turn to the right. The aim is to produce a plastic composition with each pose and incorporate the intermediary space of the background into the composition.[50]

Using the rather primitivising format of the Javanese shadow puppet, Huszár placed the De Stijl idea of abstraction in a contemporary cinema context. The audience was seated in a darkened room, watching the movements of a figure against a brightly lit screen. With a narrative framework abolished, all that remained were the jerky actions and static poses of an animated painting. By allowing the head to turn, Huszár disrupted the bodily symmetry that the flat projection of the human figure may have otherwise encouraged. The mechanical dancing figure was the literal representation of the modernised vision put in practice by Mondrian and Van Doesburg.

All the attempts of later commentators to interpret De Stijl as an outpouring of Puritan feeling or the search for mystical explanations for existence have obscured its striking modernity. The role that abstraction played in the months I have described in this chapter was not as a restorative or as an escape from a chaotic situation

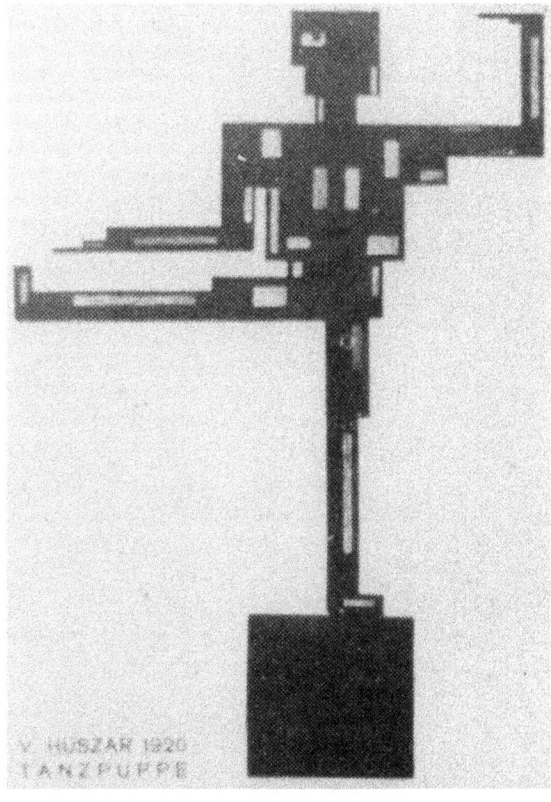

10 Vilmos Huszár, *Mechanical Dancing Figure*, 1917–20

but as a participant in a process of destruction, a shattering of the image of the world. As I shall go on to describe in the subsequent chapters, this aspect of modernism found its place in a series of environments where fine art and mass culture collided. We began this chapter with stained glass and ended with a virtual cinema experience. *Gemeenschapkunst* was unravelled and transformed into critical language to address a new situation, and utopia became a dynamic rather than static experience.

Notes

1   De Stijl did not introduce abstraction to the Netherlands, however. Several artists, such as Jacob Bendien and Janus de Winter, had produced abstract paintings, largely inspired by Kandinsky, from 1913 onwards.

2   The first manifesto is quite specific that 'the new plastic art' was at the forefront of cultural development. See 'Manifest I of De Stijl', *De Stijl* 2: 1 (November 1918), pp. 236–9.

3   Mark Cheetham, *The Rhetoric of Purity: Essentialist Theory and the Advent of Abstract Painting* (Cambridge: Cambridge University Press, 1991).

4   See Rudolf Oxenaar, 'Bart van der Leck tot 1920: een primitief van de nieuwe tijd' (Ph.D. dissertation, Rijksuniversiteit Utrecht, 1976), pp. 112–13 and Cees Hilhorst, 'Bart van der Leck', in C. Blotkamp (ed.), *De Stijl: The Formative Years* (Cambridge MA and London: MIT, 1986).

5   Rudolf Oxenaar observed in his thesis on Van Der Leck that the painting could have been a window, i.e. that it was designed to give the effect of stained glass but also respond to an architectural setting. See Oxenaar, 'Bart van der Leck tot 1920', p. 112.

6   Hilhorst, 'Bart van der Leck', p. 159.

7   'De gedachte dringt zich op dat Van der Leck het harde bestaan van de mijnwerkers heeft geassocieerd met het voorbeeld bij uitstek van menselijk lijden, de passie van Christus. De mijningang, waar alle aandacht naar toe wordt getrokken, is aangeduid door een T-formig kruis samengesteld uit een zwarte horizontale en een gele verticale streep. De mijn kan geïnterpreteerd worden als een moderne versie van de plaats van de kruisiging, de Calvarieberg, onderwerp van taalloos vele triptieken, vooral uit de 15de en 16de eeuw.' Carel Blotkamp, 'Triptieken in Stijl', in T. van Kooten (ed.), *Bart van der Leck* (Otterlo: Kröller-Müller Museum, 1994), p. 157.

8   Blotkamp, 'Triptieken in Stijl', p. 157.

9   Blotkamp, 'Triptieken in Stijl', p. 157.

10 A. J. Barnouw, *Holland under Queen Wilhelmina* (New York and London: Scribner's Sons, 1923), p. 150.

11 Hilhorst, 'Bart van der Leck', p. 165.

12 'Geen illusie, geen stemming, geen fascinatie, maar een monumentale klaarte staat mij voor den geest.' Bart van der Leck, letter to Mrs Kröller-Müller 18 October 1916, quoted in Van Kooten (ed.), *Bart van der Leck*, p. 47.

13 Lieske Tibbe, *R. N. Roland Holst 1868–1938: Arbeid en schoonheid vereend, Opvattingen over Gemeenschapkunst* (Amsterdam: Architectura and Natura, 1994), p. 88.

14 Bart van der Leck, 'De plaats van het moderne schilderijen in de architectuur', *De Stijl*, 1: 1 (1917), pp. 6–7.

15 Adriaan Roland Holst, *Bezielde Dorpen* (The Hague: Bakker, 1957).

16 Blotkamp, 'Triptieken in Stijl', p. 159 and also in Carel Blotkamp, *Mondrian: The Art of Destruction* (London: Reaktion Books, 1994), p. 101.

17 Blotkamp, *Mondrian: The Art of Destruction*, p. 101.

18 See Joop Joosten, 'De sporen van het penseel: Textuur in het werk van Mondriaan', *Jong Holland*, 9: 4 (1993), pp. 44–9.

19 The recent appearance of the Mondrian *catalogue raisonné* has marked the climax of a lifetime's work by Joop Joosten in putting together the transitional period, see Joop Joosten and Robert Welsh, *Piet Mondrian: Catalogue Raisonné* (New York: Abrams, 1998). The intellectual parameters of this work were put in place by Joosten's seminal essay 'Mondrian: Between Cubism and Abstraction', in Solomon R. Guggenheim Museum, *Mondrian* (New York: 1971), pp. 53–66.

20 In correspondence with Van Doesburg, Mondrian shows his awareness not only of how he would like his own work to be illustrated in the journal but also how Van der Leck is to be illustrated. Letter from Mondrian to Van Doesburg, 7 July 1917, Van Doesburg Archive, RKD.

21 Piet Mondrian, 'De Nieuwe Beelding in de schilderkunst', translated as 'The New Plastic in Painting', in Harry Holtzmann and Martin James (eds), *The New Art – The New Life: The Collected Writings of Piet Mondrian* (London: Thames and Hudson, 1987), p. 29.

22 One of the most quoted passages from the essay is the following: 'Ancient wisdom represented the fundamental inward-outward relationship by the cross. Neither this *symbol*, however, nor any other symbol can be the plastic means for abstract-real painting: the symbol constitutes a new limitation, on the one hand, and it is *too* absolute on the other.' Mondrian, 'The New Plastic in Painting', pp. 45–6.

23 Blotkamp, *Mondrian: The Art of Destruction*, p. 55.

24 'Slechts vaag is die bij Mondriaan's "Evolutie," al moest de bedoeling daarvan vermoedlijk veel scherper onder woorden te brengen zijn.' Giovanni (J. Kalff) *Algemeen Handelsblad*, 16 October 1911, quoted in Joop Joosten and Robert Welsh, *Piet Mondrian: Catalogue Raisonné*, vol. 1, p. 422.

25 Els Hoek, 'Piet Mondriaan', in Carel Blotkamp (ed.), *De vervolgjaren van De Stijl 1922–1931* (Amsterdam and Antwerp: L. J. Veen, 1996), p. 138.

26 Other regular guests at these events were the composer Jacob van Domselaer and his future wife Maiaike Middelkoop, the writers Martinus Nijhoff and Adriaan Roland Holst. Laren, fifteen miles to the south-east of Amsterdam, had grown ever more popular with artists, since the late nineteenth century, who were attracted to its more varied landscape surroundings.

27 Theo van Doesburg, letter to Anthony Kok, 7 February 1916, Van Doesburg Archive, RKD.

28 'Mijn persoonlijk denken ervaar ik als door-en-door katholiek en tevens als door-en-door anti-kerkelijk en speciaal anti-roomsch. Ik durf met allen nadruk beweren: ik ben katholiker dan de roomsche kerk, katholiker dan de paus.' M. H. J. Schoenmaekers, *Beginselen der Beeldende Wiskunde* (Bussum: Dishoek Uitgeverij, 1916), p. 203.

29 Schoenmaekers, *Beginselen der Beeldende Wiskunde*, p. 7.

30 To this date every interpretation of Mondrian's debt to theosophy has laid stress on the importance of inwardness, rejection of the material world and the development of an inner, non-ocular, vision. See Mark Cheetham, *The Rhetoric of Purity*, p. 50. *The*

New Plastic in Painting makes repeated comments concerning the importance of the interaction of the internal and the external which directly contradict this. The most recent insistence on the significance of Mondrian's Protestant background can be found in Susanne Deicher, *Piet Mondrian. Protestantismus und Modernität* (Berlin: Reimer, 1995), which does not pay attention to the dissident nature of Schoenmaekers' ideas.

31 Joop Joosten and Robert Welsh, *Piet Mondrian: Catalogue Raisonné*, vol. 2, p. 111.

32 'Hoe komt het dan, dat vele moderne beeldende kunstenaars over hun werk gaan spreken en schrijven? – Een nieuw inzicht in het betrekkelijke objectiviteit is krachtig groiende in tegenwoordige menschheid. Dat nieuwe inzicht moet eerst gezegd worden in woorden, die de direct-breede natuurgegevens nieuw verklaren. Dan gaat onze cultuur de relativeering ervan nieuw aanschouwen in fijne levensbijzonderheden. En dan zal een nieuwe beeldende kunst de aanschouwing ervan gebaren . . . zonder worden.' Schoenmaekers, *Beginselen der Beeldende Wiskunde*, p. 53.

33 An undated letter from Mondrian to Slijper (inv. no. 150, Slijper Archive, RKD) mentions, 'Het zelfportret krijg je voor het pak.' (You will get the self portrait for the suit.) Intriguingly the same letter discusses Slijper receiving the *Evolution* triptych and instructions on how to hang it. A letter from Mondrian to Slijper dated 17 December 1916 (inv. no. 152, Slijper Archive, RKD) mentions that the triptych has been sent to Slijper's Amsterdam address. In a subsequent letter dated 4 May 1917 (inv. no. 181, Slijper Archive, RKD) Mondrian describes getting a suit from a tailor in Amsterdam and encloses a copy of a letter to the tailor asking for credit or payment with a painting.

34 'Na afloop gingen wij veelal naar het Hotel Hamdorff, waar Roland Holst zich gewoon en Mondrian geometrisch aan de gezelschapsdans wijdden.' (After dinner we often went to the Hotel Hamdorff where Roland Holst and Mondrian devoted themselves to the social dancing, in a normal and geometric style respectively.) J. Greshoff, *Afscheid van Europa* (The Hague: Nijgh and Van Ditmar, 1969), p. 109.

35 'Dat dansen was een hoogst serieuze bezigheid voor hem. Hij danste rechtop, met zijn hoofd schuin naar boven en maakte 'gestileerde' passen.' M. van Domselaer-Middelkoop, 'Herinneringen aan Piet Mondrian', *Maatstaf* 7: 5 (1959), p. 284.

36 An oft-made observation of Mondrian's later Neo-plastic paintings is that they seem to have both a centrifugal and centripetal force. They can be read as isolated objects but also seem to extend infinitely beyond their boundaries.

37 'Wat het blauw betreft heb je ook gelijk hoewel 't licht in Suasso de kleurwaarden schijnt te veranderen. Op mijn – te klein – atelier deed 't anders. Het is ook maar een technische questie: ik voel zoo, dat mijn werk op de plaats en in verband met de plaats zelf moest gemaakt worden. Ik beschouw mijn werk ook als de nieuwe decoratieve kunst, waarin de picturale met de decoratieve ineen smelt.' Piet Mondrian, letter to Theo van Doesburg, 16 May 1917, Van Doesburg Archive, RKD.

38 'Het is in een woord overweldigend. Het geheel komt tegen de lucht uit. De kleuren compositie staat geheel los in de ruimte.' (It is in a word overwhelming. The whole thing stands out against the sky. The colour composition is completely free in space.) Theo van Doesburg, letter to Anthony Kok, 9 September 1917, Van Doesburg Archive, RKD.

39 J. J. P. Oud, 'Glas-in-lood van Theo van Doesburg', *Bouwkundig Weekblad* 34: 35 (31 August 1918), p. 202.

40 The first and still most detailed description of this project is given by Jane Beckett, '"De Vonk", Noordwijk: An example of early De Stijl co-operation', *Art History* 3: 2 (1980), pp. 202–17.

41 Beckett, '"De Vonk", Noordwijk', p. 208.

42 Allan Doig, *Theo van Doesburg: Painting into Architecture, Theory into Practice* (Cambridge: Cambridge University Press, 1986), p. 63.

43 The discussion of colour in architecture which takes place in De Stijl distinguishes it from the general trend in modernism towards whiteness. It is for this reason that Mark Wigley has only a marginal place for De Stijl in his otherwise intriguing book *White Walls, Designer Dresses: The fashioning of modern architecture* (Cambridge MA and London: MIT, 1995). Nevertheless, I am indebted to this text for the attention it draws to Semper's discussion of clothing in relation to architecture.

44 'Hier mag es wohl zum ersten Mal gewesen sein, daß in Wirklichkeit die Türen in einem Raum untereinander verschieden gestrichen wurden mit der Absicht, eine räumliche Farbkomposition entstehen zu lassen. Außerdem sollte dadurch eine lösende Aktivität einsetzen als Gegensatz zum Gebundenen, das zur Eigenart der Architektur gehört. Die Starrheit der Konstruktion würde durch die auflösende Wirkung dieser Art Bemalung für das Auge aufgehoben werden können.' J. J. P. Oud, *Mein Weg in 'De Stijl'* (1960), quoted by Giovanni Fanelli, *Stijl – Architektuur* (Stuttgart: Deutsche Verlags-Anstalt, 1985), p. 14.

45 Beckett, '"De Vonk", Noordwijk', p. 216.

46 'Het zijn schilders als Picasso and Mondriaan, het zijn beeldhouwers als Archipenko en Brancusi, het zijn bouwkunstenaars als Olbrich en Behrens in Duitschland, Berlage en van 't Hoff ten onzent, Sullivan en Lloyd Wright in Amerika, die met al hun indivi-dueele verschillen in hun werk doen kennen den nieuwe tijd, die gekomen is, den nieuwe tijd van de nieuwe mensch! Daarom verheugen wij ons . . . en slechts één wensch bezielt ons: om allen naar krachten mee te bouwen aan dat jonge gebouw van de schoonheid in de nieuwe maatschappij.' Jan Wils, 'De Nieuwe Bouwkunst: bij het werk van Frank Lloyd Wright', *Levende Kunst*, 1 (1918), p. 210.

47 A 1985 Huszár retrospective at the Gemeentemuseum in The Hague was subtitled 'de grote onbekende van De Stijl' (the great unknown [figure] of De Stijl). The catalogue which accompanied the exhibition did much to rectify the situation but Huszár is still the least recognised of the De Stijl painters outside of the Netherlands.

48 Sjarel Ex, 'Vilmos Huszár', in Blotkamp, *De Stijl: The Formative Years*, p. 93.

49 'Hij heeft iets geheel nieuws uitgevonden, bewegende schilderkunst.' Theo van Doesburg, letter to Anthony Kok, 14 July 1917, Van Doesburg Archive, RKD.

50 'Deze mechanische dansfiguur verschijnt op een vit [sic] doek als schaduw (schim). De vlakken op de figuur zijn doorzichig, groen en rood. De beweging geschiedt van achter onder de plank, door middel van toetsen (er zijn er tien), die verbonden zijn door snaren. Elke beweging is recht hoekig berekend, en er is niets toevalligs bij. Het hoofd kan ook naar rechts draaien. De bedoeling is bij elken stand een beeldende compositie te geven, en de tusschenruimten op het fond in die compositie op te nemen.' Vilmos Huszár, 'Mechanische Dansfiguur', *Merz* 1 (January 1923), p. 13.

2

The monumental image of the city

In the previous chapter I gave a privileged position to the discussion of abstraction in De Stijl both in terms of practice and the appearance in the journal of theoretical articles by the likes of Mondrian and Van der Leck. I concentrated on highlighting the destructive aspects of the vocabulary of De Stijl and indicated ways of imagining its utopian elements as an internal critique of the modernist project initiated by *gemeenschapkunst*. This chapter begins a consideration of the interaction between De Stijl's abstract aesthetic and the process of modernisation in the Netherlands. As shall be shown in a variety of contexts, De Stijl participated directly in the transformation of everyday life. While in several instances the models of the future it threw up were never realised, they frequently made way for others that did. The reorientation of urban planning in the post-war period is one such instance and it is with this topic that I will begin.

The very first issue of De Stijl was dominated by Mondrian's *The New Plastic in Painting* and Van der Leck's *The Place of Modern Painting in Architecture*. The contribution from Oud was no less significant, however. His short article *Het monumentale stadsbeeld* (The Monumental Image of the City) clearly defined the architectural ambitions of the journal and established its target as the total transformation of the urban scene. As we saw in the first chapter, during its formative moments, De Stijl projects were occurring in rather peripheral locations, such as Noordwijkerhout and Alkmaar. Oud did not try to excuse this situation but drew attention to the equal task of a building such as *De Vonk* and modern city planning, namely the achievement of monumentality. By using this term, Oud clearly invoked the tradition of *gemeenschapkunst* and the revival of the monumental arts which was key to it. Oud also mentioned Berlage as the originating force behind the emergence of a modern monumental idiom in the Netherlands. Monumentality was, for Oud, a quality that had little to with size but rather to do with style and could be achieved only when architecture expressed its own means. Describing architecture as 'the art of the definition of space', Oud argued that its role in determining the cityscape was concerned more with the grouping of buildings to create streets than with the layout of streets to create squares on which might be located buildings of monumental proportions. As we shall see, this redefinition of monumentality was to have a major impact on planning and the way that the modern city actually looks.

For Leonardo Benevolo, a prominent historian of modern architecture and planning, the crisis of Baroque urban form apparent in Oud's rejection of the square as a primary structure of city life has a direct connection to the turn away from perspective in the contemporary visual arts. In his book *The European City* he makes a very swift connection between the formal artistic experimentation that led to Mondrian's abstract paintings and the scientific urban planning which emerged at the end of the nineteenth century and gathered pace at the beginning of the twentieth.[1] The type of planning that results in the scale of garden cities, for example, is no longer made from ground level; the viewpoint has moved way above. At the same time Benevolo also comments that the ambition of artists to provide a model of future life can be connected to the growing intervention of public bodies to free large areas in and around cities for development. As he states, 'the design of an overall plan became possible, without the obstacle of property lines' so that 'urban space opened up to a new sort of planning in which there was again a place for artistic culture, itself finally freed of the constraints of the past'.[2] The end result of this convergence Benevolo sees in the *Algemeen Uitbreidingsplan* (General Expansion Plan) of Amsterdam Council, the largest urban development venture to take place in Europe in the interwar period.

Conceived between 1928 and 1934, the Amsterdam expansion took until the 1950s to complete. Instrumental in the design of the plan was Cor van Eesteren who, as I shall describe in more detail later, worked side by side with Theo van Doesburg in Weimar and Paris and was a central participant in the 1923 De Stijl exhibition at Léonce Rosenberg's *Galerie de l'Effort Moderne*. The temptation is great, therefore, to read elements of the General Expansion Plan as De Stijl realised in urban form. What will become clear, however, is the fact that De Stijl was not the sole advocate of modernisation in the Netherlands by any means. Nor did it have sole claim to a utopian position in the Netherlands. The image of the city was a highly contested topic in the period and the antagonistic vocabulary of De Stijl was pitched against clearly defined competitors. The redefinition of monumentality that Oud proposed at the outset of De Stijl was directed specifically against rival architects from Amsterdam, for example.

Another factor in determining the exact correlation between De Stijl and the urbanisation of the Netherlands comes into greater focus when we consider how resistant it has been to the types of analysis now common in the study of modernism. Although De Stijl collaborators such as Wils, Oud and Van Eesteren participated in urban design to a scale only dreamed about by their contemporaries in other European countries, it is extremely difficult to identify De Stijl with any single metropolitan area.[3] Similarly the Netherlands has chosen over the years to project an image of itself as a country of flowers and windmills largely untouched by the concerns of modern life. Yet, for Peter Hall, the region encompassed by the western provinces of the Netherlands is 'one of the world's most complex urban areas' and 'one of the most important city regions of the European continent'.[4] As far back as the 1920s one observer predicted that the Netherlands would become 'the promised land of city planning and housing development'.[5] Population density had already forced the country to become urbanised to a far greater extent than Britain, France or Germany but the conditions which created the great metropolitan centres of London, Paris and Berlin were not replicated.

The dislocation of De Stijl from the pattern of modernisation familiar to scholars of the French or German modernism is exacerbated by the very problem of placing it within any one particular city. However, this lack of location may well be the key to the significance of the city for De Stijl. Where, for example, Haussmann's Paris preserved the importance of the capital city by redefining the city centre and transforming it into a site of recreation and public display, De Stijl left the historic centre virtually untouched and took place on the periphery in a form that can perhaps be read as a suburban, or better as polycentric. Quite distinct from similar modernist groupings, De Stijl did not emerge from a café culture, and was not linked to dealers and studios in particular locations.[6] It is very telling to list where we can find the members of De Stijl during its early years. They were in fact dispersed in a variety of locations: Van Doesburg and Oud were living in Leiden: Mondrian and Van der Leck were both resident in the small village of Laren to the north of Utrecht: Huszár, Vantongerloo and Wils were in The Hague: Van 't Hoff and Rietveld were in Utrecht. There was never any pressure or desire on the part of the original participants, or any subsequent ones, to group together in one city. If anything De Stijl became even more dispersed as time went on and members moved abroad. The only consistent feature is a negative one; the place most obviously missing from this list given above is Amsterdam, then and now the largest city in the Netherlands.

How then can we describe De Stijl from the viewpoint of urban modernity? Where was the thrill of boulevard or the alienation of the crowd? This is what Mondrian would seek when abandoning the Netherlands for Paris and ultimately New York but how was it ever realised by the Dutch at home? The discussion I want to develop will need to use a distinction between the city as understood in this physical, literal manner and the image of the metropolis which emerges at the turn of the century and finds greatest expression in the 1920s. The metropolis was created by the rationalisation of economic and social relations. It placed the Renaissance model of the city as a political order into crisis partly because it was not visible in the same way. As I will demonstrate, De Stijl has the tension between city and metropolis at its heart and it is precisely its initial alienation from Amsterdam that guaranteed its lasting impact in the Netherlands.[7] For in the 1920s the Dutch produced an urban form quite different to anything seen elsewhere before. They realised the creation of a giant conurbation encompassing the provinces of North and South Holland and reaching to Utrecht in the east. The *Randstad* (rim city), as it came to be known, offered a brand new model of a decentralised urban landscape which bound together all of the most important political and cultural centres in the country but left them dispersed, as independent units.

The previous chapter treated the appearance of De Stijl as a sudden confluence of energies which sought to instantly reorder the common language of Dutch modernism. There was space in the journal though for reflection on more gradual processes of transformation. This is a feature of Mondrian's second major article in De Stijl, an experimental text titled *Natuurlijke en abstracte realiteit* (Natural Reality and Abstract Reality), serialised over numerous issues between 1919 and 1920. The article took the form of a three way discussion between a layman, a naturalistic painter and an abstract painter who engage in debate while walking from the country to the city. Over seven scenes their conversation describes a journey from flat landscape into the built environment, to arrive finally at the abstract artist's studio. Over the course of the trip, the abstract painter convinces his companions that the development of abstraction in painting is a necessary consequence of the process of modernisation, here tied firmly to a narrative of urbanisation. The final scene was written following Mondrian's return to Paris and contains his first comments on the realisation of his painterly aesthetic on a grand architectural scale. The previous six scenes have their own fascination, however, in that the sites through which the characters are apparently walking are in fact descriptions of motifs repeatedly painted by Mondrian himself. From the flat landscape already mentioned, the characters then behold a tree silhouetted against a moonlit sky, stars above a beach, a windmill, a house and then a church facade. The deliberate confusion created between reality and its depiction befits the abstract painter's explanation that the real and the visible are not identical. Reading the 'trialogue' one also experiences the sensation that its characters are not walking at all but it is the landscape in front of them which is transforming. From painting to painting, the world changes before their eyes as the natural and rural becomes the manufactured and urban. As such, *Natural Reality and Abstract Reality* is quite an accurate reflection of Mondrian's own circumstances over the years he lived in and around Amsterdam, before his first move to Paris in 1912. During this time he witnessed the initial stages of the expansion of the city Van Eesteren was later to complete. It is well worth briefly considering this period, which was to have a significant impact on the direction taken later by De Stijl.

It is only in recent years that serious scholarship has been directed at Mondrian's earlier naturalistic period but certain features of it have now been well established. The first of these is his interest in the landscape immediately on the edge of Amsterdam. The area he frequented the most, to the south and south-east of the city, was largely comprised of polders (reclaimed land below sea-level) which had been used for many years for a combination of farming and light industry. This unspectacular landscape was seen at the time as an undesirable location for residence by the wealthier middle classes. By the end of the nineteenth century they were taking advantage of improved rail connections to move out of the city centre either eastwards beyond the polders to the more picturesque landscape around Hilversum, or westwards to the dunes beyond Haarlem. The waterways crossing the polders were also of a functional rather than recreational nature and had been part of Amsterdam's vital trade connection to the Rhine. As more of that traffic was now on its way to the fast-expanding port of Rotterdam, the small industries reliant on the flow of goods and services through these channels were in decline. It was far from a rural idyll but in fact a landscape created from a set of economic circumstances that had now been superceded by steam power and the railways. A section of this polder land close to the city boundary repeatedly visited by Mondrian was an area of known as *Schinkelbuurt* (after the Schinkel canal running through it), a place where old and new technologies had come face to face. Mondrian's painting *Wingless 'Paltrok' Mill in the Schinkelbuurt* of 1898 (Figure 11) had previously been interpreted by Michel Seuphor as a view of a village. It has in fact been identified as one of many traditional mills that used to occupy the area on the outskirts of the city which were used for sawing timber.[8] The mill that Mondrian depicted had already lost its sails and fallen into disrepair and was to be completely demolished soon after he painted it.[9] Encroaching in the background are the chimneys of the new factories which had spelled its fate. Between the viewer and this distant threat, lies a strip of small houses around the old mill, no doubt also in danger. These old mills attracted Mondrian for more than their bold shapes. They were an easily rec-

11 Piet Mondrian, *Wingless 'Paltrok' Mill in the Schinkelbuurt*, c. 1898

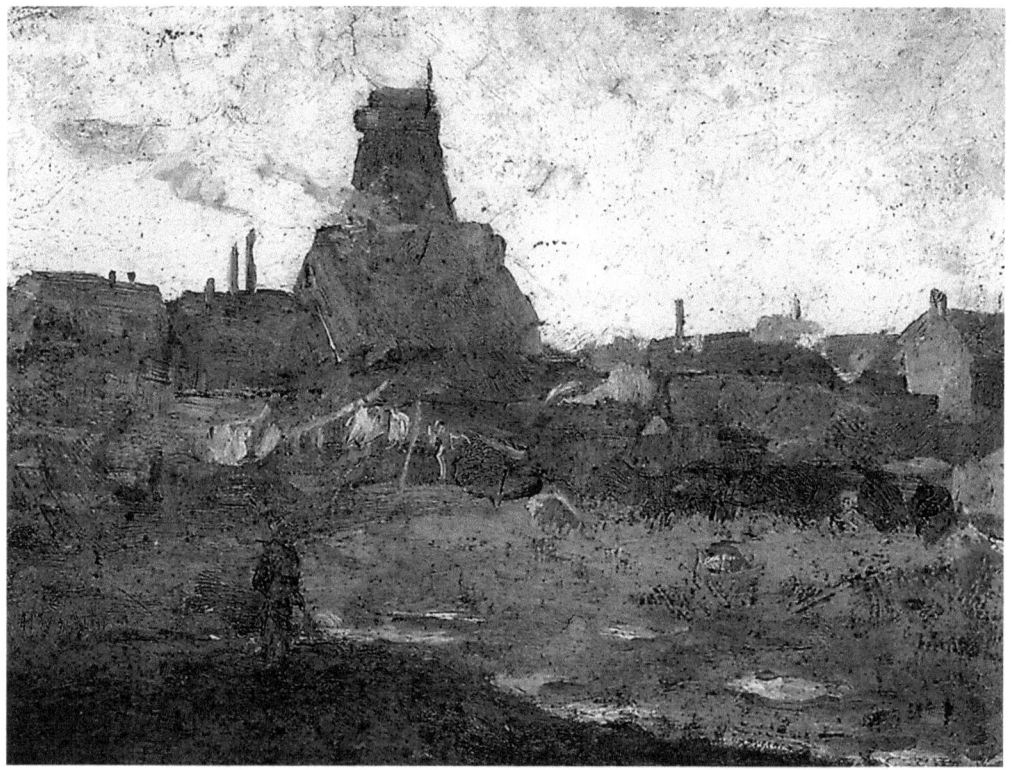

ognisable image of a way of life being eradicated by the pressures of modernisation. He regularly used to meet friends (and perhaps lived for a short time) in
another derelict site, 'The Mill without Sails', close to the Amstel river just outside
the city boundaries.[10] Once again, what had only shortly before been an integral
part of the local economy was now a playground for artists and other disaffected
types.

For most of his Amsterdam years, Mondrian occupied numerous studios and
rooms predominantly located in the south of the city. Several were in the notorious
District YY or *De Pijp* (The Pipe) as it is still commonly known to this day, a nick-
name derived from its dark narrow streets and mix of the poorest classes, students
and prostitutes. Ruysdael Straat and Albert Cuyp Straat, two of Mondrian's
addresses at this time, may sound pleasant enough, and suitably artistic, but they
formed part of a series of developments hastily thrown up by speculators on the
edge of the city to profit from a fast-expanding population. From this part of
Amsterdam Mondrian was able to quickly access the polder land and on his bicycle
could cover a considerable range in a day trip. As Robert Welsh has pointed out
these forays away from the city were quite distinct from an escape into the pas-
toral.[11] Although Mondrian lived with poverty and deprivation on his doorstep, his
view of the countryside did not conform to the sentimental depiction of rural life
practised by the so-called Hague School artists with whom he has often been associated. The repeated characteristics of Mondrian's paintings of the early 1900s
include use of brownish tonalities, adoption of a frontal viewpoint, often close up
and looking upwards, and a choice of subjects representative of a process of transformation. According to Welsh, these can all be identified with an aesthetic developed by Amsterdam artists such as George Breitner and Willem Witsen, who
applied it to the depiction of the gritty side of modern city life. There were very
few occasions when Mondrian chose to represent factories, dock sides or commercial activity, as Witsen and Breitner often did, but by viewing the polders through
their eyes he very clearly revealed the manmade nature of the local landscape.

The confusion of the rural and the urban in Mondrian's naturalistic period has
considerable resonance with the subsequent emergence of regional planning in the
Netherlands. Before we can move on to this issue, however, it is necessary to
describe a little further the peculiar manner in which Amsterdam expanded in the
early twentieth century. For it was the poor conditions of the very type of accommodation Mondrian occupied at this time which resulted in legislation that would
radically alter the architectural landscape of the entire country. In 1901 the government drew up a law which made local authorities directly accountable for the
standard of new buildings constructed within their boundaries. It also obliged
every council with a population over 10,000 to draw up a plan for expansion and to
revise the plan every ten years. This law, which came into force in 1902 also provided local authorities with massive powers of expropriation intended to alleviate
habitual construction problems in the fast-expanding parts of the Netherlands.
Much of the land on which new building was taking place was reclaimed and quite

obviously had extremely sandy soil. Councils were entrusted to ensure that land was properly prepared for construction before releasing it to developers. Not only did this do much to quell unwanted speculation, it encouraged the emergence of consortiums and housing associations, many of which still exist to this day.

The demand for an Amsterdam expansion plan was also prompted by the difficulty of making alterations to the medieval structure of the city centre. Haussmann-style demolitions were impeded by the network of canals, whose function was much reduced but whose proliferation made changes inconvenient. The addition of grand new public buildings was taking place, then, outside of the centre. The process was begun with the completion of the Rijksmuseum in 1883, soon to be followed by the Stedelijk Museum a few hundred metres down the road. The Rijksacademie and Concert Hall were also erected in the same district, accompanied by new recreational spaces such as the Museumplein and Vondelpark. The problem faced by Amsterdam was how to negotiate the meeting of this grand cultural development and the slum areas bordering it.

The architect to whom Amsterdam city council turned to assist in solving their problems was Berlage. He was already engaged in the construction of the Stock Exchange building on the Damrak, the largest modern building to be constructed in the city centre after Cuypers' Centraal Station, and had been working on plans to prevent the space in between the Museumplein and the Vondelpark suffering unsympathetic infilling. Impressed by his ideas, the municipal authority commissioned him to plan a much larger expansion of the city and find a solution to housing problems in Amsterdam without continuing the concentric rings of canals which formed its seventeenth-century structure. However, his plan shocked the public by announcing the redundancy of the picturesque canal house, calling instead for residential massing and the construction of large blocks of buildings. While this may have been acceptable for low-cost social housing, part of Berlage's commission was to provide the conditions to prevent the continuing exodus of the middle classes to the countryside, which they could now easily reach by train.[12] Berlage's plan integrated large green spaces, elegant walks and substantial boulevards with areas of high-density housing in order to produce a compromise between the demands of the different classes destined to occupy the area. The cultural ambience of the district was to be reflected in the 'artistic' nature of buildings themselves and is preserved in the names of the streets which continued to be named after seventeenth-century Dutch artists.

Berlage's Amsterdam expansion plan was the first major piece of modern urban design in the Netherlands and followed a model of the city as a work of art derived largely from the writings of Camillo Sitte. His *Der Städte-bau nach seinen künstlerischen Grundsätzen* (City Building According to Artistic Principles) of 1889 was a great influence on Berlage, who saw his task as the creation of the image of a grand city. His tree lined boulevards replaced the picturesque canal street, supplanting its fragmentary nature with unified masses. The charm that today's tourist still finds along the canals is produced by the constant variation amongst the houses which line them and the play of reflections in the water. Berlage compensated for the loss of visual interest by making his roads turn in unpredictable ways, revealing in the process his lack of concern for function. Sitte had highlighted the aesthetic problem created by straight roads that, although more practical, the loss of a focal point in the middle distance can be disorientating (as can be experienced in the 'canyons' of New York's grid plan, for example). Berlage took on board Sitte's appreciation of Baroque planning where such vistas are closed off by significant buildings and the city dweller is always drawn towards something. In the early stages his plan ran into practical difficulties, however, as it encroached beyond the administrative boundaries of Amsterdam council. Conflicts with neighbouring authorities, such as Watergraafsmeer and Nieuwe Amstel, were not to be fully resolved until after the First World War, when the Netherlands took the next step in city planning, before many other European countries, and began regional planning. By that time Amsterdam had returned its first Socialist-dominated council chamber and this left-wing group, under the enlightened leadership of F. M. Wibaut, would give the plan a very particular inflection.

Under the 1902 Housing Act municipal authorities had become responsible for the quality of new buildings erected within their jurisdiction and were required to draw up a building code.[13] Amsterdam went further and instituted a *Schoonheidscommisie* (Aesthetic Committee) which controlled the actual look of the buildings to an unprecedented degree, way beyond their structural integrity. Mediating between newly formed housing associations which had sprung out of the Housing Act and a particular group of architects who would later become known as the Amsterdam School, the socialist council oversaw the rapid construction of some of the most spectacular social housing to be found anywhere in the twentieth century. Using traditional materials such as brick and tile, combined with energetic forms derived from Art Nouveau, the architects created what Maristella Casciato has described as 'the true appearance of "the city within the city"'.[14] Where only some years previously Mondrian and his friends had congregated in 'The Mill without Sails' now stood *Takbuurt* (which translates literally as Tak District and was named after the socialist councillor P. L. Tak), a conglomeration of one thousand six hundred dwellings in a thirty-acre site comprised of six different housing associations and including Michel de Klerk and Pieter Kramer's extraordinary *De Dageraad* (The Dawn) estate with its waves of brick (Figure 12).

What Casciato means by 'the city within the city' can be felt by anyone who approaches *De Dageraad*. Its two grand corners are situated right at the centre of the development and overlook a small square. Their imposing height gives an incredible feeling of containment but their oblique setting on the corner does not make them oppressive. The rest of Amsterdam is cut off from view but, following the model proposed by Sitte and Berlage, the effect is not one of alienation. In fact, the opposite sensation is produced, one of inclusion within a large organic form. Throughout *Takbuurt* can be found squares or courtyards, often decorated with statues or plaques celebrating significant figures of the socialist movement which

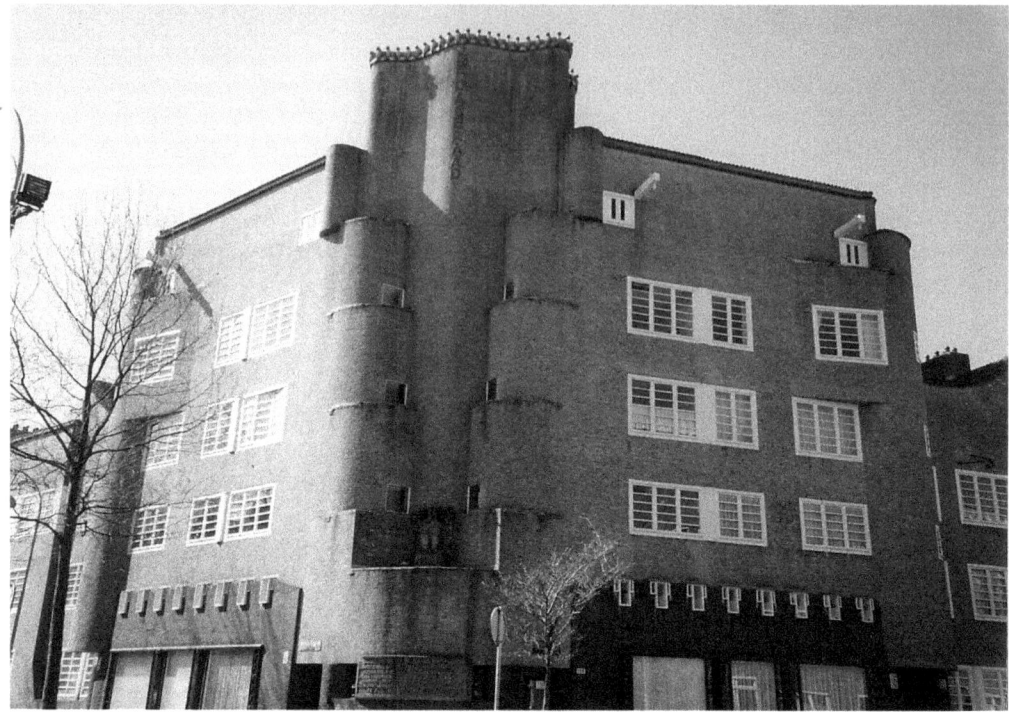

12 Michel de Klerk and Pieter Kramer, *De Dageraad*, Amsterdam, 1923

imply activities of congregation and social interaction outside of the family home. In fact, from the exterior of *De Dageraad*, for example, it is impossible to guess how its apartments might be divided up into separate units as the eye is kept wandering over the lively brick surfaces. This was one very important way of resolving the problem introduced by Berlage of linking the visual experience of the canal street with the modern form of the housing block. It was predicated on the idea of urban space as continuity, linking the old and the new but in a modern monumental fashion. Thus *De Dageraad* is positioned away from the waterside but conjures up the feeling of waves in its flowing shapes. It also peculiarly combines forms reminiscent of turrets with those derived from farm buildings, linking together the old city walls and the surrounding countryside. As with many buildings of the Amsterdam School, *De Dageraad* tried to reinvent a type of pictorial architecture which expressed the changes brought about through modernisation but did so through a comforting historical vernacular.

As stated above De Stijl was not included within this pattern of development in Amsterdam although the timing of its foundation, 1917, coincides with the period of greatest building activity the city had seen in two hundred years. The *Manifesto of De Stijl*, proclaiming the dawning of a new era in which the individual would be reconciled with the universal, contains nothing which at first sight appears contradictory to the ambitions of the Amsterdam council to provide an environment in which community spirit would win out over urban isolation. The collective activity of painter, architect, designer which formed the backbone of De Stijl policy in its early years was also practised by the Amsterdam School, which also shared a reforming vocabulary derived from the Arts and Crafts tradition. Yet, during the 1920s the two would become the most bitter rivals who saw virtually no common ground between themselves. De Stijl criticisms of the Amsterdam School often made accusations of individualism (the expressionistic nature of certain buildings), decadence (disregard for cost) and nostalgia. What I want to demonstrate is that these criticisms are also tied up with a larger argument regarding the city itself. The 'city within a city' engineered so successfully by the socialist council of Amsterdam could not have existed without a notion of a political constituency. In the De Stijl metropolis, as we shall see, such forms of belonging are eradicated.

Returning now to Oud's *Het monumentale stadsbeeld* (The Monumental Image of the City), we can see now where his argument is derived from. Oud's concern for the development of a modern monumental urban form sprang directly from Berlage's Amsterdam expansion plan and the activities of the Amsterdam School therein. In fact Oud went so far as to suggest that the Amsterdam School had departed from Berlage's scheme to the point where 'the monumental has been corrupted into what is essentially decadent'.[15] The future of the cityscape was dependent on the design of the modern housing block, according to Oud, and on 'the acceptance of modern materials'. The consequence of these new requirements in Oud's view necessitated the disappearance of the square as a planning unit in favour of the street; his article envisions long horizontals (emphasised by flat roofs) as the basic components of the urban scene. As we just saw, *De Dageraad* was constructed around a square at which point it reached its greatest vertical thrust. It was this old-fashioned concept of monumentality, derived from largely from size, as well as a symbolic language, that Oud set his stall out against. As we shall see, it was very difficult at the time to imagine what De Stijl proposed in its place. If the title of Oud's article emphasised a concern for what a city actually looked like, he was reluctant to go beyond vague suggestions of 'rhythmic arrangement of planes and masses'. The search for the monumental image of the city was in fact to become the undoing of the city of monuments, a process we can see emerging in Oud's projects for the *Woningdienst* (Housing Department) of Rotterdam Council.

Like Amsterdam, Rotterdam had a fast-growing population drawn by its expanding port which, prominent on the Rhine delta, had benefited from the expansion of Germany's industrial belt in the Ruhr. Also like Amsterdam, Rotterdam Council had cleared large areas for housing projects. In contrast to the exuberance of the Amsterdam projects, Oud's designs at Spangen, Tusschendijken, Oud-Mathenesse and Kiefhoek were far more restrained, regular, repetitive even. Economy was far more of a determining factor for Oud, who was keen to test the possibilities of standardisation although initially he was forced to use conventional materials. He relied on subtle geometric patterns in the arrangement of windows and doorways to relieve the monotony of flat facades reduced to minimal decorative appeal (Figure 13). As we consider the Rotterdam developments in turn, it will become clear how they departed ever further from Berlage's 'city as a work of art'.

Spangen was a polder in the north-west of Rotterdam which by the time of Oud's appointment had already been laid out to accommodate large perimeter housing blocks. Several architects were involved with the project and the building most discussed in the architectural press was a large block of experimental gallery maisonettes designed by Michel Brinkman. This was the first appearance in the Netherlands (if not Europe) of the 'street in the air', where access to apartments was gained from raised walkways. In comparison to Brinkman, Oud's designs for blocks I, V, VIII and IX at Spangen were far more regulated and geometric. The site was bordered on one side by a canal known as the *Spaanse Bocht* (Spanish Curve) because of its elegant shape. This created problems for the architects who wished, for the sake of economy, to standardise the individual units as much as possible but were hindered by the irregularity of the ground plan caused by the curved shape. Where permitted, Oud designed extensive runs of identical units and closed them round an inner court. Other blocks had been devised to make novel use of the

13 J. J. P. Oud, Spangen block VIII, Rotterdam, 1920

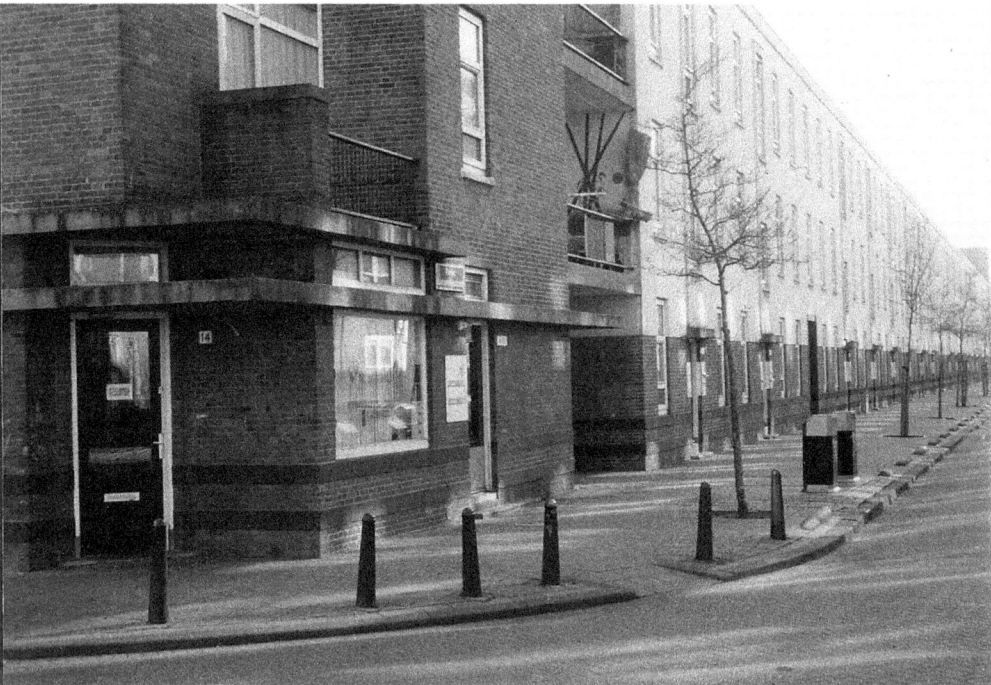

courtyards for schools but this does not appear to have been to Oud's taste. Compared to his colleagues, Oud was much keener to separate public and private space. It is interesting to compare two commentaries on Spangen in *Bouwkundig Weekblad* (Architectural Weekly), first by Brinkman and then Oud, to see how their emphasis changes.

In his account Brinkman carefully explained the rationale behind the gallery blocks in terms that were almost entirely concerned with social use. He discussed installing lifts to allow bakers' carts to reach the galleries and sell their wares along the streets in the air. He also mentioned his decision to run a street through the centre of the perimeter block to allow easy access (including police visibility) 'so that nobody will have the idea that they are living in a little courtyard. Also the concept of tenement housing is eliminated because you can clearly see everybody's front door from the public street.'[16] For Brinkman, then, the modern housing block could provide its residents with a sense of their own property by providing a separate front door for each dwelling while dispensing with the closed nature of the traditional house.

In contrast, Oud began his article with an image of an interior, a photograph of a show apartment decked out with Rietveld furniture. He did not discuss at all how these spaces were actually to be used, but concentrated on the aesthetic problems of unifying the district, down to the level of individual dwellings. Street facades were not to call attention to themselves but rather be a mechanism for binding together the units with the larger urban fabric.[17]

In accordance with De Stijl principles of collective activity, Oud commissioned Van Doesburg to design colour schemes for his housing blocks. On the exterior this included the painting of doors and window frames and in the interiors the painting of walls and the design of fireplaces. Responding to the demand of the *Manifesto of De Stijl* that its aesthetic be realised within an everyday environment, these colour solutions are the first attempt to map the principles of abstract painting onto the urban scene.[18] Just as Oud was attempting to use as many standard items in the construction of the blocks, so Van Doesburg sought to use a fittingly simple range of colours. The painting of interior walls was intended to dispense with the need for wallpaper and the use of similar colours on the interior and exterior woodwork gave a sense of the continuity between them. The difference from the Amsterdam School is clear. There, as we have already seen in one example, housing blocks were monumental but highly individual, distinguishable from each other by moments of architectural bravado. Each development was intended to develop its own sense of belonging. Not only did Oud reduce variety to a minimal level but hardly thought about expressing the perimeter block as a social unit. He attempted to relate the individual dwelling to a far larger object which in his mind went beyond the immediate exterior. The rhythms of the facades emphasised by Van Doesburg's colour patterns are difficult to experience by standing at a certain point. They have assumed proportions which relate to passage, movement, the street as bearer of traffic rather than element of social

unification. In terms of urban planning, we have moved from the chain, house –
street – square – town, to cell – district – city.

The collaboration between Oud and Van Doesburg is interesting to follow as it
combines debates concerning standardisation and the rationalisation of housing
problems with questions concerning the realisation of abstract painting in an architectural context and the role of the avant-garde in general. In 1918 Oud had
declined to sign the *Manifesto of De Stijl* because he felt its rhetoric was too extreme
(and too open to interpretation as communist), and that it may have jeopardised his
career. Within the space of two years he was applying some of its principles to the
housing of thousands of working-class families and permitting Van Doesburg, who
had no architectural or design training, to decorate the interior and exterior of these
imposing blocks and all at public expense. However, in 1921 the collaboration
between the two men came to a dramatic end. The cause of the split was ostensibly
Van Doesburg's insistence on using black in his latest colour designs for the facade
of the final blocks in Spangen. Oud feared that black would give an illusionistic
appearance of recession in his otherwise flat facade and accused Van Doesburg of
producing a destructuring effect. Van Doesburg's refusal to change his design led
to Oud's official split from De Stijl, although he maintained contact with many of
its other members.[19]

The basis of the quarrel between Van Doesburg and Oud, in terms of the group,
was an ongoing rivalry between the painters and the architects; Van Doesburg
wished to be more than a glorified decorator, while Oud considered architecture to
be primary and colour an additional complement to it. At a much deeper level what
was emerging was a difference in how the city is thought in De Stijl. As we have
seen, urban planning in the Netherlands was closely connected to the ongoing discourse around the concept of monumentality. Oud had used his Spangen buildings
to distinguish his notion of the monumental from that being practised in
Amsterdam. In place of imposing size, symbolic vocabulary and individual flair,
Oud suggested that a monumental effect could be produced from standardisation,
modern materials and geometric rhythms highlighted by the use of colour. The
horizontality of the housing blocks would then create a city dominated by long,
straight streets. Thus the flatness of the facade in Oud's blocks is the natural expression of this new emphasis on the street rather than square and, as in *De Vonk*, discussed in the previous chapter, it reads as a skin separating two spaces rather than
an architectonic object in its own right. Van Doesburg's threat to perforate the
facade was seen by Oud as a danger not only to his attempt to produce monumentality but also to the relationship he had established between exterior and interior
space. He intended each individual dwelling to feel directly connected to the cityscape without needing to be seen as part of an intervening unit (as was the case with
the Amsterdam School). If *De Dageraad* had been based on the idea of producing a
continuity with the historical architecture of the city, Oud conceived of continuity
in a very different way, as highlighted in a fascinating commentary by the architectural critic J. P. Mieras, serialised in *Bouwkundig Weekblad* in 1923.

Mieras's article, *Een Uithoekje van een Wereldstad* (A Far Corner of a World City), was written in a partly satirical tone and gave an account of the new Rotterdam building projects in connection to the identity of the city itself. The *uithoekje* of the title suggests a far flung place, already a comment on the pattern of development in Rotterdam which, unlike Amsterdam, never had a clearly defined centre. The projects at Spangen do not cohere to a consistent plan of concentric growth, nor did Rotterdam have the same definite shape of other Dutch towns, which were commonly built around a medieval marketplace. Mieras began his article with the surprising claim that it is precisely for this reason that Rotterdam had a metropolitan feel lacking elsewhere in the Netherlands, even in Amsterdam. As he comically stated, someone straight from the provinces can think 'Amsterdam is big but in five minutes I can still be in the meadows with the cows.' However, he continued, 'there is an element in Rotterdam that makes its predestination as a world city even more pleasant. Because you do not think, you do not fear, you do not hope that in five minutes we are with the cows but, and that is the wonder of Rotterdam, you are standing in front of the cows, in front of the meadow.'[20] Here Mieras referred to the district of Hoboken, which was kept as farmland well into the twentieth century despite its central location. It allowed him to make the point that not only did the decentralised nature of Rotterdam give it an advantage over its rivals but that the contrast of urban and rural that could be had right at its heart intensified the sensation of its modernity.

After this preamble, Mieras moved on to discuss the Spangen development about which he was not entirely positive. He compared it to similar projects in Amsterdam and found it compromised in its ambitions; the numerous architects involved had all aimed for slightly different things leaving a rather confused impression. The article concluded, however, by commenting on Oud's more recent housing projects at Tusschendijken, where he had not been forced to blend his designs together with those of other architects. Begun in 1921 the Tusschendijken blocks were completely standardised perimeter constructions enclosing a courtyard of part private, part communal space. Where previously, at Spangen, Oud was obliged to incorporate traditional gables and pitched roofs, these latest buildings had flat roofing allowing for a far simpler transition to be made at the corner. Mieras observed that the minimal decoration permitted by Oud was restricted to an emphasis on the play of verticals on the facades to counterbalance the extended horizontality produced by the flat roofs. Other than this, the facades had become flat planes. Yet, for Mieras, the peculiarity of the geometry was that 'the blocks are buildings where, while one stands in front of the main facades, the side facades appear to have priority. And given that walking through the perpendicular intersecting streets one is continually able to notice this, the architecture is thus typically characteristic of the street, that is the road comprised of houses, along which men move.'[21] Once again the tone has a satirical edge to it but, even if Mieras is mocking the prosaic nature of Oud's architecture, the point remains that at Tusschendijken monumentality, in Oud's terms, has the effect of disorientation.

The main facades of the housing blocks disappeared, as did an entrance clarified by architectural detail. In their place had come the new components of repetition, standardisation and a spectator constantly on the move.

Having pushed the concept of monumentality to its limit at Tusschendijken, Oud appears to have put aside the housing block as the basic unit of urban design and the accompanying scale of city planning derived from Berlage. His next projects at Oud-Mathenesse, and most famously Kiefhoek, were made up of small terraces with the former earning itself the popular name of the *Witte Dorp* (White Village) such was its miniature feel in comparison to what had preceded it. The transplanting of a village into the heart of the city fulfils the destiny that Mieras saw for Rotterdam to combine the rural and the urban in a shockingly modern way. In this case Oud was once again faced with an irregular site but took advantage of its triangular shape to set his buildings off against each other at peculiar angles. The spaces between buildings began to take on more and more significance and the estate closed itself off against the rest of the city. As one writer has put it: 'He designed these small neighbourhoods as one building, as a delimited architectonic object, that would not let itself be used with impunity as a model for the entire city.'[22]

The effect described of delimitation can also be felt by anybody walking into the Kiefhoek estate (Figure 14). This is very different to the 'city within the city'

14 J. J. P. Oud, Kiefhoek, Rotterdam, 1929

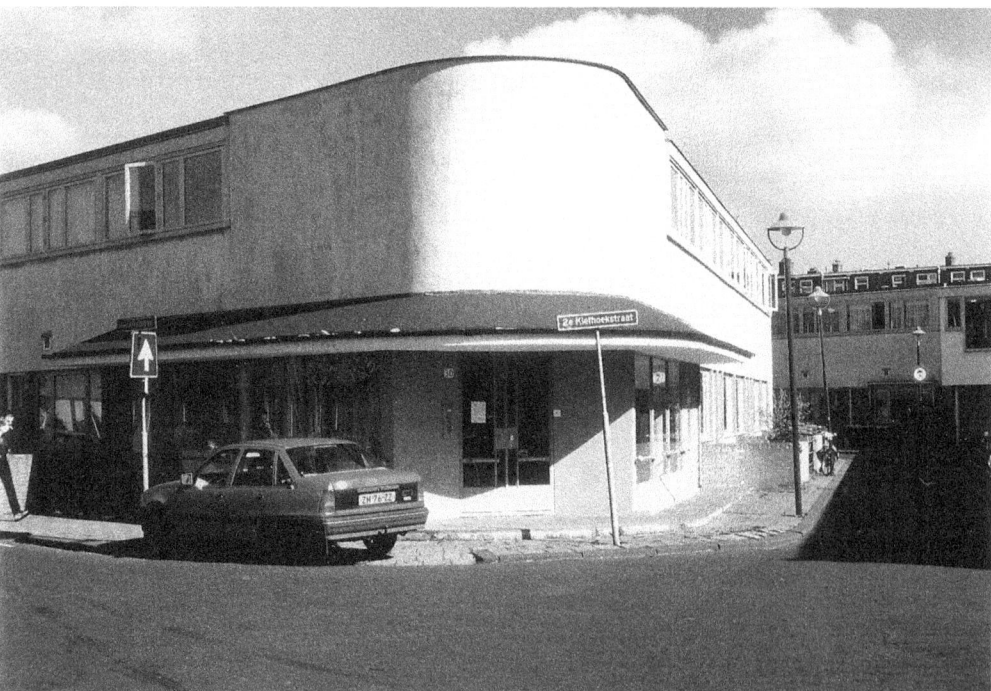

discussed above in connection to Amsterdam because, in this example, there is nothing to remind you that you are in Rotterdam, no visual association, no points of collective activity. Not only did *De Dageraad* try to match the visual sensation of the canal street in its flowing forms, it had also closed itself around a small square in which were placed monuments to local socialist councillors. Kiefhoek has no similar points of identification. Interestingly, the only break in its shell occurs where Oud constructed a church for the estate. Currently occupied by the Salvation Army, it was originally planned as a Reformed Church, the denomination reflected in the simplicity of its form, which is a plain white box. While this causes it to blend in with the rest of Kiefhoek, it is set perpendicularly to one of the main streets, which helps to disengage it from the houses. The message given is difficult to interpret. Is it that the church connects the estate to the wider community? If so, the manner in which this is expressed architecturally is very different to that traditionally adopted by church building. As Richard Sennett has described, the church at the centre of a medieval town was a visibly ordered space distinct from the muddle of streets around it.[23] Asymmetric to the terraces of Kiefhoek, the only visual quality that the church seems to serve is a change in scale between the two-storey houses of the estate and the taller canal houses that encircle them. It is no longer placed at the centre of the community and cannot be seen from most points of Kiefhoek. It does not provide what churches have offered through the ages, a stable point of reference in the midst of change, and there is no evidence to show that it was so conceived. As a conclusion to Oud's involvement with urban design, though, it leaves one very clear message; the city of monuments had given way to the monumental image of the city.

We left Van Doesburg above at the point where he was attempting, in Oud's terms, to 'destructure' the facades of Spangen blocks VIII and IX. In his correspondence Van Doesburg claimed that his use of colour was partly to produce some variety to counteract the monotonous effects of standardisation. Either way there is little difference between this procedure and the effects produced for *De Vonk* and the first Spangen blocks, where he also experimented with asymmetrical patterns. Oud's concerns about 'destructuring' are in my view a displaced reaction to something else that Van Doesburg was beginning to introduce to his conception of colour in architecture. The overall effect that Van Doesburg stated he was after was that of 'dissonance'. The musical analogy was not accidental but developed from a lengthy period during which Van Doesburg tried to match colour relations to musical scales. When applied architecturally, Van Doesburg theorised, colour could take on a temporal dimension. In the first Spangen collaboration Oud had been quite prepared, and was keen to accept, the spatial consequences of the application of vibrant colour. However, for his notion of monumentality to be sustained, the facades of his housing blocks had to be perceived as complete. Van Doesburg's desire to fragment the perceptual experience temporally was totally at odds with the type of monumentality Oud hoped to produce at this point. Van Doesburg would explore the consequences for urban space of this break with the monumental with a new sparring partner, a young Dutch architecture student by the name of Cor van Eesteren.

At the time of his split with Oud, Van Doesburg was living in Weimar desperately trying to secure himself a job at the Bauhaus. Contact with the likes of Walter Gropius and Adolf Behne convinced him of the path De Stijl was pursuing architecturally, while new friendships with Dadaists such as Hans Richter, Raoul Hausmann and Kurt Schwitters increased his daring. In 1922 Van Eesteren passed through Weimar as part of his Prix de Rome tour which he had transformed into a study of German planning.[24] Advised to pay a visit to Van Doesburg, he found himself in the middle of the events which led up to the International Congress of Dadaists and Constructivists staged in September of that year. This was the start of a few years of intense collaboration between Van Doesburg and Van Eesteren, where the former offered the radical ideas, the latter the architectural know-how. The first project the two embarked upon was in fact Van Eesteren's final student work, a design for a new university complex planned as part of the Amsterdam South expansion. Van Eesteren had won the Prix de Rome with a design for a Royal Academy of Sciences which, although recognisably modern, had preserved classical qualities of symmetry and balance; the main entrance was clearly defined and a diminishing hierarchy of masses arranged. The design for the new university was of a completely different order. For a start, its relation to the street was totally transformed, with no main facade facing directly onto it. Dramatic diagonals led from the exterior through into a central building of unusual octagonal shape, designed to contain a great hall whose novel structure was further confused by Van Doesburg's startling colour compositions. Needless to say this design did not find favour back in the Netherlands. Van Eesteren was refused his Advanced Architectural Diploma and the committee of the Prix de Rome discontinued his grant.[25]

Undaunted, Van Eesteren continued to work with Van Doesburg and followed him to Paris in 1923. There they worked together on the famous models that were shown at Léonce Rosenberg's *Galerie de l'Effort Moderne* (Figure 39). Eshewing any concern for traditional architectural distinctions between interior and exterior, expression of a main facade, or clarification of stories, the Paris models presented De Stijl architecture as the realisation of colour in three dimensions and little else. Specific functions were apparently abandoned in favour of mobile and continuous spaces. It is at this point that Van Doesburg made his first mention of the city in any of his writings, stating:

> Do you know, gentlemen, what a city is? A city is a tension in depth and a tension in height. Nothing more. Two straight wire connections form the city. Each individual attempts to find a common mid-point through these two tensions either on foot, by train, by tram or explosions (the transport of the future).[26]

Written under his dadaist pseudonym I. K. Bonset, this is a slightly tongue-in-cheek comment but indicative of the way Van Doesburg was approaching urban planning not from the point of view of practical issues such as housing, industry and environment but solely in terms of a contradiction between depth and height, or density and traffic. His correspondence with Van Eesteren at this time shows he was having these discussions with the most unlikely people and a letter of July 1924 finally mentions the 'Tzara Doesburg idea' for urban planning. As he continues:

> It will be splendid if we can elaborate that viaduct construction of mine and Tzara's. Tzara will be satisfied if we call it the 'système Tzara'. He doesn't have to be mentioned as the architect. I shall start to work out the sketches. It could become a gigantic design. Very big – in colour including traffic and everything. By having uniform blocks sawn which I colour, we can have have a splendid big model cheaply.[27]

Leaving to one side the bizarre proposition of Tristan Tzara as an architect, we should duly note the nihilistic strain emerging in the De Stijl discourse on the city. If Oud's work in Rotterdam, based on repetition, standardisation and a concern for monumentality, had established the street as the main unit of urban planning, Van Doesburg extended the eradication of civic space into abstractions of colour and shape with almost no consideration of function beyond the movement of traffic.

Van Doesburg's letter to Van Eesteren quoted above also contains information regarding the destination he had in mind for his enormous model: the 1925 *Exposition Internationale des Arts Décoratifs et Industriels Modernes*. Two months after writing this letter, however, Van Doesburg was to find himself and De Stijl effectively barred from participating in the exhibition (and especially from representing the Netherlands as he had hoped to do). Instead, to his horror the Amsterdam School architect J. F. Staal was commissioned to build the Dutch pavilion which became a fantastical brick construction combining forms derived from churches, ships and Javanese vernacular architecture. The contents of the pavilion were dominated by decorative arts produced by designers associated with the Amsterdam School, much to Van Doesburg's disgust and humiliation.

While De Stijl was not represented collectively as part of the Dutch entry to the exhibition, there was one dramatic example of its incursion in a most unexpected place, this being Frederick Kiesler's contribution to the Austrian pavilion. Van Doesburg had met Kiesler in Berlin in 1922 and invited him to join De Stijl. A theatre designer of great originality, Kiesler had early success at the *Internationale Austellung neuer Theatertechnik* (International Exhibition of New Theatre Design) in Vienna in the autumn of 1924, an event Van Doesburg had also attended. On the strength of this, Josef Hoffmann had given him free hand to design the theatre section of the Austrian pavilion. What Kiesler exhibited was a *City in Space* whose connection to theatre was only of the most tenuous nature. Raised entirely from the ground, Kiesler's city was comprised of extended strips intersecting at right angles. Of differing widths and colours, the components of the city refer not to buildings, it would seem, but rather to the tensions in depth and height described earlier by Van Doesburg. Kiesler would later recollect how, the day after the opening of the exhibition he had discovered Mondrian and Van Doesburg standing in front of his model. Van Doesburg was to greet him with the words: 'Your deeds, what we all ever hoped to do. You have done it.'[28]

Little or no evidence remains of Van Doesburg's urban planning schemes of this period but he backdated a series of drawings made in 1929, entitled the *Cité de Circulation* (City of Circulation), to 1924, suggesting that they were the based on ideas conceived at this moment. Here we see tension in height and tension in depth expressed in the repetition of standardised tower block units raised on pilotis allowing for maximum use of ground space (Figure 15). Density of population, requiring elevation, is played off against traffic demands in a frighteningly dehumanising fashion. The 'Tzara Doesburg' viaduct system was transformed into a cable car transporting people at a mid-level, a common theme in 1920s city schemes. The presence of pilotis here should alert us to the most famous urban design of the period, however, Le Corbusier's *Ville Contemporaine* (Contemporary City) published in his 1924 book *Urbanisme* (Urbanism). The 1925 Paris *Exposition*, where Van Doesburg wanted to present his model, was also the site at which Le Corbusier exhibited his *Plan Voisin* for the centre of Paris, which proposed its complete demolition and replacement with enormous skyscrapers.

Allan Doig, one of the few commentators to have made any significant mention of the *Cité de Circulation* has suggested that it be seen in its dating as a deliberate reference to the publication of Le Corbusier's *Urbanisme* and even more so as 'an attempt to make good the shortcomings of the "City of Tomorrow"'.[29] As has been

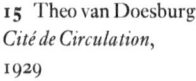

15 Theo van Doesburg,
Cité de Circulation,
1929

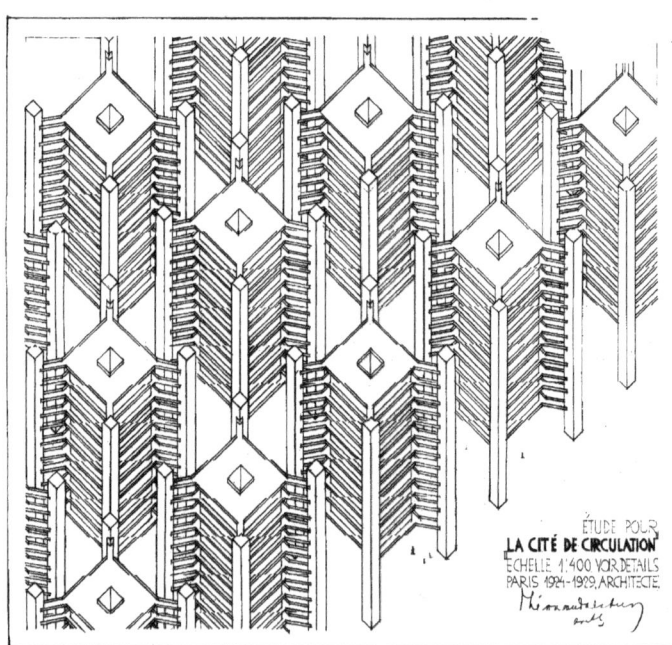

demonstrated there are perhaps other reasons for the 1924 inception date but it is worth looking at specific criticisms made by Van Doesburg of *Urbanisme* at the time. In early 1925 Van Doesburg reviewed Corbusier's book for a Dutch architectural journal. While accepting the urgency of the problems Le Corbusier set out to tackle, Van Doesburg ultimately rejected the *Ville Contemporaine* (Le Corbusier's model of an ideal city for 3 million inhabitants) on the grounds that it not only retained but emphasised the city centre, a zone to be occupied by vast skyscrapers constructed around a central station and airport. As Van Doesburg describes:

> In the centre, the highways run into an enormous square of 2400 x 1600m . . . For a decentralized city plan the notion of a square is equally untenable as that of a street tube. For a systematic development of the city's three main elements, production, distribution and consumption, integration of the countryside (agriculture etc.) and the city is a prerequisite.[30]

Hardly 'making good', Van Doesburg opposed Le Corbusier on a basic issue; where the latter was extremely concerned to preserve the boundaries of the city, to abolish suburbs and urban sprawl, Van Doesburg produced a formula for total decentralisation, merging of city and country and loss of definite shape. The parallels here with Mieras's *Uithoekje van een Wereldstad* are interesting to consider.

Van Doesburg's return to the *Cité de Circulation* in 1929 was prompted by his belief that he had invented a building type that could truly be set into a decentralised scheme. In an article for *Het Bouwbedrijf* (The Building Trade) he gave a short history of building technology leading predictably from brick walls bearing floor loads through to contemporary concrete pillar systems which freed exterior walls from internal construction. Finally, he introduced a fifth type which necessitated the removal of all structural elements to the exterior, turning the modernist framework inside out. Van Doesburg saw this as directly connected to urban planning:

> Then we can envisage a technically well realisable metropolitan traffic architecture as a sound solution for city planning, wherein the traffic problems find a radical solution by the fifth technical possibility: the shifting of supporting elements to the *outside*. Since the street tubes which obstruct traffic have disappeared, traffic can flow without hindrance.[31]

The drawings for the *Cité de Circulation* provide a picture of how this was to operate. Each building has four pillars through which access to the building is gained and services provided. Suspended between the pillars is the habitable space, raised from the ground. On no side are we presented with a main facade. In fact it has become difficult to judge where the building begins and ends. The architecture shrugs off a traditional task of mediating between two spaces, public and private, which have become mutually interchangeable. The main purpose of the design was to abolish the street, understood as a thoroughfare between houses, an end contributed to by the dispersive effect of the grid plan. Standardisation, which had been discussed early on in De Stijl and was the backbone of Oud's housing projects, was taken to an extreme in the *Cité de Circulation* and, accompanied by decentralisation, no one building is permitted to appear of greater value. This is a plan for indefinite expansion which recognises no boundaries and can be viewed from any direction with similar effect. Drawn in axonometric projection, it was quite literally a view from nowhere.

As we have seen repeatedly now, decentralisation was the key concept for the emergence of the Dutch metropolis. Van Doesburg's *Cité de Circulation* may appear unfeasible but it emerged directly from practical considerations. For example, the last collaborative venture between Van Doesburg and Van Eesteren had taken place in 1924, a design for a shopping arcade on the Laan van der Meerdevoort in The Hague (Plate 3). This is still a major road which links together the city centre with the suburbs and at the time connected with new estates, such as Jan Wils' *Daal en Berg*. It also drew into the city what were formerly outlying villages such as Kijkduin. What appears to have attracted Van Eesteren to the competition for the commission for this project was the diversity of uses the arcade would have to accommodate. Not only shops were required but residences above them. In addition the client wanted a restaurant, meeting hall and billiard club integrated into the scheme as well.

The competition was for a very new type of construction. It was neither the covered arcade of the nineteenth century nor the department store which had come to dominate the central locations of most modern cities. The size of shop planned for is that of the family business which may have occupied the ground floor of a traditional town house. In their design Van Doesburg and Van Eesteren make a clear distinction between commercial activity on street level and the residential space above. A new aspect to the use of the building is suggested by the disparity between the division of the shop fronts and that of the flats above; shop owners no longer live where they work and urban residences can be in mixed-use spaces. The horizontal run of shops and flats is then played off against the block at the corner, which was to contain the restaurant and other spaces of association and entertainment. The closed box of the billiard room contrasts with the large windows of the restaurant and with the staircase located behind at the side. The whole complex of housing, work and entertainment becomes a sequence of openings and closures, private and public occupying the same space. Striding out from the scene is a single figure, a photomontage of a highly fashionable modern man, tailored in a sporty English manner. His difference from the Parisian flâneur is important. While he shares a concern for dandyish clothing, he is no longer the man on the edge of the crowd nor does he stop to look, browse or collect the ephemera thrown up by the energetic commerce of the city. Instead he experiences urban space solely as emptiness, as the possibility for free movement.

As I mentioned at the beginning of this chapter, Dutch town planning differed from the model established by Baron Haussmann in that it left the historic centres of its major cities largely intact. However, the future of the city centre was still of great concern, an issue explored in detail by Van Eesteren. In 1924 he entered a competition set by Amsterdam city council for the redesign of the Rokin, one of the major arteries in the medieval core running between the Dam and the Muntplein. The council had planned to fill one the most attractive canals in the city centre, the Reguliersgracht, to make it suitable for motor vehicles and relieve congestion on the Rokin. Massive public opposition had forced the council to consider how else to deal with increased traffic, leading Van Eesteren to submit a proposal which would have redeveloped the entire street, partially filling the canal for car parking but also regularising the building line. The increased impact of horizontal spans was to be balanced by a tall tower block placed at the junction with the Spui. His plan was rejected in the first round, no doubt because of the abstract way in which it was presented. No consideration was given to the facades themselves, no specifics of construction or decoration mentioned. Calling the plan *Elementair* (Elementary), Van Eesteren suggested that urban planning concern itself only with the broadest distribution of masses in space.

Van Eesteren's next competition entry, however, won first prize. This was for the development of another famous street, Unter den Linden in Berlin, which he presented in a very similar way. As Vincent van Rossem has commented, however, these schemes are far less revolutionary than they otherwise appear:

> The design [for Unter den Linden] was justifiably honoured, for it probably consti-
> tuted the epilogue to a tradition: a final ingenious attempt to reconcile the traditional
> street facade, the problems of tall buildings and the irresistible pressure to centralise
> business functions at the expense of residential ones, within the physical constraints
> of the historic city.[32]

Van Eesteren's plans, which were discussed in De Stijl, combined Oud's consideration for monumentality with Van Doesburg's efforts to represent the city as a spatio-temporal abstraction.[33] What began as resistance to the socialist city of Amsterdam council transformed itself by the mid-1920s into a consideration of new commercial and traffic demands. As will be shown next, this parallelled the moment at which the Dutch metropolis first became visible.

In 1924, at the point when Oud was working at Oud-Mathenesse and thinking ahead to Kiefhoek, when Van Doesburg first conceived the *Cité de Circulation*, at the moment Van Eesteren would begin drawing up his scheme for the Rokin, the annual congress of the Town Planning and Garden Cities Association was held in Amsterdam. The congress took place at the beginning of July and was attended by luminaries such as Raymond Unwin and Ebenezer Howard, along with 435 delegates from 25 countries. It became a major point of discussion among Dutch architects and raised the international profile of Dutch planning considerably. Berlage was present as one of the leading members of the Association and Oud attended all of the proceedings. Van Doesburg did not attend but reports in his correspondence that he discussed the event at length with Jean Badovici, editor of *Architecture*

Vivante. As he related in a letter to Van Eesteren, Badovici 'gained the impression of Holland that a Roman had of Greece', so impressive were advances in Dutch architectural thinking.[34] This is the same letter in which he first proposed designing a city model for the Paris exhibition of 1925. Oud also mentioned the congress in his correspondence, stating that its primary concern was with 'decentralization of the city as well as regional growth plans'.[35] An editorial in the *Tijdschrift voor Volkshuisvesting en Stedebouw* (Journal for Social Housing and City Planning) reporting on the congress commented that these were indeed the main points of discussion but that they were not particulary novel for the Dutch participants: 'the question was thrown up if the metropolis should carry on growing, then should it be decentralised and that a regional plan should be designed for the areas which form an economic unity without yet possessing a nucleus of predominating significance, but it was not particularly new to us. Regional planning had already received attention in our circles.'[36]

The section of the report on the congress that remains most gripping, however, is the description of the tours that delegates were taken on. These were conducted in such a variety of means of transport it is quite bewildering. On Saturday 5 July the delegates met on the Dam, the ancient heart of Amsterdam. They were then bussed along the seventeenth-century canal streets to the Amstel river and from there to the sites of extension to the south, returning back to the centre via the Vondelpark. From there they were driven to Michel de Klerk's *Eigen Haard* (Own Hearth) estate next to the station. The groups were then divided and some took the ferry across to Amsterdam North while others went to Schiphol airport and boarded KLM planes to survey the scene from the air: 'Amongst these aeroplanists was Dr Berlage who was able to confirm in this manner that the drawing he had made of the expansion plan fitted very well with its actual execution, at least that which related to the bird's eye-view.'[37] The following day the parties were taken, again in buses, this time out of the city to the new developments around Hilversum, 15 km to the south-east. They then went on to Utrecht and after refreshments in the restaurant of the *Jaarbeurs* (Trade Exhibition Centre) took the train to The Hague where further tours were conducted. The following day further trips took place in and around Rotterdam, to its new airport and to Delft. Not only was much of the time spent getting on and off buses, trains, boats and planes, but there are not many countries in the world where you might imagine being able in one day to visit three or four different towns or cities to inspect new developments and still have time for a nice lunch along the way. Consider that we are still in a pre-motorway age here and the feat becomes even more impressive. What had been demonstrated was not only that a great range of planning enterprises were taking place in diverse locations but that these places were already exceptionally well linked together.

The first article to draw attention to the untypical relationship between urban centres in the Netherlands came just one year after the congress. It was written by Th. K. van Lohuizen, who would later work with Van Eesteren as part of the

Amsterdam planning team. Published with the article was a map of *Stedelijke Invloedssfeer* (Urban Spheres of Influence), which was effectively the first map of the *Randstad* (Figure 16).[38] Providing a large range of statistics, Van Lohuizen was able to show that the fastest-growing areas of the western Netherlands were not, as expected, its largest cities, but that in recent times the suburbs or neighbouring villages were leading the way. Even more unexpected for the time was Van Lohuizen's account of the forces of centralisation and decentralisation. He discovered that Amsterdam, for all the attempts of the council to preserve growth from the centre, was now fast losing population to the periphery or further. Rotterdam, on the other hand, keen on decentralisation, was growing faster than its surroundings. Perhaps the most shocking statistic of all, however, was that the city that had the largest growth proportionally between 1869 and 1920 was The Hague. What is so astonishing about this fact is that not only has The Hague been largely missing from my account of housing development but that it lacked either the commercial vitality of Amsterdam or the industrial muscle of Rotterdam. Apart from a growth in governmental bureaucracy there is little to explain such a large expansion in population. Van Lohuizen's article clearly identified a new feature in urban development, that population and work opportunities were not following each other in a predictable way. His explanation for the popularity of The Hague is straightforward; a combination of good transport connections and the availability of recreational landscape. The exodus from Amsterdam was to the coast or to the woods. Rotterdam was growing centrally because these areas were not so easily accessible from it. The

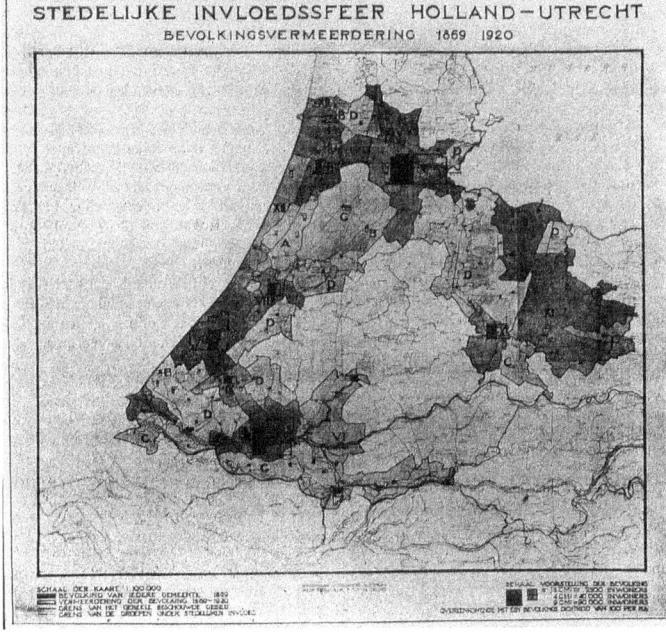

16 Th. K. van Lohuizen, *Urban Spheres of Influence*, 1925

Hague, however, could offer a beach less than five kilometres away at Scheveningen and attractive woods within the city boundaries. The Dutch city dweller of the early twentieth century had greater flexibility in deciding where to live than ever before and was taking leisure amenities well into account. The modern-day commuter was born early in a country where travelling distances were short and transport connections efficient.

Another witness to the birth of the polycentric metropolis at this time was the German architectural critic Karl Scheffler, who published an account of Dutch building in 1930 written in the form of a travelogue. This book, simply entitled *Holland*, provided a new vision for the old circumstances. Scheffler, as Vincent van Rossem describes, 'clearly saw that this old metropolis [seventeenth-century Holland] was really the perfect embodiment of the modern city planning ideal. His travelogue is an almost hallucinatory description of a city of millions in which a perfect balance has been achieved between a highly developed cultural landscape and a circle of independent urban nuclei.'[39]

Van Eesteren's plans for the Rokin and Unter den Linden appeared in De Stijl and also in a new journal called *i10*, founded by the anarcho-syndicalist Arthur Lehning and published in Amsterdam between 1927–29.[40] Combining radical politics with constructivist aesthetics and critical theory, *i10* threatened to, and partially succeeded in, usurping De Stijl as the most radical journal in the Netherlands. Oud, Mondrian, Van Eesteren and Huszár all decamped to it. In fact, Mondrian's debut contribution to *i10* should definitely attract our attention; appearing in the very first issue, his most extended meditation on the translation of abstract painting to the built environment, *Neo-plasticisme: De Woning – De Straat – De Stad* (Neo-plasticism: Home – Street – City).

As promised in the title of the article, Mondrian focused on the relationship between the private interior, the immediate exterior and then from there to the total image of the city. Illustrated with a photograph of his studio arranged along Neo-plastic lines, the article suggests that the 'disharmony' of the city can be overcome by extending the principles of painting (balance of contrasts) into architecture and urban design. Most important for him is that 'a balanced opposition of buildings, constructions and empty spaces' be created, so that man may be 'as satisfied indoors as outdoors'.[41] By making the individual 'part of the whole' Mondrian suggests 'well being, moral and physical, thus healthy, will be spread by the balanced oppositions of relationships, of size and colour, matter and space, which will be supported by the relationships of position. With a little good will, it will not be so impossible to create an earthly paradise.'[42] If all this seems a little outlandish, it must be understood that these statements would be followed in later issues of the journal by Van Eesteren's very focused plans but also given intellectual weight by some of Lehning's contacts. Two pages on from Mondrian's article can be found a Dutch translation of the preface of Ernst Bloch's *Spirit of Utopia*. Proclaiming the necessity of the wish principle for any revolutionary movement,

Bloch defended utopianism against the orthodox Marxist practise of unmasking utopias as merely reactionary ideologies.

When considered in the context of urban planning as outlined so far in this chapter, Mondrian's vision of an ideal Neo-plastic city begins to appear more and more realistic. He was in contact with people who were actually considering the wholesale reconfiguration of city life. There is also no doubt that some of the contradictions of contemporary thought about the city are present in his text. The first is the conflict between the modern neutral environment whose particularities have been annihilated, to use Mondrian's own terminology, and his celebration of individualism. Another way this is expressed in the text is in his call for difference and diversity but that it should be harnessed into equilibrium. The language is still that of his painterly theory but the object has taken on new dimensions. As Mondrian describes it, the interior, the home, should be continuous with the street and the street with the city at large: 'The idea of the "home" – "Home, Sweet Home" – must be destroyed at the same time as the conventional idea of the street.'[43] Mondrian's desire was to make the twentieth-century metropolis visibly present at every point, even in the shelter of the private house, but he was faced with a phenomenon that did not settle into a clear image. It could only be made present as the push and pull between centrifugal and centripetal forces, the imposition and unravelling of a grid, the sensation of fullness in the empty spaces at the centre of so many of his paintings.

Mondrian's utopianism can be understood as an accurate reflection of the circumstances that were tugging at the fabric of the Renaissance city. Where previously the economics of the market square or the institutions of the law and government could be seen in wood and stone, the metropolis only showed itself as flows: the movement of population from one district to another, the passage of traffic through any particular street, the exchange of information or commodities. With this in mind I will now return to Benevolo's comparison of abstract painting and the General Expansion Plan of Amsterdam.

As mentioned at the start of this chapter, Van Eesteren was responsible for the design of an expansion plan for Amsterdam which would take the city far beyond the boundaries established by Berlage. He began his work in 1928 after being offered a post by Amsterdam Council as architect in the newly formed *Afdeling Stadsontwikkeling* (City Planning Department). The reasons for the change of direction on the part of the council are complex but worth outlining.[44] As mentioned previously Berlage's plans had already thrown up problems of local authority boundaries and led to regional planning schemes. Amsterdam council was also dogged by internal disputes between the *Dienst der Publieke Werken* (Office for Public Works) and the *Woningdienst* (Housing Department) concerning who should lead urban planning decisions. These had been partly been solved by the institution of the *Commissie Groot Amsterdam* (Commission for Greater Amsterdam) in 1921. The plan which emerged from this commission failed to impress the *Nederlands Instituut voor Volkshuisvesting en Stedebouw* (Netherlands Institute for Social

Housing and Town Planning), which criticised the perpetuation of Berlage's aesthetic formula. Radical change was to come only after elections in 1927 when the
socialists temporarily lost control of the council for the first time since 1914. During
this period the *Afdeling Stadsontwikkeling en -uitbreiding* (Department of City
Development and Expansion) was created on the initiative of the new liberal dem-
ocrat councillor responsible for public works. The architectural group *De 8* (The 8)
also seized the opportunity to launch a protest against the Amsterdam School
architects and the *Schoonheidscommissie* of the council who together had kept a
closed shop on architectural projects in the city for so long. The outcome was that
the new planning department would take on a clear functionalist identity. This was
apparent in Van Eesteren's very first scheme for Amsterdam West. The change of
geographical direction is important for a start. His concern was to link up the new
residential districts of the south with what was still Amsterdam's most industrial-
ised area, the docks to the west of the centre. He showed a far greater concern for
developing the efficient movement of people and goods than Berlage had ever considered, setting in place the ring roads which still cut through the outer districts of
the city.

It was not only traffic that Van Eesteren considered – his plans also involved the
creation of a wood the size of Haussmann's Bois de Boulogne and an enormous
lake to the south-west of the city. These still serve as recreational areas and a screen
against the airport. As Manfred Bock describes, moving from Berlage's *Plan Zuid*
to the *Algemeen Uitbreidingsplan* (General Expansion Plan) is like stepping through
an invisible barrier:

> Two worlds collide: the layout of the street versus its use; image versus structure; the
> private space of the street and square carved out of the city, versus continuous space
> subdivided and determined by the opened masses . . . The geometrical city plan
> opposes the harmonious spatial order of urban elements in time.[45]

According to Bock, between Berlage and Van Eesteren we find De Stijl. That is
certainly true chronologically but what does it mean in practical terms? As this
chapter has shown it was only Oud who managed to realise his conception of a
modern monumental urban architecture, which he actually saw as the continuation
of Berlage's propositions. Both Mondrian and Van Doesburg were restricted to
fantasies of ideal cities but in each case they extended Oud's essential concern with
standardisation. In Mondrian's writings this appears in the guise of 'neutralisation'
and 'annihilation', and in Van Doesburg's *Cité de Circulation* as a celebration of the
thoroughly dehumanising potential of modernity. In Mondrian's *Home-Street-
City* he discussed the 'tragedy' of modern life as an imbalance between novelty and
equilibrium. Neo-plasticism had resolved this problem in painting, to his view, by
defeating repetition but also managing to express unchanging harmony. In the context of the city, Mondrian asserted that 'Neo-plasticism is more at home in the
Métro than in Notre Dame' while also projecting an image of 'an earthly paradise'
as a stable resolution to the endless novelty the city creates.[46] Van Doesburg's *Cité*

de Circulation, based as we saw earlier on tensions in depth and height, played with the elements of standardisation and freedom of movement. Mobility and normalisation were again projected onto the city as underlying contradictions to its image as the resolution of individualism and community, accompanied by decentralisation which eradicates the formal boundaries of the city itself.

Van Eesteren's appointment in Amsterdam was not as presumptuous as it may seem from my presentation above. He was one of only very few of his contemporaries to have researched urban planning in any significant depth. Even before meeting Van Doesburg, he had studied Berlage's theories and gained practical experience in designing extension plans for his home town of Ablasserdam. He had also transformed his Prix de Rome tour into a study of German cities and their development. While in Paris, he had collaborated with Georges Pineau, a graduate from the *Ecole des Hautes Etudes Urbaines* (School of Advanced Urban Studies), the only place in Europe at the time to offer training in urban design. Pineau showed him how to construct a *dossier urbain*, the collection of statistics necessary to predict population growth, traffic demand and other environmental considerations. This resulted in a design for a business district of 1926, illustrated in the tenth anniversary edition of De Stijl the following year. Such a background led to his employment in 1927 by the *Staatliche Bauhochschule* (State Building Academy) in Weimar specifically to teach town planning.

During his teaching years Van Eesteren devised a lecture, *Eine Stunde Städtebau* (An Hour of City Planning), which he presented widely in Germany. One review of the lecture reported that: 'It was limited principally to pithy brief comments on a long series of photographs, plans and statistics, a movie that filled the whole evening.'[47] Van Eesteren did indeed show ninety slides in the single hour and his notes indicate that he spoke curtly about each. The images, which are also recorded in these notes, varied as the review suggested from plans to photographs and even photomontage. Responding to the idea that the lecture was more like a movie, Van Eesteren stated, when repeating the lecture in Berlin in 1928, that a film would have been an excellent alternative to a traditional lecture.[48] His attitude towards urban planning was intimately connected to the visual consumption of space. 'Experience everything in images' was to become his motto for his students when teaching in the Netherlands, a practice that seems at first antithetical to the functionalism with which he was later to be associated. However, this was also an important part of his inheritance from De Stijl in which, as we have already noted, the city quite literally came to be seen differently.

Van Eesteren's Greater Amsterdam was not completed until the 1950s. This parallels the reception of De Stijl culturally, which achieved widespread public recognition after the publication of Hans Jaffé's 1956 monograph. While De Stijl came to dominate the Dutch museums and the history of Dutch modernism, reaction to the new urban situation was manifested in the mass squatter movement which aimed to preserve the centre of Amsterdam as a residential area, opposing the flow to the new suburbs and the occupation of the centre by business. After years of persistent resistance, the squatters succeeded in maintaining Amsterdam Centrum as a densely inhabited area. The illusion of Amsterdam, however, is that the contest between centre and periphery exists at this local level. In a fascinating comparison of Amsterdam and Los Angeles, Edward Soja has recently tried to contrast the bounded historic European city with the urban sprawl we associate with the formless American autopia.[49] He starts from the position that between Amsterdam and LA there could be no greater difference. Then, as he points out, Amsterdam is now merely part of the *Randstad*, the rim city created by the simultaneous expansions of Rotterdam, The Hague, Leiden and Utrecht, which have merged to become a 100-mile stretch of urbanised landscape. To catch the train from Rotterdam to Amsterdam is to experience what Van Doesburg had suggested as the integration of city and country; although you may see cows and sheep, you never feel that you have left the city. De Stijl did not cause the *Randstad* to come into existence but was deeply ingrained in the circumstances which surrounded its emergence.

Notes

1 Leonardo Benevolo, *The European City* (Oxford: Blackwell, 1983), p. 197.
2 Benevolo, *The European City*, p. 197.
3 There are numerous interesting contacts between the De Stijl architects and their counterparts across Europe. A key example is the interaction between Oud and Bruno Taut who took on the role of *Stadtbaurat* (City Building Officer) in Magdeburg in 1921 and subsequently worked with Martin Wagner on housing projects in Berlin from 1924. See Ernst van der Hoeven, *J. J. P. Oud en Bruno Taut: Ontwerpen voor een nieuwe stad. Rotterdam-Berlijn* (Rotterdam: NAI, 1994). Van Doesburg also followed developments at the Bauhaus closely and would have been well aware of the expansion projects for Dessau designed by Gropius and his students. In France, Le Corbusier was very restricted in the plans he was able to realise. His housing project at Pessac of 1922 is the single example of extensive planning and design constructed by him during the 1920s. It is fair to say that the Dutch modernists were given far greater responsibilities far quicker than elsewhere at the time.
4 Peter Hall, *Urban and Regional Planning* (London: Routledge, 1992), pp. 197 and 202.
5 'Senator Vinck beantwoordde's Minister's toesprak namens de vele vreemdelingen, die als dragers eene groote idee, van alle oorden der wereld waren toegestroomd om met eigen oogen te aanschouwen wat Nederland reeds tot stand heeft gebracht op het gebied der volkshuisvesting. Spreker meende reeds thans te kunnen voorspellen dat Nederland binnen een kwart eeuw het beloofde land van stedebouw en woningbouw zal zijn' (Senator Vinck answers the Minister's speech on behalf of the many foreign visitors who had streamed from all corners of the world, as bearers of a single great idea, to witness what The Netherlands had already managed to bring about in the field of social housing. The speaker intended already at this time to predict that The Netherlands would, within a quarter of a century, become the promised land of town planning and housing.) Report on the 1924 Congress of the International Town Planning and Garden Cities Association by L. S. P. Scheffer, 'Het Internationaal

Stedebouw-Congres II', *Tijdschrift voor Volkshuisvesting en Stedebouw* 15: 11 (November 1924), p. 251.

6   It is possible to create subsets of De Stijl according to personal friendships and areas of residence. The close association of Wils and Huszár, for example, is based on the artistic milieu of The Hague and their joint activities within the *Haagsche Kunstkring*. I also explore the role of cultural institutions such as museums and exhibiting groups to the formation of De Stijl in the final chapter. In general, though, there was little of the associative activity familiar to comparable avant-gardes.

7   I have derived this distinction between city and metropolis from Massimo Cacciari, *Architecture and Nihilism: On the Philosophy of Modern Architecture* (New Haven and London: Yale, 1993).

8   For the identification of the windmill see Joop Joosten and Robert Welsh, *Piet Mondrian: Catalogue Raisonné* (New York: Abrams, 1998), vol. 1, p. 230.

9   In chapters 3 and 5 I discuss the patronage offered to De Stijl by Cornelis Bruynzeel jr. who was the leading exponent in the Netherlands of modern wood manufacturing methods. Mondrian's attraction to the delapidated wind powered saw mills around Amsterdam can be offset against the factory Jan Wils designed for Bruynzeel at Zaandam in 1920 and the involvement of Vilmos Huszár, Van der Leck and Piet Zwart in designing the company advertising and various products.

10 Charles C. M. de Mooij and Maureen Trappeniers, *Piet Mondriaan: Een Jaar in Brabant 1904/1905* (Zwolle: Waanders Uitgeverij, 1989), pp. 8–9.

11 Robert Welsh, 'Mondriaan in Amsterdam: The Artist at Work', in Robert Welsh, Boudewijn Bakker and Marty Bax, *Piet Mondriaan: The Amsterdam Years, 1892–1912* (Bussum: Thoth, 1994), p. 59.

12 See Vincent van Rossem, 'Berlage and the Culture of City Planning', in Sergio Polano (ed.), *Hendrik Petrus Berlage: Complete Works* (New York: Rizzoli, 1988), p. 46.

13 Maristella Casciato, *The Amsterdam School* (Rotterdam: 010, 1996), p. 21.

14 Casciato, *The Amsterdam School*, p. 7.

15 'Zij sluit daarin aan bij de Berlage-school en stelt zich principieel tegenover de z.g. Amsterdamsche school, waarin het monumentale verworden is tot het in beginsel decadente.' J. J. P. Oud, 'Het Monumentale Stadsbeeld', *De Stijl* 1: 1 (1917), p. 10.

16 'Doordien een openbare straat midden door het terrein gaat, beidt dit ook zijn groote voordeelen voor politietoezicht, levendigheid voor de bewoners enz.; zoodat de gedachte van "op een hofje" te wonen al niet licht bij iemand op zal komen. Ook wordt het idee "kazernewoning" weggenomen doordat men hier vanaf de publieke straat de voordeur van elke woning afzonderlijk ziet.' Michel Brinkman, 'Volksbewoning te Rotterdam in den Polder "Spangen"', *Bouwkundig Weekblad* 41: 8 (February 1920), p. 47.

17 J. J. P. Oud, 'Gemeentelijke Volkswoningen, Polder "Spangen", Rotterdam', *Bouwkundig Weekblad* 41: 37 (September 1920), pp. 219–22.

18 It is worth noting that the stained-glass windows Van Doesburg designed for the lights above the entrance doors in Spangen blocks I and V were based on street and dock scenes painted shortly before. See Els Hoek (ed.), *Theo van Doesburg. Oeuvre Catalogus* (Bussum: Uitgeverij Thoth, 2000), p. 242.

19 A useful account of this argument can be found in Hans Esser, 'J. J. P. Oud', in Carel Blotkamp (ed.), *De Stijl: The Formative Years 1917–1922* (Cambridge MA and London: MIT, 1986), pp. 140–8.

20 'Er is nog een element in Rotterdam dat de praedestinatie van Rotterdam voor wereld-stad nog aannemelijker maakt. Want je denkt niet, je vreest niet, je hoopt niet over 5 minuten zijn we bij de koeien, maar, en dit is het wonder van Rotterdam, je staat voor de koeien, je staat voor de wei.' J. P. Mieras, 'Een Uithoekje van een Wereldstad', *Bouwkundig Weekblad* 44: 33 (August 1923), p. 363.

21 'De blokken zijn bouwwerken, waarvan de zijgevels hoofdzaak zijn, zoolang men voor de voorgevel staat. En aangezien men bij het wandelen, door de rechthoekige elkaar snijdende straten steeds zulk een beschouwingsmogelijkheid heeft, karakteriseert deze architectuur dus typisch de straat, di. De met huizen behoorende weg, waarlangs zich menschen bewegen.' Mieras, 'Een Uithoekje van een Wereldstad', p. 384.

22 'Hij ontwierp deze kleine woonbuurten als een gebouw, als een afgebakend architecto-nisch object, dat zich niet ongestraft als model laat gebruiken voor de hele stad.' Sjoerd Cusveller, *De Kiefhoek: een woonwijk in Rotterdam* (Laren, V+K Publishing, 1990), p. 39.

23 Richard Sennett, *The Conscience of the Eye: The Design and Social Life of Cities* (New York and London: Norton and Company, 1990), pp. 11–19.

24 Van Eesteren made numerous drawings and watercolours during his trip including views of Dresden, Freiburg, Regensburg and Nürnburg, which reveal his interest in the structure of different cityscapes. He also met with Fritz Schumacher in Cologne who was at the time the leading planner in Germany. See Vincent van Rossem, *Cornelis van Eesteren, The Idea of the Functional City: A Lecture with Slides 1928* (Rotterdam: NAI Publishers, 1997), pp. 9–11.

25 Allan Doig, *Theo van Doesburg: Painting into Architecture, Theory into Practice* (Cambridge, Cambridge University Press, 1986), p. 141.

26 'Weet ge, mijnheeren wat een stad is? Een stad is een spanning in de lengte en een spanning in de hoogte. Anders niet. Twee rechte ijzerdraad-verbindingen beelden de stad. Elk individu probeert door middel van: beenen, trein, tram of explosies (de verplaatsing der toekomst) het gemeenschapelijke middelpunt, dezer tween span-ningen te vinden.' I. K. Bonset, 'Tot een Constructieve Dichtkunst', *Mécano* 4/5 (1923), n.p.

27 'Het is ook prachtig als we die viaduktbouw van mij en Tzara meer uitwerken. Tzara is tevreden wanneer we het "système Tzara" noemen. Zijn naam behoeft niet als archi-tect vermeld te worden. Ik zal beginnen de schets beter uit te werken. Het zou een reuze ontwerp kunnen worden. Heel groot – in kleuren met verkeersmiddelen en alles er bij. Door uniforme blokken te laten zagen die ik kleur, kunnen we eens prachtig groot model van weinig geld kunnen laten maken.' Letter from Van Doesburg to Van Eesteren, 12 August 1924, Van Eesteren Archive, NAI, Rotterdam.

28 F. St. Florian, 'Frederick Kiesler, Architekt der Unendlichkeit 1890–1965', in Vienna, Hochschule für Angewandte Kunst in Wien, *Frederick Kiesler: Architekt 1890–1965* (1975), p. 9. One of the few photographs which survive of the *City in Space* shows a group of people gathered in front of it amongst whom can be found both Van Doesburg and Tzara.

29 Doig, *Theo van Doesburg*, pp. 213–14.

30 Theo van Doesburg, 'Vernieuwingspogingen in de Fransche Architectuur', *Het Bouwbedrijf* 2: 1 (January 1925), pp. 32–38, translated in Theo van Doesburg, *On European Architecture: Complete Essays from Het Bouwbedrijf 1924–1931* (Basle, Berlin, Boston: Birkhäuser Verlag, 1990), p. 37.

31 Theo van Doesburg, 'Kunst- en architectuurvernieuwing in Italië', *Het Bouwbedrijf* 6: 17 (August 1929), pp. 341–4, translated in Van Doesburg, *On European Architecture*, p. 252.

32 Van Rossem, *C. van Eesteren*, p. 15.

33 See Cor van Eesteren, 'Moderne Stedebouwbeginselen', *De Stijl* 6: 10/11 (1924–25), pp. 162–8.

34 'Sprak we over het congres in Holland. Hij kreeg van Holland de indruk, zooals een romein van Griekenland.' Letter from Van Doesburg to Van Eesteren, 24 July 1924, Van Eesteren Archive, NAI, Rotterdam. The same letter proposes that Van Doesburg and Van Eesteren present a model of a city at the Paris *Exposition*: 'Kunnen wij van des tijd nog iets maken. Ik heb 'n idee een groot model met weenig kosts, van een stad te maken, alles van de nieuwe verkeersmogelijkheden te manifesteeren.' (Can we make something else at the same time? I have an idea to make a large model cheaply of a city representing everything to do with the new traffic possibilities.)

35 'On attend en hollande que le congrès international des urbainistes sera très important; j'entendrais aussi quelques collèques bien connus de l'angleterre, d'allemagne et de la belgique qu'ils visiteront le congrès. On discutera spécialement la question de la décentralisation de la ville aussi que la question des plans d'extension régionals.' Letter from Oud to Badovici, June 1924, Oud Archive, NAI, Rotterdam.

36 'Ook dat wij in een nieuwe phase zijn getreden, dat de noodzakelijkheid is gebleken niet de stad alleen, maar de stad met haar omgeving, het geweest, te beschouwen, dat de vraag is opgeworpen of de groote stad moet blijven groien, dan wel of zij moet en kan worden gedecentraliseerd, dat ook voor gewesten, welke een ekonomische eenheid vormen, zonder nochthans een kern van overwegende beteekenis te bezitten, een gewestelijk plan behoort te worden ontworpen, het was ons niet geheel vreemd. Het gewestelijk plan had in ons kringen reeds de aandacht.' Editorial, *Tijdschrift voor Volkshuisvesting en Stedebouw* 5: 7 (July 1924), p. 161.

37 'Nadat de heeren Howard en de Miranda hadden geantwoord, werd de tocht voortgezet, ditmaal echter gesplitst, aangezien een gedeelte van de congresleden gebiruk maakte van de geboden gelegenheid om per vliegtuig van de K. L. M. van Schiphol een tocht boven de hoofdstad te maken. Tot deze vliegtuisten behoorde ook Dr. Berlage, die zich op deze wijze ervan kon overtuigen dat de voorstelling die hij zich bij het ontwerpen der uitbreidingsplannen had gemaakt, althans wat de vogel-perspectief betrof met de werkelijke uitvoering zeer goed overeenkwam.' L. S. P. Scheffer, 'Het Internationaal Stedebouw-Congres II', *Tijdschrift voor Volkshuisvesting en Stedebouw* 5: 11 (November 1924), p. 247.

38 Th. K. van Lohuizen, 'Concentratie en Decentralisatie', *Tijdschrift voor Economische Geographie* 16 (1925), pp. 341–50.

39 'Toen de Duitse architectuurcriticus Karl Scheffler twintig jaar later door de Randstad reisde, zag hij zodoende direct dat deze oude metropool eigenlijk een perfecte belichaming was van moderne stedebouwkundige idealen. Zijn reisverslag, getiteld *Holland*, is een bijna hallucinerende beschriving van een miljoenenstad waarin een perfect evenwicht is bereikt tussen een hoogontwikkeld cultuurlandscap en een ring van zelfstandige stedelijke kernen.' Vincent van Rossem, *Randstad Holland* (Rotterdam: NAI, 1994), p. 41.

40 Cor van Eesteren, 'Over het Rokin-Vraagstuk', *i10* 1: 3 (1927), pp. 82–8.

41 'Hij zal steden maken, die hygienisch en schoon zijn door een evenwichtige tegenstelling van gebouwen, constructies en leege ruimten. Hij zal dan even tevreden binnen als

buiten zijn.' Piet Mondrian, 'Neo-plasticisme: De Woning – De Straat – De Stad', *i10* 1: 1, p. 12.

42 'Vreugde, moreele en physieke, dus die van gezondheid, zal zich verspreiden door evenwightige tegenstellingen van verhoudingen, van maat en kleur, materie en ruimte, die gesteund worden door de verhoudingen van stand. Met een beetje goeden wil zal het niet zoo onmogelijk zijn een aardsch paradijs te scheppen.' Mondrian, 'Neo-plasticisme: De Woning – De Straat – De Stad', p. 17.

43 'De idee "tehuis" (Home, sweet home) moet verloren gaan. Eveneens de convention-eele idee "straat".' Mondrian, 'Neo-plasticisme: De Woning – De Straat – De Stad', p. 18.

44 The following account has been summarised from that given in Vincent van Rossem, *Het Algemeen Uitbreidingsplan van Amsterdam*, which is the second volume of Manfred Bock (ed.), *Cornelis van Eesteren. Architect Urbanist* (Rotterdam: NAI, 1993), pp. 120–39.

45 Manfred Bock, 'De Stijl and the City' in Mildred Friedman ed., *De Stijl: 1917–1931. Visions of Utopia* (Oxford: Phaidon, 1982), p. 198.

46 'De Neo-plastiker is meer op zijn plaats in de "métro" dan in de Notre-Dame en hij houdt meer van den Eifeltoren dan van den Mont-Blanc.' Mondrian, 'Neo-plasticisme: De Woning – De Straat – De Stad', p. 18.

47 Württemburger Zietung, 14 October 1927, quoted in Van Rossem (ed.) *Cornelis van Eesteren*, p. 39.

48 Van Rossem (ed.), *Cornelis van Eesteren*, p. 39.

49 Edward Soja, 'The Stimulus of a little Confusion: A Contemporary Comparison of Amsterdam and Los Angeles', in Michael Peter Smith (ed.), *After Modernism: Global Restructuring and the Changing Boundaries of City Life* (New Brunswick and London: Transaction Publishers, 1995), pp. 17–38.

3

Advertising as fine art

To this point I have argued that the abstract aesthetic of De Stijl was a reformulation of the discourse of *gemeenschapkunst* in the Netherlands and I then placed that discourse in the context of urban planning. In each case, we have seen how the vernacular forms of monumental art were negated in the hope of creating a new idiom. Thus in Oud and Van Docsburg's Spangen collaboration, hundreds of working-class Rotterdammers lived with abstraction literally on their doorsteps. They were no doubt blissfully unaware that the colour compositions they encountered on a daily basis were supported by complex and esoteric theories published in a small-circulation journal. Yet that does not discount the fact that De Stijl was as much attuned to a mass audience as it was to the tiny readership it actually managed to reach. This chapter will explore the field in which such concerns came most into focus by examining some of the overtly commercial work engaged in by De Stijl artists. Van der Leck, Van Doesburg and Huszár all readily accepted advertising and graphic design commissions. Although their motivations in carrying out these commissions may have differed slightly – Van Doesburg saw it as a more profitable field than fine art while Huszár was committed to a public art form – their approaches had much in common. Once again it is clear that the use of abstraction has little to do with the purification of fine art. Not only did all of the De Stijl artists maintain a distinct element of figuration in their graphic works but, more significantly, constantly tested and exposed the boundaries of fine art.

Over the last quarter of a century a significant literature has built up on what is often called 'The New Typography'. Within this literature De Stijl has come to occupy a central place and is seen as a key moment in the formation of a modern graphic design idiom.[1] The methodologies adopted by the standard accounts of typography and graphic design owe much to dominant art historical descriptions of modernism. Firstly they tend to construct a history of typography as technical innovation. Despite the fact that the half-tone printing process had been in use since the 1880s, it is frequently implied that only the experimentation of futurism, dadaism and constructivism unleashed the potential of photo-mechanical reproduction and allowed it to supercede letterpress and lithography. The second tendency is to carry over into discussions of typography a concern for surface or picture plane parallel to the developments in abstract painting. This is used to explain both the chaotic look of dada journals and posters, and the clarity of layout

aimed for in constructivism. I do not discount that there is some merit in these
approaches and that they can be usefully applied to the history of De Stijl. What I
want to combine them with here, however, is a discussion of more mundane issues
such as commercial viability, interaction with a mass audience and the emergence
of modern commodity sign production.

It has not gone without previous mention that the very first image to appear within
the pages of De Stijl was an advertisement. The same image, which promoted the
parquet flooring of Cornelis Bruynzeel Jr.'s wood manufacturing company,
appeared in the first six issues in an identical position, taking up the whole page of
the inside front cover (Figure 17). The designer responsible for the advertisement
was Vilmos Huszár and he placed his signature prominently on it. Huszár lived
close to the Bruynzeel family in the Voorburg district of The Hague and had
installed a stained-glass window in their home the previous year. Over the next
decade he was to have far more contact with the family and their business, redeco-
rating and furnishing residences, redesigning the company trademark and

17 Vilmos Huszár,
advert for Bruynzeel,
1917

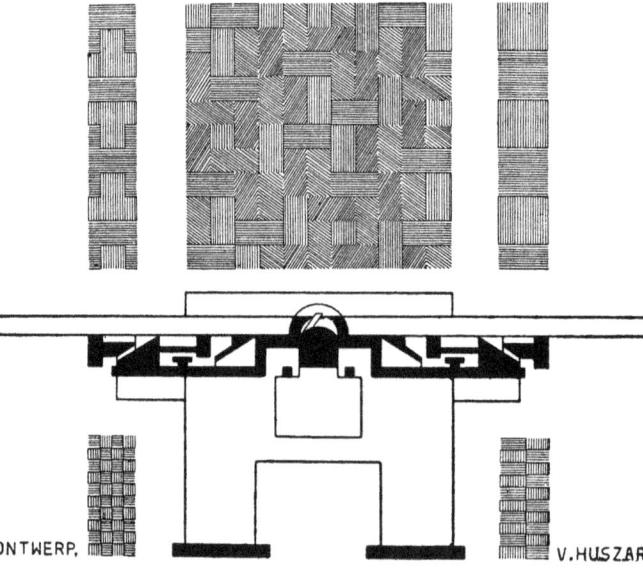

C.BRUIJNZEEL & ZONEN

ROTTERDAM

PARKETVLOEREN

EIKENVLOEREN MET KOPSCHE GROEF EN MESSING

OM DIRECT OP DE BINTEN TE SPIJKEREN

ONTWERP.   V.HUSZAR.

stationery, and producing a trade stand to display the firm's wares. Over the first quarter of the twentieth century the Bruynzeel business grew into the most techni- cally advanced wood finishing company in Europe and Huszár refashioned its image accordingly. The advert in De Stijl was extremely simple and direct; using the patterns of parquet, Huszár divided the page up into blocks broken by text set in a plain sans-serif font. Text and image were kept relatively separate although the justification of the type served to indicate the edges of the page without the use of any further border. The one flourish of the design was the rather ornamental shape at the bottom, which seems to have been derived from the company logo of an eagle. What was very striking for the period, however, was the prominence granted to the artist's signature, which was also made into a distinct feature of the composition. It is also impossible to overlook the way in which Huszár integrated his own mono- gram of an H into all areas of the page.[2]

Readers of De Stijl would have encountered the Bruynzeel advert directly after the front cover of the journal on which another design by Huszár featured. In chapter 1 I described the square, black and white vignette, which appeared between the title and the subheading, and discussed how it was closely related to Huszár's concerns with the interaction of figuration and abstraction (Figure 9). A painting he was working on at the same time as the vignette, *Portrait in Three Dimensions*, explicitly decomposed a figure into small blocks which were then set against each other to emphasise movement on the horizontal and vertical axes. The third dimen- sion was given not by the illusion of depth so much as what formalist theory would later describe as the 'push and pull' of the colours in relation to the picture plane. As I described earlier, in the De Stijl vignette one can still clearly see the profiles of two figures, or perhaps one figure rotated (facing up and down), with the third dimension now understood as the balance between the black figure and white ground. While it may be true that the Bruynzeel advert was less formally ambi- tious, it must be said that it is very comparable in the effects it produced. Both the vignette and the advert share an extreme orthogonality and a tendency to produce an 'all over' effect equalising figure and ground. Both take the square as a basic unit; in the case of the advert, one occupies the focal area of the design. It is quite clear that Huszár has tried to transfer the De Stijl 'look' to Bruynzeel's products. At the same time, Bruynzeel's enthusiasm for a modern image allowed De Stijl to reveal from the very start its suitability for a commercial idiom.

Along with the vignette, the cover of De Stijl was also notable for the unusual appearance of its typography, which was also appended to an extensive range of additional stationery, including headed letter paper, envelopes, compliment slips, receipts, visiting cards and press cards. The common feature of all these items was the format of the words *De Stijl*, which were composed from disjointed blocks and avoided any previous typographic association. One interesting precedent does exist, however. In 1908, the Dutch architect, J. L. M. Lauweriks had launched a journal called *Der Ring* (The Ring) and used circles to make the letters of the title. The blocks of De Stijl function in a similar punning way; they play on the word *stijl*, which in addition to its main meaning of style also has additional connotations of post, rafter, jamb and, as Paul Overy has pointed out, a type of crossing joint in carpentry.[3] De Stijl was represented as a manufactured object like a building or a piece of furniture.[4] The formation of the title also recalls the brick mosaics that Van Doesburg produced for the exterior of *De Vonk*, where standard units were given a surprising variety and concealed patterns. Although the blocks which made up the words De Stijl were not totally regular in length, each letter fitted into a square. A dot was placed in the top right-hand corner of the title to close off the L and give the heading itself a block-like form.

The total effect of the De Stijl title was modern but at the same time extremely primitive. Rather than producing associations with advanced printing methods or luxury, collectable lithographs, the closest visual connections of De Stijl were with the cheapest wood block printing of the previous century or with stencils. A rival Amsterdam publication, *Wendingen* (Turnings), commissioned a different cover for each edition from a renowned artist. In contrast, the format of De Stijl bore association with forms made familiar by the indiscriminate fly-posting of city centres. As has been recently pointed out, the sans-serif form that derived from woodblock printing was based as much on affordability as legibility.[5] The simplicity of the De Stijl title was not necessarily equalled by its clarity. This may have been part of a different strategy, to attract attention precisely by being difficult to read.[6] In any case the look which resulted was similar to the one which had also attracted the cubists and futurists; De Stijl was given the image of anonymity, syntheticism and mass production.

Some practical decisions concerning the graphic look of De Stijl must also have been made, however. It must be recalled that De Stijl appeared at a very difficult moment economically. Although the Netherlands was neutral during the First World War, it did not remain untouched by hardship. In 1917 shortages of food and fuel reached their peak and there was also a national paper shortage. *Het Getij* (The Tide), a literary magazine to which Van Doesburg contributed regularly, was forced to use packing paper for its 1918 editions. Until 1921 De Stijl was printed on a rough text paper. Illustrations had to be printed separately and then loosely inserted. The publisher of the early issues of De Stijl, Harms Tiepen in Delft, also needed a basic level of advertising revenue to make the printing of the journal financially viable. At the outset Van Doesburg imagined a monthly edition of one thousand copies, although throughout its existence De Stijl never exceeded a few hundred subscribers. The simplicity of the Bruynzeel advert was partly born of necessity (the paper could only take woodcut or letterpress) and its prominent placement functioned as an advertisement for advertising through De Stijl, as much as for the company itself. The techniques used looked restrained and economical. As Schwitters would print on the cover of an edition of his magazine Merz in 1924, 'Good advertising is cheap.'[7]

The links established between fine art and advertising on the first pages of De Stijl were not at all disconnected from the discourse of *gemeenschapkunst*. In fact, as

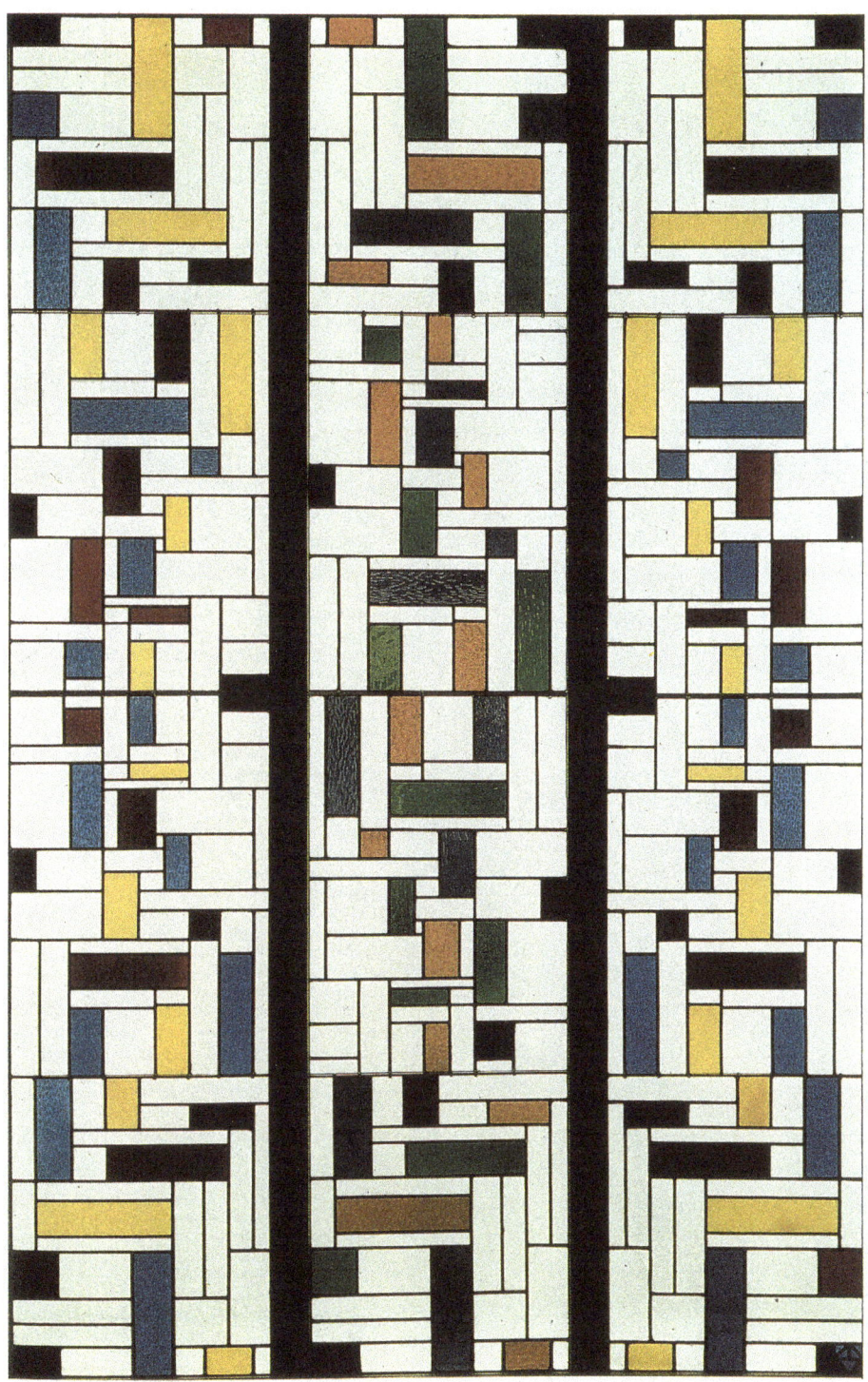

1 Theo van Doesburg, *Stained-Glass Composition IV*, 1917

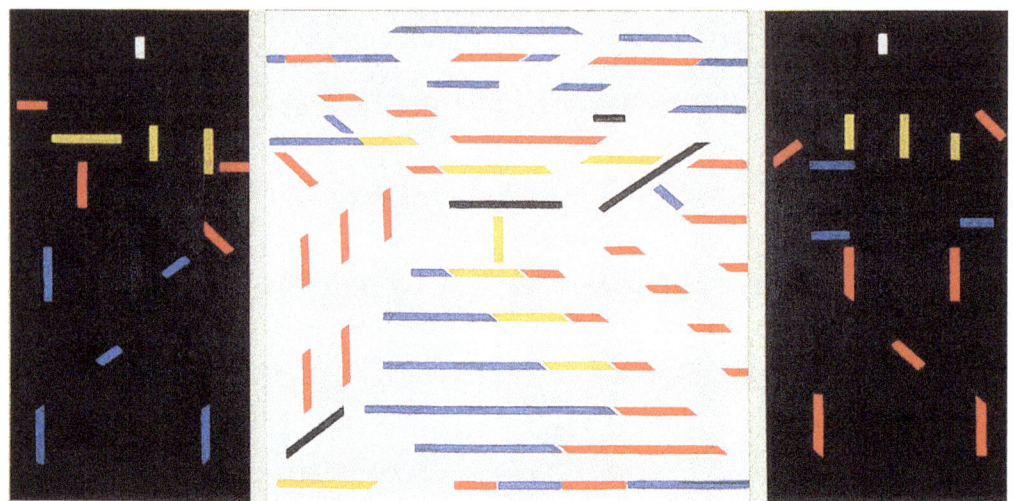

2 Bart van der Leck, *Composition 1916 no. 4*, 1916

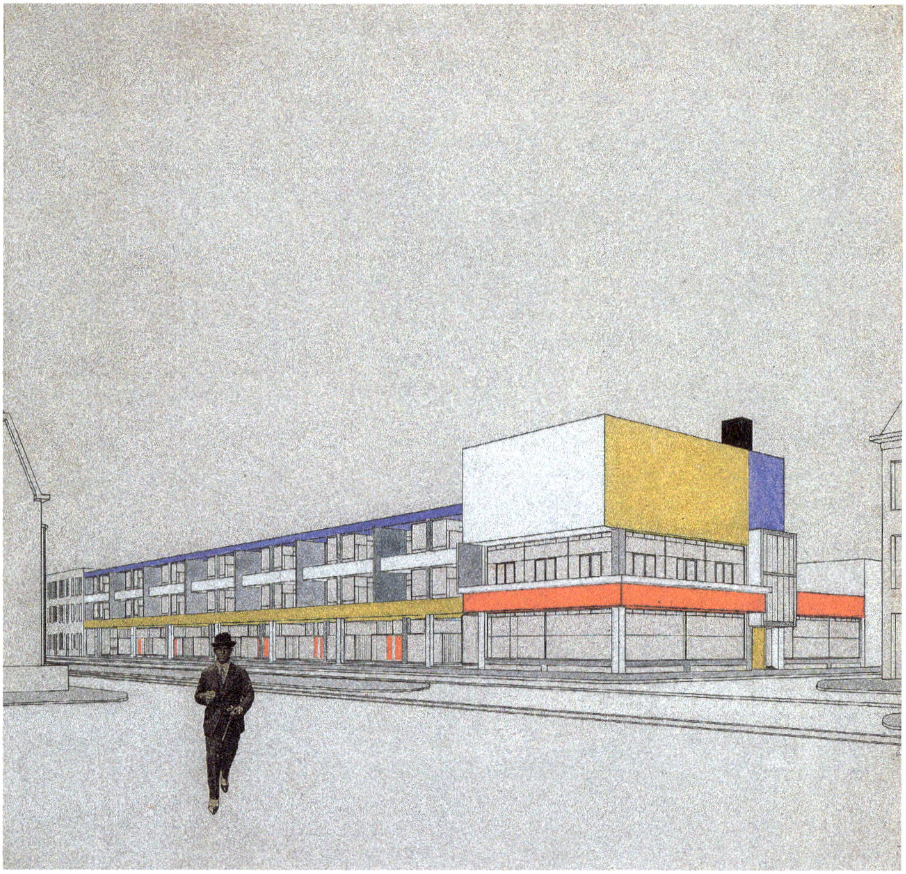

3 Theo van Doesburg and Cor van Eesteren, *Colour Design for a Shopping Parade and Café-Restaurant*, 1924

I will discuss in greater detail shortly, several of the leading representatives of this tendency had produced advertisements. If we take the basic motivation of *gemeenschapkunst* to be the connection of fine art with a large public, advertising offered an ideal means of achieving this goal. Today advertising is viewed as entirely manipulative. Such negative views of advertising were only just surfacing at the beginning of the twentieth century and were spurred on by the crossovers between advertising and propaganda during the First World War. The use of abstraction in advertising, as we have just seen in the Bruynzeel example, was based on the desire to appeal to as large an audience as possible but at the same time to avoid looking over-indulgent. Psychophysical theories of emotional response to colour and form had already penetrated advertising practise in the late nineteenth century. By combining such concepts of empathetic reaction to form with economical production values, De Stijl was able to maintain a universalist agenda and carry on the tradition of an 'art for the people' sponsored by business. To focus these issues it is useful to turn once again to Van der Leck, who became active in this area during the war years.

Significant mention has already been made of Van der Leck's activities on behalf of Müller & Co. and their importance for the emergence of De Stijl. In addition to his stained-glass window for the company headquarters and colour schemes for Holland House (the London office of the company), he also produced a poster for the Batavier-Line, a North Sea ferry service operated by the firm (Figure 18). For this commission, Van der Leck transferred the social realist painting style he had developed over the previous decade to the slightly different format demanded by the medium, in this case lithography. He used a very limited range of colours – red, green, blue, brown and black – against a white background and simplified the objects he depicted into very basic shapes. Smoke billowing from the stack of a steamship is drawn as three sausage-like forms, for example. Obviously the printing technique could have coped with far more subtlety but Van der Leck made a deliberate feature of the separation of colours into distinct, unmodified blocks. Furthermore he divided the whole poster into a series of boxes in which he placed images relating to the service on offer. The top left- and right-hand sides represent the loading of cargo and passengers respectively. The figures are composed to reflect each other in a way that recalls Roland Holst's murals in the Amsterdam Stock Exchange and Van der Leck's *Mine Triptych*, discussed in the first chapter. The smartly dressed man in black on the right is mirrored by a large black trunk on the left, and the young girl dressed in blue is counter-weighted by small blue barrels. Underneath these vignettes lies a rather fetching image of a large steamship, leaving adequate space to put the company name and service in simple sans-serif text.

What is eye-catching about the poster is the modern look of Van der Leck's Egyptianised figures and the neat composition, which uses every corner of the space offered. Also of note is the careful placement at the very centre of the poster of the M logo of Müller & Co. on the smoke stack of the boat. This standard had been adopted several years before when Müller & Co. had purchased the ferry service from the

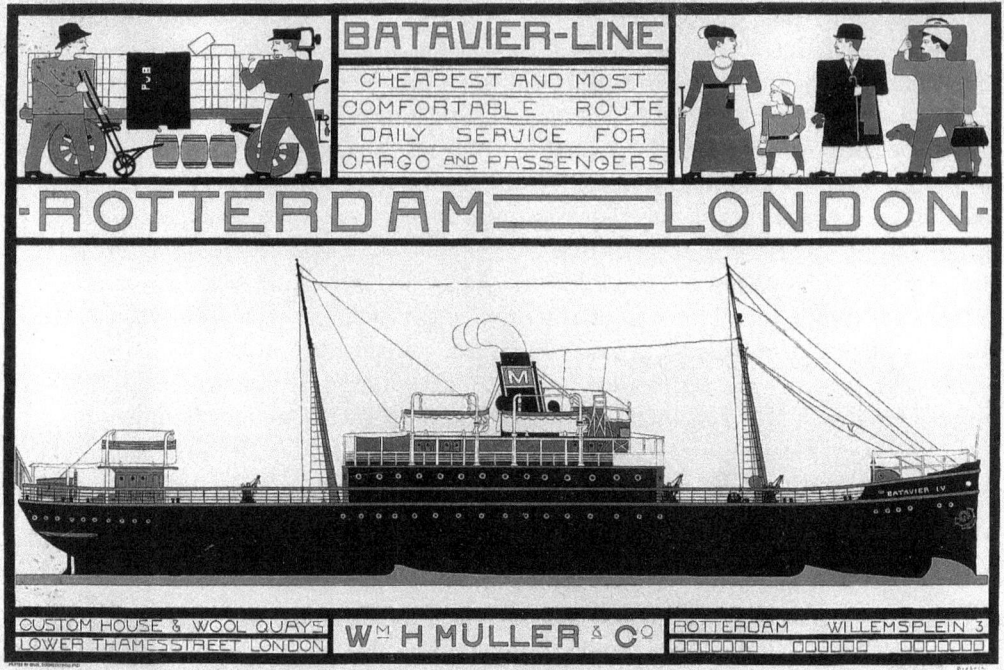

18 Bart van der Leck, *Batavier-Line*, 1915–16

Nederlandsche Stoomvaart Maatschappij (Dutch Steamship Company). What makes
it especially interesting on Van der Leck's poster is the circumstances of the First
World War. As I outlined earlier, Müller & Co., through the activities of Anton
Kröller, was heavily involved with the Netherlands Overseas Trust, an organisation
which managed all foreign trade on behalf of the Dutch government. All goods in
and out the Netherlands had to be carried on vessels operated by the Trust. Given
that Müller & Co. had the largest commercial fleet in the country at the time, advertising was a little superfluous. Van der Leck's poster says more about the perception
of the firm than its need to drum up business. While the smoke pours out from the
stack above the large M and the waves break over the bow of the ship, at the stern the
Dutch national flag hangs completely slack. The choice of the title *Batavier-Line*
had been made to evoke patriotic association with the Batavians, the ancient tribe
from which Dutch people have sometimes claimed descent. As Van der Leck's poster
makes clear, however, in the search for a monumental, national style, big business
had taken the lead from government, just as it was concurrently directing
foreign relations.

The close connections between Van der Leck's fine art and commercial production can be highlighted by his next commission, which again came through Müller
& Co. On this occasion, Hélène Kröller-Müller invited Van der Leck to design a
poster for the *Volksuniversiteit* (Open University) in The Hague where she was a

board member. Here he came up with an even more simplified and abstracted design. In the sketch for the poster it can be seen how he planned to represent the students as a series of schematic bodies reduced to simple black lines. The lettering above and below them was to be made from lines of exactly the same thickness and quality. The figures, as much as they can be discerned, are represented either writing (pens and paper can just about be made out) or reading. Not only were the students depicted engaged in the production and consumption of text, but their very substance had become the lines they were reading or writing. This rather subtle pun was perhaps too well concealed and the *Volksuniversiteit* poster was rejected by the other board members. However, Van der Leck went on to use exactly the same process of figural decomposition for his first abstract painting of 1916, titled simply *Composition 1*. This painting had as its basis the frontal portrait of a female figure which Van der Leck 'decomposed' to a few lines.[8]

Finally, one other poster designed by Van der Leck is important for this discussion. He was commissioned in 1919 by the *Nederlandsche Olie Fabriek* (Dutch Oil Factory), based in Delft, to advertise their salad dressing. In this instance, Van der Leck chose a scene of a shopkeeper offering a bottle and a square tin of the salad dressing over a counter, and again subjected it to his customary process of reduction to basic shapes and primary colours (Figure 19). As in the *Volksuniversiteit* poster, the text above and below the main image was also made up of the same broken blocks as the figure. The most interesting feature of the design, which again failed to win over all the directors and be published, is the limits of legibility Van der Leck tested. The bottle and the tin virtually disappeared in his final sketch but what was preserved was the vestigial trace of the company badge, a crest which was simplified into a black square surmounted by a inverted trapezium. True to his long-standing interest in realist subjects, Van der Leck chose the shop counter as the theme for his advert. However, the image he came up with did not so much proclaim the qualities of the product as the strength of its brand identity. How easy was it to spot this particular salad dressing on a shelf alongside other products? As he demonstrates, even after much reduction of detail it was still clearly visible as *Delftsche Slaolie*. By association Van der Leck also tested the strength of his own personal style. The poster was designed shortly after his split from De Stijl. Although he continued to use the same vocabulary of primary colours and geometric forms, he was keen to demonstrate that his work could be easily distinguished from that of his former colleagues.

In this short sequence of posters, then, we have seen a number of interlocking issues raised: the role of advertising in bringing art to a mass audience, the use of abstraction to engage with this audience, simplification as a means of demonstrating affordability and avoiding accusations of waste, the production of a collective style and the opposite desire to preserve an individual style. Ultimately, Van der Leck's residual concern for his own artistic identity followed a pattern established in the nineteenth century. Posters had in fact become commodities in their own right, as much as the products they were intended to sell. It is well known how

19 Bart van der Leck,
Delfsche Slaolie, 1919

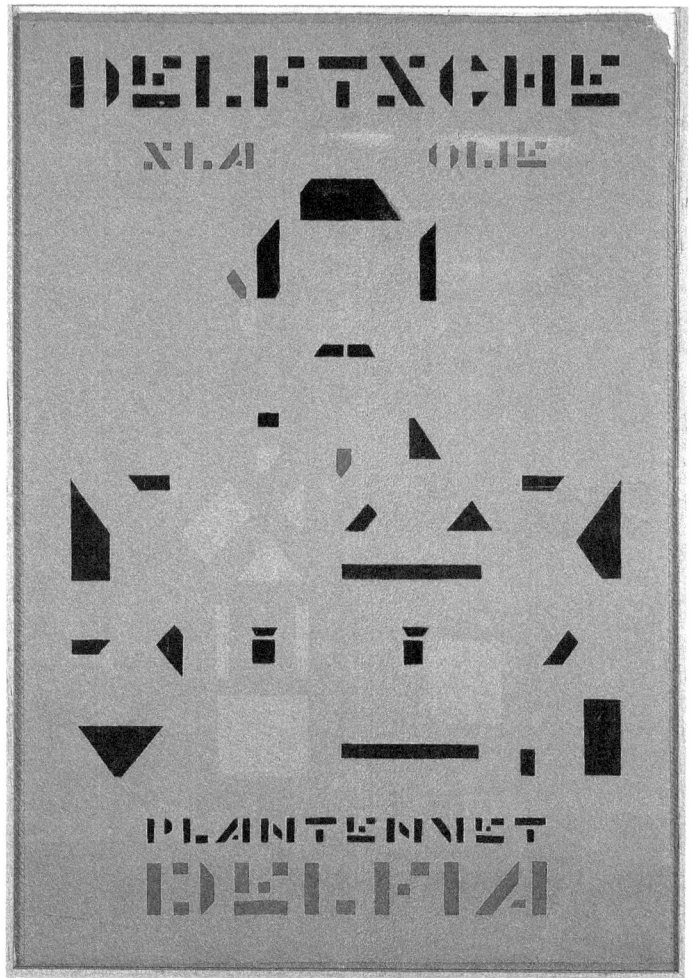

French artists such as Jules Cheret and Henri Toulouse Lautrec made their careers
in commercial work which was appreciated for its artistic qualities and avidly collected. In the Netherlands the debate concerning the boundaries between fine art
and commerce had centred around the ambitions of the *Nederlandsche Olie Fabriek*
to use leading contemporary artists in the promotion of their products. The
director of the company, J. C. van Markens was active in the socialist movement
and wished to bring the best of the fine arts to a mass audience. From the 1890s
onwards he worked with, among others, Theo Nieuwenhuis, Jan Toorop, George
Breitner, Richard Roland Holst and Anton Pieck. Van der Leck was just one of a
long line of artists involved in what was seen by his time as a prestigious commission. So successful was the brand and its 'artistic' identity that for many years Art
Nouveau was known in the Netherlands as 'salad dressing style' after Toorop's
wavy-lined poster of 1894.

However, it was a poster produced by George Breitner for the salad dressing in 1905 that caused most controversy. Where previous artists, such as Toorop, had made specially designed lithographs, Breitner asked printers to produce a lithographic copy of one of his paintings. The reproduction appeared on the poster surrounded by a border carrying the company name. A wave of hostile criticism greeted the publication of the poster, although two different concerns were expressed.[9] For most critics, the primary issue was the seeming lack of relationship between the image and the product. Breitner's painting depicted two white horses next to a building site, a subject seemingly of total irrelevance. Although previous posters had been far from realistic, there had always been some attempt by the artists to integrate the product somehow with the image, such as Jacob Zon's 1895 poster, now looking rather ridiculous, which represents a knight bringing salad dressing to a damsel in distress. A different issue was raised by Richard Roland Holst, who was very sensitive to ethical questions concerning the production and dissemination of art. For him it was the process by which the poster was made that was most scandalous. As a copy of a painting, the lithograph had neither value as a print nor did it do justice to the quality of the original work.[10] Significantly, Roland Holst also criticised the translation of painting into lithography for having introduced too much complexity rather than the simplicity and honesty that poster production should aim for. Although fine artists in the Netherlands had been producing commercial work for many decades, the Breitner incident drew attention to a boundary many had been unaware of before. Breitner had associated his painting directly with a commercial product in order to transfer to it artistic qualities such as sensibility, originality and taste. High art could be brought into contact with commerce to give it an auratic touch. What neither Breitner nor his clients had bargained for, however, was the reverse effect whereby art itself could suddenly become visible as yet another commodity which could be mass produced.

The problematic relationship between modern art and modern commerce introduced to the Netherlands by Breitner's 1905 poster remained unresolved and lingers in the graphic work of De Stijl artists. Although to my knowledge there is no parallel incidence in the Netherlands of a painting simply being reproduced to support a commercial product, there are many subsequent examples of the use of an image with no illustrative link to a product. The theory of the autonomy of visual experience from textual reference, which underpinned the theorisation of abstract art, was closely linked to contemporary advertising techniques where colour and shape were expected to persuade consumers as much as any written content. This can be seen in a fascinating piece of packaging designed by Van Doesburg in 1919 for a major export company in Amsterdam.

Van Doesburg worked for the firm Hagemeijer & Co. on several different graphic design and typographic projects. The company traded mainly in Southeast Asia (Indonesia was still a Dutch colony at this time) and as part of his commission Van Doesburg produced the packaging for a Gouda cheese made especially for export (Figure 20). Here he utilised the same rotational symmetries he had adopted in his

20 Theo van Doesburg, *Prima Goudsche Kaas*, 1919

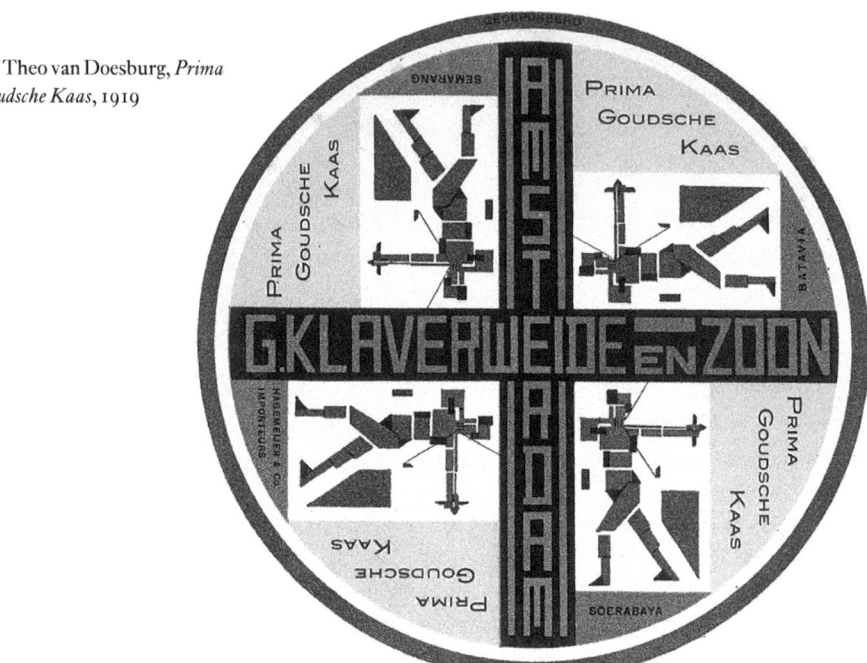

stained-glass windows and created a cartwheel effect with the image of an archer repeated four times around the intersection of the company name horizontally and the word Amsterdam vertically. It appears that Van Doesburg was entirely responsible for the image of the archer which seems to have little relevance to the product. In fact, in his correspondence he expressed concern that his design was going to be rejected precisely for this reason.[11] His fears were unfounded and the firm was won over by the dynamic form the archer created. Its total irrelevance to cheese, the name of the cheese maker or even agriculture in the broadest sense was not seen as a hindrance.

The triumph of the visual qualities of Van Doesburg's archer over any symbolic meaning the figure may have possessed can be compared to the contemporary use of the same motif by Roland Holst. In 1919 Roland Holst designed the cover for a programme of events celebrating the achievement of an eight-hour working day by the *Algemeene Nederlandsche Diamantwerkers Bond* (General Dutch Diamond Workers Union) (Figure 21). He used the image of an archer with the slogan '16 uren voor uw doel' (sixteen hours for your own aim). The figure of the archer was in fact recycled from a wall painting he had made six years earlier, installed in a show room built by H. P. Berlage exhibited in Leipzig. The collaboration between Roland Holst and Berlage extended the reforming ideology of the Stock Exchange building and the archer was captioned *Erwartung* (Expectation). In both incidences, the archer represented progress. In the first case, the archer was placed in the context of the unified collaboration of art, architecture and design, pointing the way to social equality through the production of an appropriate modern style. In the second instance, the archer stands in for the purposefulness of the union in pursuing the rights of the workforce. I have no evidence to show that Van Doesburg deliberately used the image of the archer to mock Roland Holst's symbolism but he would have been very aware of the symbolic heritage of such a figure. On the cheese carton the archer lost all of his lofty meanings. Even the simple aspect of shooting into the future was confused by Van Doesburg's rotations; the figure was represented turning with legs facing one direction and shoulders the other. This seems to me a deliberate reference to the polemic between the two artists at precisely this time.

In 1918 Roland Holst had taken over the directorship of the Rijksacademie from Antoon Derkinderen and used his inaugural speech to attack abstract artists

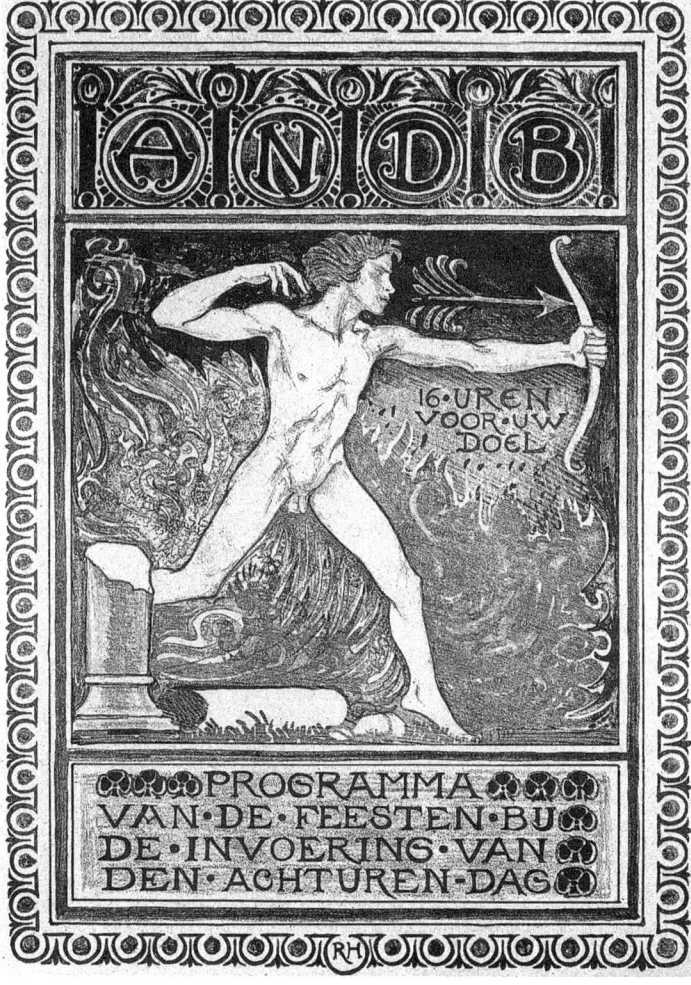

21 Richard Roland Holst, cover of *Programma van de feesten bij de invoering van de achturendag* 1919

for enslaving themselves to the machine. For many years Roland Holst had promoted monumental art as a means of restricting the commodification of the art
object. His antagonism to abstraction was based on its seeming eradication of the
artist's craft and in his lecture he analogised this to a 'mechanisation of the spirit'.
As he continued:

> It [the mechanisation of the spirit] also makes the spirit into a mass product. It abol-
> ishes individuality without achieving a collective unity and because it has no high
> spiritual ideal, its effect is merely a levelling.[12]

Roland Holst had been a definite target of criticism in De Stijl before this speech but
his comments raised the temperature of debate considerably. Van Doesburg reviewed
the speech in De Stijl and accused Roland Holst of representing the end of bourgeois
culture, likening his words to a funeral oration. Where Roland Holst used the analogy
of geometry and the machine, Van Doesburg countered by describing the twists and
turns of the former's decorative style as directionless and decadent. Both men
accused each other of leading culture into decline. Their use of the motif of the
archer was bound up with its symbolic connotations of progress. Perhaps Van
Doesburg also chose the motif because of the challenge of transforming an obviously curved shape, a bow, into straight lines. Moreover, by doing so he also registered a different relation between word and image to that practiced by the leading
lights of *gemeenschapkunst*. Roland Holst's archer acted out the literary associations
with which he was captioned in a very traditional way. Van Doesburg's archer was of
the same order as the text which surrounded him. It could well be that Van Doesburg
chose the archer because his pose created the shape of the letter K, this being the first
letter of the word *kaas* (cheese) and the name of the brand, *Klaverweide*. Where
Roland Holst was keen to maintain a definite connection between the artist and a
public, Van Doesburg, under the aegis of abstraction, is involved in the development
of signs that link consumers to products and processes, rather than producers.

Experimentation with typography and graphic design was connected not merely to
abstraction in the visual arts but attitudes to literature as well. The second manifesto of De Stijl, published in 1920, was concerned solely with literature and
demanded a new role for the word to reinvest it with meaning and free it from the
clichés of journalistic prose. In the issues of De Stijl which followed the manifesto,
Van Doesburg published experimental texts by Mondrian and himself, notably the
X-beelden (X-images) and *Letterklankbeelden* (Lettersoundimages) written under
his dadaist pseudonym I. K. Bonset. The first of the X-images included words set
diagonally and phrases which could have been taken from adverts, features Van
Doesburg no doubt adopted from futurist poetry and the writings of Guillaume
Apollinaire.[13] The *Lettersoundimages* were, as the name suggests, concrete poems to
be read either phonetically or just admired for their look on the page. Each format
fulfilled the requirements of the manifesto that literature be rejuvenated through
the application of 'syntax, prosody, typography, arithmetic, orthography'.[14]

As De Stijl began to feature more and more experimental poetry, Van Doesburg decided to redesign the look of the journal itself. By 1920 he had managed to take personal control of the journal's publication, initially with financial support from Van 't Hoff but later relying on his own personal resources. The following year, the new look De Stijl appeared with a modified subheading of 'international monthly for new art, science and culture' (Figure 22). The international outlook was reinforced by the addition to the title page of the names of cities where De Stijl had some foothold, such as Weimar, Paris, Rome (the list constantly changed). The emergence of De Stijl as an international phenomenon was accompanied by a new look for the title itself; the block typography discussed above was replaced by standard sans-serif font. The most striking addition, however, was a large NB printed in red behind it. This stood for *nieuwe beelding*, although it is doubtful how many readers from outside the Netherlands, or even native readers, would have guessed that immediately. In fact it is a rather paradoxical strategy to re-launch the journal in an international format with text that would have been indecipherable to a non-Dutch speaker. The NB is more likely to have been read by somebody without inside knowledge as the Latin *Nota Bene*. This befits the task of a front cover to grab attention. The journal as a whole was reorientated from portrait to landscape format and the cover redesigned asymmetrically. Correspondence between Van Doesburg and other contributors reveals that this was intended to be both

22 Cover of De Stijl, 1921

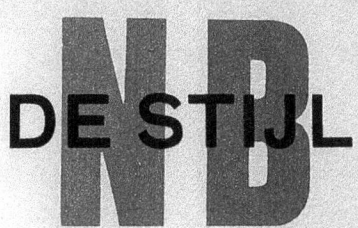

eye-catching and practical. Mondrian wrote to Van Doesburg in the summer of
1920 with a variety of suggestions to make the NB 'jump in the eye'.[15] Van Doesburg
himself explained in detail to Oud that the new format would be much easier to
fold to put into the post without damaging the spine. It could also be carried around
in the pocket in the same way.[16] The same reasoning lay behind the design of
Mécano, Van Doesburg's Dada journal launched the following year, which comprised one large sheet folded into eight. This could be viewed in a variety of per-
mutations while being similarly easily distributed and transported. De Stijl was
very self-consciously marketed, therefore, for an urban audience who might not
just read the journal at home and preserve it on a bookshelf but who would carry it
around to read on a train or in a café. Its peculiar shape and off-centre cover would
also help it to stand out against other journals on a rack and the title, set to the left,
could be left visible when the journal was stacked.

Van Doesburg reutilised the new look of De Stijl to publicise other events tan-
gential to it. In 1923 he participated in the Dada tour of Holland with Nelly van
Doesburg, Kurt Schwitters and Vilmos Huszár. To advertise their first performance Van Doesburg designed a poster using many of the same features (Figure 23).
This time, rather than NB, the word Dada appeared in red under black text, making
it clearly visible in what was otherwise a totally chaotic composition. The other sections of text on the poster described sections of the programme for the *Kleine Dada
Soirée* (Little Dada Evening) to be held at the *Haagsche Kunstkring*. It was the task

23 Theo van
Doesburg, poster for
Kleine Dadasoirée, 1923

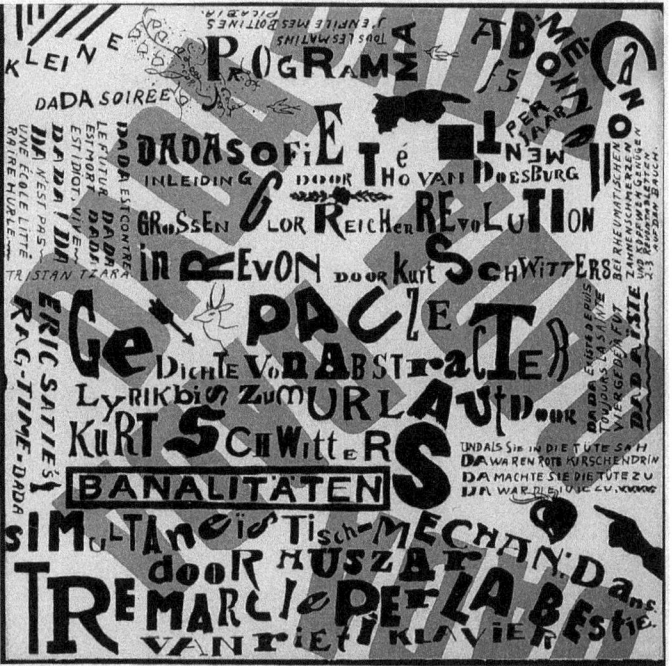

of the viewer to unravel all the pieces from each other and deduce the useful information from the trash. One person who almost certainly attended the Dada evening was Piet Zwart, a member of the *Kunstkring* who was collaborating with Huszár at the time on interior design projects. He immediately demonstrated the applicability of the Dada poster for commercial advertising with a poster design for a nut-based fat produced by Pomona, a vegetarian enterprise based in Utrecht. His 1923 poster for 'Nutter', which claims to be 'handy, tasty and clean' (*nut* in Dutch means utility or benefit), similarly used two-colour type, this time red and green. On the right-hand side Zwart printed the name Pomona vertically in reverse underneath another section of type. Such an irreverent treatment of the client's name would normally be unthinkable but Zwart used the antiauthoritarian associations of Dada to promote a product from a rather alternative manufacturer that was supposed to appeal to consumers for its rejection of convention. Although more orderly than the Dada poster, it was still impossible to judge where exactly to begin reading. Short statements made claims in all directions and ultimately the poster looked as if it was arguing with itself.

Zwart was taken to task for such excesses by Machiel Wilmink, the editor of the journal *De Reclame* (The Advert), who wrote of the dangers of what he termed 'jazz effects'.[17] While accepting the need to be modern, Wilmink considered the restless and confused look of adverts, such as that for Pomona, to be a sign of mental instability. Nor could he see any advantage in the production of adverts which would, as he put it, need Sherlock Holmes to decipher. Zwart had shown, however, that legibility was not the only goal of the new advertising; intrigue, excitement and interaction were also important ingredients. This was especially the case where adverts would have to compete with other illustrations and text in magazines, and also with each other in the case of outdoor advertising. The ability of colour and form to stimulate the spectator was an important concept for both advertising and abstract art and it is hardly surprising that the two crossed over in the early 1920s. By the end of the decade, however, De Stijl would have produced two very distinct reactions to this situation; Theo van Doesburg combined advertising theory with abstract painting while Vilmos Huszár threw himself wholeheartedly into advertising as an 'art for the people'.

In 1925, on a visit to Hanover for the opening of his exhibition at *Der Quader* gallery, Van Doesburg was taken by Kurt Schwitters, with whom he was staying, to visit the studio of a young abstract artist by the name of Friedrich Vordemberge-Gildewart. As the latter recalls:

> I will never forget the moment when Theo van Doesburg came into my studio. He stared at my picture 'K' (no. 9/1924) and asked if I regarded it as a 'painting'. It was not until I had explained that it was a painting and not an advertising poster that he actually greeted me and showered me with compliments for being so courageous in my designs. He seemed very impressed by my work and this was confirmed when he made me a member of *De Stijl* and invited me to Paris.[18]

The narrative recounted here is ambiguous. At first sight it reads as if Van Doesburg rewarded Vordemberge-Gildewart with membership of De Stijl only when he declared the fine art value of his painting, suggesting that he would have had no interest in it had it turned out to be a poster. However, the inability of this leading figure of the avant-garde to distinguish fine art from advertising clearly demonstrates how close the two were to each other at the time. He has it only on Vordemberge-Gildewart's word that what he is looking at is a painting. Read in this way, Van Doesburg could just have easily been impressed by the 'courage' Vordemberge-Gildewart expressed in flirting with a commercial idiom.

Unfortunately the painting that Van Doesburg saw in Vordemberge-Gildewart's studio has been lost. From descriptions of it and contemporary sketches it is possible to deduce that in addition to being called 'K', it had that letter inscribed large upon it.[19] As a founder member of the *Gruppe K* (K Group), a collective of abstract artists in Hanover, Vordemberge-Gildewart could very well have intended the letter to stand as a statement of identity, and this in turn could have lead to Van Doesburg's anxiety over the status of the work as painting or advertising. Was it a poster for an exhibition, for example? Similarly the ambiguity of the associations of the letter k come into play here. The most obvious signification is that of *Konstructivismus*. From 1925 on Vordemberge-Gildewart used the letter k to prefix the titles of all of his paintings. He only later revealed, however, that it stood for *komposition*. But it should also not be forgotten that k is also the first letter of *Kunst* (Art), and was used in this abbreviated form by El Lissitzky the very same year in his essay *K. und Pangeometrie* (A. and Pangeometry).[20] The use of a letter, an extrapictorial device, to draw attention to the value of the object as pure art is an extremely contradictory enterprise. The K painting may also have reminded Van Doesburg of Mondrian's *Composition in Oval with Colour Planes 2* (1914) in which he integrated the lettering from an advertising hoarding for Kub bouillon cubes, as Picasso had shortly before in his *Landscape with Posters* of 1912.[21]

The place that Van Doesburg saw the K painting is also not insignificant to Vordemberge-Gildewart's story. The young German artist was occupying the studio in the Kestner-Gesellschaft recently vacated by El Lissitzky, who had moved to Switzerland to recover from tuberculosis. In his haste to depart, El Lissitzky left behind some eighty sheets of sketches and designs which Vordemberge-Gildewart would use as a visual resource for the rest of his career. They included preparatory drawings for the Proun paintings and proofs of El Lissitzky's major typographic and advertising work, including the designs for the futurist opera *Sieg über die Sonne* (Victory over the Sun), magazine covers for *Broom* and *Veshch-Gegenstand-Objet* and posters for the Pelikan Ink Company, whose director Fritz Beindorff was a major patron and later director of the Kestner-Gesellschaft.[22]

Van Doesburg was well acquainted with El Lissitzky and had published his typographic picture story *Tale of Two Squares* in De Stijl in 1922. Prompted by his encounter with Vordemberge-Gildewart, Van Doesburg wanted to produce an equivalent and coopted Schwitters into a collaboration whose inception is recalled by Kate Steinitz:

> Hardly was *Paradise Fairy Tales* finished when Nelly and Theo van Doesburg came to visit. We talked about typography and architecture, about the journals *Stijl* and *Merz*, about many other matters. Suddenly Theo van Doesburg pointed to the *Hahnepeter* book. Couldn't we make another picture book, an even more radical one, using nothing but typographical elements? Lissitzky had once designed a book of poems in a new typographical style. We would try for the same method but make it entirely different. 'Doesn't Kurt have another fairy-tale manuscript on hand?' asked van Doesburg.[23]

Over the next few months the two artists, Schwitters and Van Doesburg, assembled the small book *Die Scheuche Marche* (The Story of the Scarecrow), which was printed as numbers 14–15 of *Merz* by Schwitters' own Aposs publishing house. It was, as desired, made almost entirely of typographical elements and told a very simple tale of a farmer's annoyance at the inability of his scarecrow to frighten off the birds who continually ate his seed (Figure 24). In a reversal of the ancient Greek fable of Zeuxis, whose painting of grapes fooled birds into attempting to eat them, Schwitters and Van Doesburg satirised the role of art as illusion. In *The Story of the Scarecrow* the birds are not fooled at all by the elementary piece of sculpture which was the scarecrow. Rather, the farmer, who in his rage at one point threatens to kill the scarecrow, is tricked into imagining it to be a real thing (the Pygmalion myth is also cunningly invoked in the simple story). Common sense is only restored to the

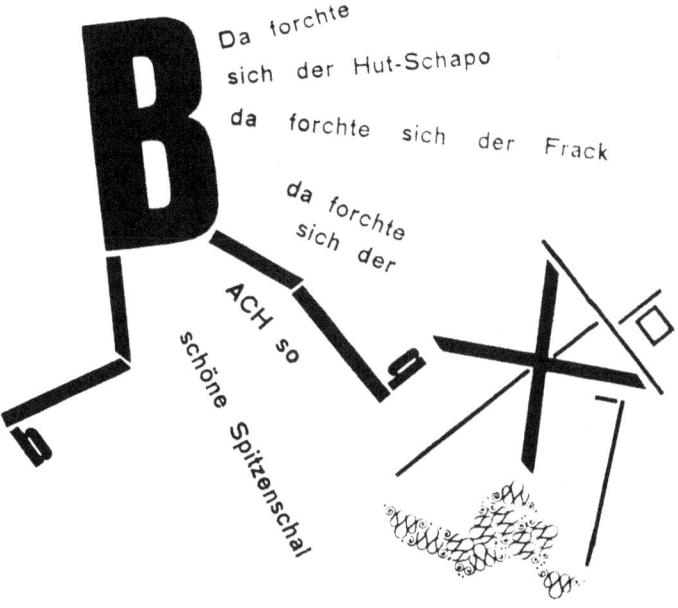

24 Theo van Doesburg and Kurt Schwitters, *The Story of the Scarecrow*, 1925

world at the end of the tale, when the former owners of the items from which the scarecrow has been made reclaim them and we can see that no essence is left over.

The use of type to make pictures can therefore be interpreted as part of the modernist rejection of pictorial illusion; the incursion of letters into painting is a guarantee of its materiality. This parallels Vordemberge-Gildewart's 'K' painting, which was certainly a composition in the modernist sense of having no exterior reference, relying on qualities of surface, colour and balance for its meaning. Yet, the 'K' painting was also an advert to the extent that it desperately tried to sell itself as precisely that, to the extent of branding itself as *Konstruktion*, *Komposition* and *Kunst*. Here we must broach the second moral of *The Story of the Scarecrow*. For the scarecrow Schwitters and Van Doesburg created was indeed the best dressed of his kind; in the story he is described as wearing a dinner jacket, top hat, cane and, an item frequently mentioned, *ein ach so schöne Spitzenschal* (an oh so beautiful lace scarf). The lazy, well-dressed scarecrow is contrasted with the active farmer, introducing an obvious class comparison. Representing fashion and modernity, the scarecrow stands for the superficiality of urban life in comparison to the rural.

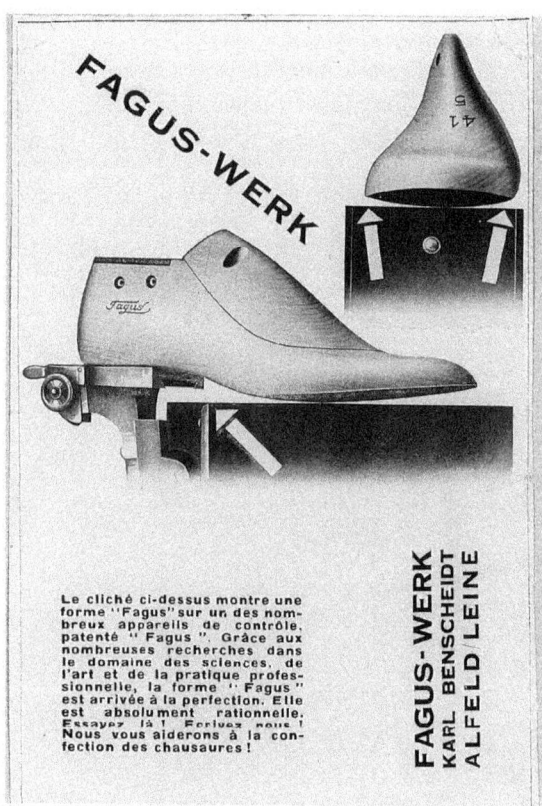

25 Theo van Doesburg, advert for Fagus, 1925

Where the farmer connotes manual labour, the scarecrow invokes the idleness of wealth. Feminised by his beautiful lace scarf, the scarecrow is unproductive and decorative, conjuring up two forms of illusion therefore: naturalistic representation and the modern commodity.

The interaction between abstraction and advertising present in *The Story of the Scarecrow* can be followed in Van Doesburg's subsequent activities during 1925. Another person Schwitters took Van Doesburg to see during the same visit to Hanover was Karl Benscheidt Jr., director of the Fagus shoe factory in Alfeld. Benscheidt was very sympathetic to modernist tendencies (the factory itself had been designed by Walter Gropius and Adolf Meyer in 1911) and had attended a lecture given by Van Doesburg at the opening of his exhibition at *Der Quader*. He commissioned Van Doesburg to produce a poster for the company, which was completed in the summer of 1925 (Figure 25). The

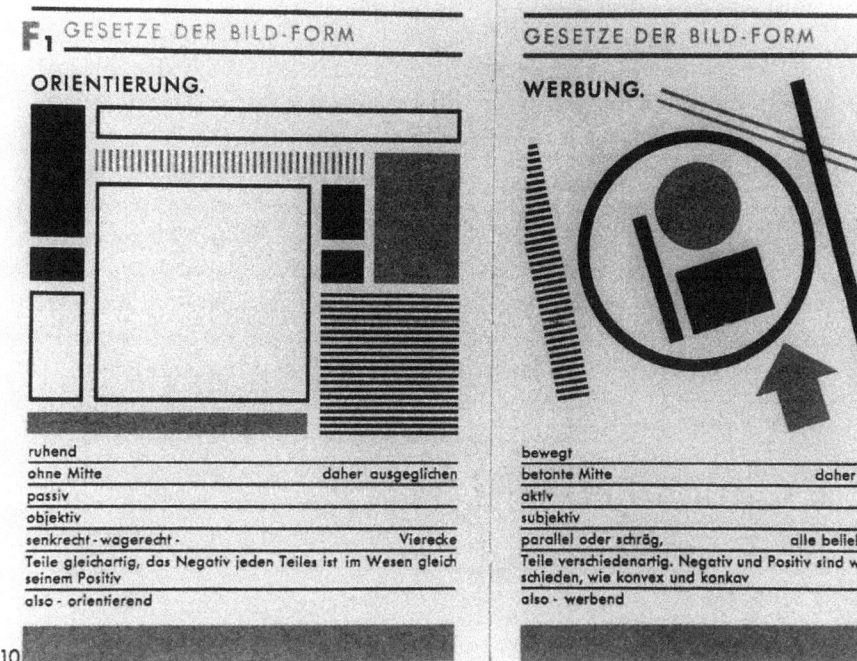

26 Kurt Schwitters, *Neue Gestaltung in der Typographie*, 1925

advert emphasised the rational scientific approach Fagus had developed in shoe production by using photographs of a perfectly designed shoe last. The purpose of the advert was to persuade the customer that readymade shoes in standard sizes were a far higher quality product than those made to order. What Van Doesburg tried to sell to the customer was a means of manufacture as much as the final product, so that he could be sure that factory production of shoes was superior to the traditional work of a cobbler. Any trace of labour is removed from the image.[24] Of particular note is the manner in which Van Doesburg placed the company name, Fagus-Werk, at an oblique angle on the page floating against a plain white field. Such effects were currently being disseminated through Schwitters' pamphlet *Die Neue Gestaltung in der Typographie* (The New Form in Typography), in which a double-page spread contrasted the objective, balanced effects of an orthogonal layout with the subjective impact of diagonals in contemporary advertising (Figure 26).

It was precisely at this moment that Van Doesburg chose to launch his new *elementarist* paintings, which he saw as having progressed beyond the classical, abstract formula of Neo-plasticism.[25] These paintings were typified by the use of diagonal lines which Van Doesburg theorised as anti-naturalistic and anti-architectural, eradicating any lingering references in art to the landscape or the human body. *Counter-composition XIII*, on which he was working contemporaneously with the

Fagus advert, is one of the first paintings he conceived and executed with internal diagonals, after he had experimented for many months with canvases orientated in diamond form. It is striking to see here the reappearance of the K shape he had discussed with Vordemberge-Gildewart. Elementarism is the direct outcome of Van Doesburg's engagement with advertising theory and was as much about grabbing the attention of an audience as it was about the eradication of naturalism in art. This can be confirmed by the cover of a book Van Doesburg planned to publish in 1925 to explain his new approach. Although the book, *Werdegang der neue Malerei* (Progress of the New Painting), never appeared, the cover design remains and shows how Van Doesburg juxtaposed *Counter-composition XIII* with an ancient Roman mosaic, the famous *cave canem* (beware of the dog) described in Petronius's *Satyricon* (Figure 27). In the ancient story Petronius recounted how guests on their way into a party were startled by the image of a large dog they encountered on a wall at the entrance. Like *The Story of the Scarecrow*, the fable seems to offer a warning about art as illusion. By contrast *Counter-composition XIII* denies any kind of representational quality. Yet the two images parallel each other in the ambition to shock and disturb the viewer. Even though Elementarism failed to reach a mass audience, Van Doesburg's attempt to revitalise abstract art by adopting advertising techniques reveals the aspirations he had for it. At the same time Vilmos Huszár had taken the De Stijl aesthetic and translated it into the most contentious of all advertising forms, the billboard.

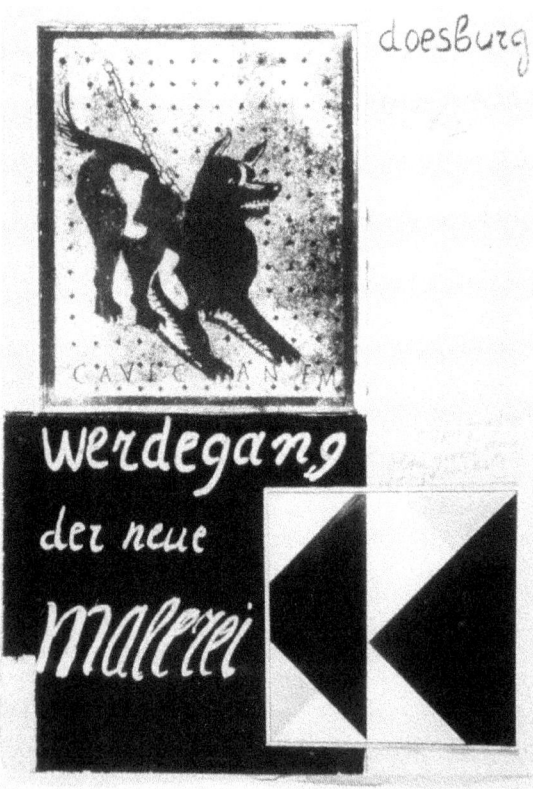

27 Theo van Doesburg, cover design for *Werdegang der neue Malerei*, 1925–26

Right on the street, right in front of the great public of whom the majority never visit an art collector or museum, right in front of them should be exhibited the highest that can be attained in art. . . . Whoever believes in 'Art for the People' has no better means of achieving his goal than advertising art.[26]

In 1927 Vilmos Huszár wrote about his recent experience in producing billboard advertising for the Vittoria Egyptian Cigarette Company of Rotterdam. His article, entitled *De reclame als beeldende kunst* (Advertising as Fine Art), was printed in the avant-garde journal *i10* and then subsequently in the trade journal *De Reclame* (The Advert) and the architectural magazine *Bouwkundig Weekblad* (Architectural Weekly).[27] Huszár made the straightforward claim that the experiments undertaken from the beginning of De Stijl in combining abstract painting and architecture could be best realised in the urban environment through the use of modernist formal devices in contemporary advertising. While Mondrian imagined the transformation of the city into a Neo-plastic environment as a gradual process, moving out slowly from individual interiors such as his studio, Huszár claimed that entire streets could be remodelled overnight. His use of the phrase 'Art for the People' referred directly to the pre-war organisation *Kunst aan het Volk* (Art for the People), set up by the interior designer Willem Penaat to promote good design at affordable prices. Penaat, and others like him, focused entirely on the domestic interior and waged a campaign against what they saw as the ills of mass-produced kitsch. The notion of advertising, the most debased form of modern imagery, coming to the rescue of taste, was total anathema to these ideals.

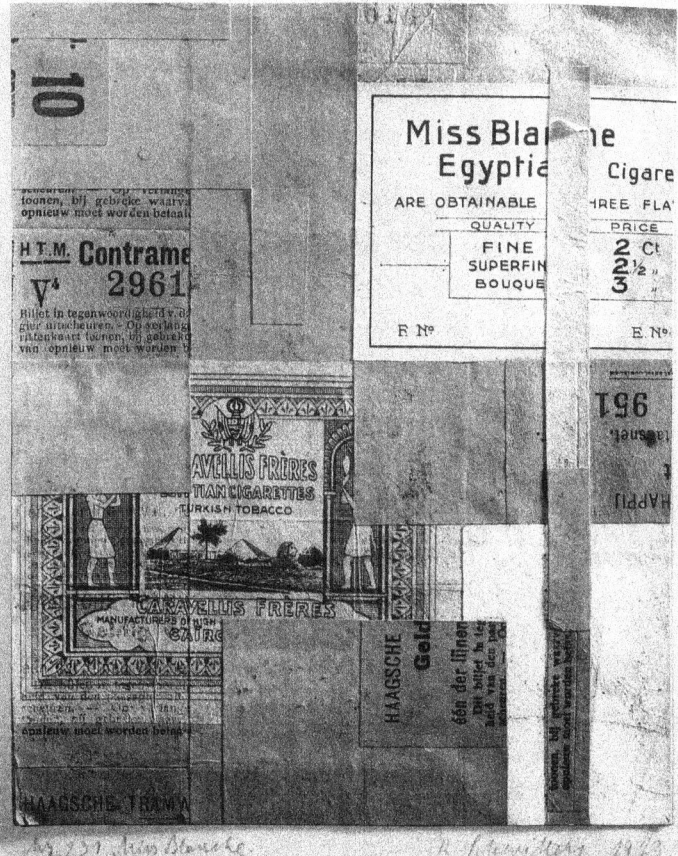

28 Kurt Schwitters, *Miss Blanche*, 1923

There is some debate as to when Huszár received the contract from the cigarette company. His first known designs date from 1925 and the advertising campaign itself began in 1926. However, a collage by Kurt Schwitters dating from 1923, the year he collaborated with Huszár and the Van Doesburgs on the Dada tour of Holland, features a small flyer for Miss Blanche Egyptian Cigarettes, one of the two varieties produced by Vittoria (Figure 28). Schwitters titled the collage *Miss Blanche* although it also featured another wrapper taken from Caravellis Frères Egyptian Cigarettes. The two brands contrast distinctly with each other in that the French brand made use of an ornate design, including a drawing of the Sphinx and statuesque figures, whereas the Dutch brand used simple type. Schwitters seems to have been attracted by this juxtaposition of old and new packaging. The French brand made a great feature of the oriental connotations of smoking which was typical of late nineteenth-century advertising, whereas the Dutch brand tried to create a more contemporary feel.[28] Also included in the collage are several tickets for the *Haagsche Tramweg Maatschappij* (Hague Tram Company), invoking associations with the prevalence of smoking in public places and the consumption of advertising while in motion through the cityscape. Repeated all over the composition is a section of text from these tram tickets which reads *opnieuw moet worden betaald* (must be paid again). This fragment, which is obviously something to do with penalties for a lost ticket, suggests in this context both the need for the renewal of the look of the cigarette adverts and also the effect of advertising to maintain demand. Although it may well have been pure coincidence, the existence of this collage, Schwitters contact with Huszár and what is known of the German artist's involvement in advertising production, make it tempting to speculate that contact had already been made with the cigarette company at this stage.

Huszár redesigned the brand image of both the Miss Blanche Egyptian Cigarette and the Miss Blanche Virginia Cigarette produced by Vittoria. Each of these featured a young woman smoking but they differed greatly in appearance. Huszár was not responsible for the choice of a female figure, which already existed in the brand name. The marketing of cigarettes at female consumers was a major phenomenon of the period, although women had begun appearing in cigarette advertising as early as the 1890s. By the 1910s cigarette companies were producing brands like Miss Blanche, named after women, of which perhaps the most successful was Manoli's Gibson Girl, released in 1911. For the Egyptian Cigarette Huszár designed an image of a woman's profile greatly stylised and abstracted to a few lines. Although by no means an imitation of Egyptian art, it did reference the hieratic stiff posture of ancient sculpture while giving clues to the modernity of the figure, who has the fashionable bobbed hair of the time. The design for the Virginia Cigarette was more striking with its young smartly dressed woman looking out directly at the spectator (Plate 4). She also had short hair, partly concealed by a trim hat, which did not quite reach her sharp collar. Perhaps as a response to the success of Gibson Girl, Huszár identified the Miss Blanche Virginia Cigarette with the look of a young, independent American woman. This image was then broken down into a De Stijl colour range; her eyes and glove were blue, jacket red, hat and hair black, sweater and cigarette white and the background yellow. No text was included on the poster other than the brand name. No claims were made for the taste, economy or effects of the product. The image itself was allowed to do all the selling and with this new design the company launched a massive nationwide campaign which made Miss Blanche a household name.[29]

Despite the boldness of the Miss Blanche image, Huszár's claims to be producing fine art for a mass audience need further elucidating. Although neatly composed and coloured, it is difficult to place these images alongside the best painting of the day, even that of Huszár himself. What was important for Huszár, however, was to banish the type of illustrative advert which was the standard until this date. In his view, the modern billboard had introduced a new form which demanded more than the expansion in size of the older advertising poster. The scale of outdoor advertising was perfect for the realisation of the long hoped for *gemeenschapkunst* and the collaborative ideal of De Stijl. Huszár's conception of advertising was intended to work in conjunction with the architectural environment as a form of monumental art. He claimed in his article that streets could be remodelled through the application of advertising to their aesthetic advantage rather than detriment. Piet Zwart supported Huszár's position and called this work *bouwkunstvriendelijk* (architec-

29 Vilmos Huszár, advert for Miss Blanche Virginia Cigarettes, illustration from *i10*, 1927

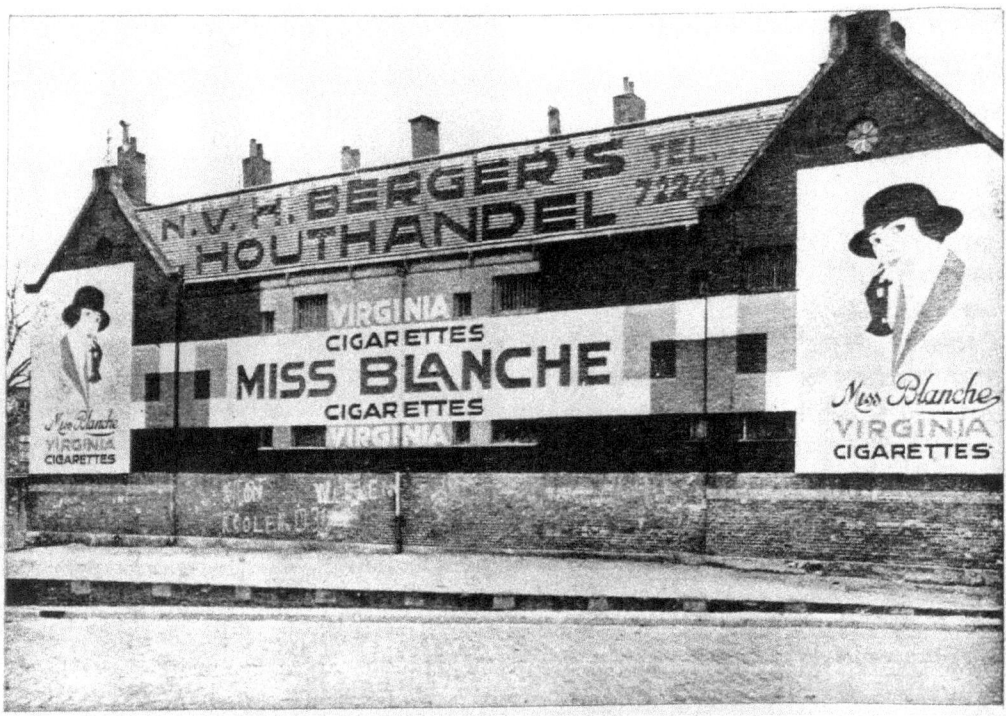

ture-friendly). In an article about the Miss Blanche campaign, Zwart compared Huszár's Miss Blanche design to a contemporary aspirin advert which also featured a young woman but in a more traditional illustrative format.[30] According to Zwart, the flatness of the Huszár in comparison did far less to disrupt the architectural integrity of the facade against which it was placed. Moreover it appears that Huszár carefully considered the placement of each of his billboard designs and made alterations to accommodate each individual situation.[31] One of the photographs he chose to illustrate his article in *i10* demonstrates his attention to detail (Figure 29). It shows a long, symmetrical facade on which was placed two large posters advertising the Miss Blanche Virginia Cigarette. The first notable adjustment is the reversal of the poster on the left so that the two figures face each other. Running between the posters is a long band on which the brand name is interspersed with simple rectangular blocks of colour. It is clear to see that Huszár cleverly integrated the windows of the facade into his composition and paid great consideration to the points at which it would be broken by the slight projection of the gable ends and the down pipe from the guttering. This was indeed then an original, unique art work, although its form has all the appearance of mass production.

As we have seen, the debate concerning the interaction between fine art and advertising in the Netherlands began with Toorop's 'salad dressing' style of the 1890s, where leading representatives of *gemeenschapkunst* were invited to use the mass-distribution facility of modern marketing to bring their work to the population at large. George Breitner chose to do this through the simple reproduction of a painting rather than specifically designing a poster. In each instance, however, the aspiration was to raise the status of advertising by association, while maintaining a clear high/low hierarchy. The intervention of De Stijl confused these distinctions and fine art became more and more informed by advertising, to the point where Van Doesburg was unable to distinguish one from another and Huszár began to make unique billboards. Along the way these artists each had to consider the identity of the new mass audience for whom advertising was being made. In the pre-war era this had clearly been the male manual worker. *The Story of the Scarecrow* and Huszár's Miss Blanche suggest that such assumptions concerning class and gender could no longer be relied upon.

Notes

1 The wellspring of the historiography of modern typography is Herbert Spencer, *Pioneers of Modern Typography* (London: Lund Humphries, 1969). Van Doesburg enjoys a prominent place in this book second only to El Lissitzky.

2 On Huszár's monograms see Sjarel Ex and Els Hoek, *Vilmos Huszár. Schilder en ontwerper* (Utrecht: Reflex, 1985), p. 150.

3 Paul Overy, *De Stijl* (London: Thames and Hudson, 1991), p. 8.

4 The design of the De Stijl's visual identity to reflect processes of production parallels a subsequent discussion in this chapter of the marketing of goods to relate consumers to products rather than producers. A much fuller and more sophisticated description of

this tendency can be found in Frederic Schwartz's brilliant analysis of the German context, *The Werkbund: Design Theory and Mass Culture before the First World War* (New Haven and London: Yale, 1996). There are distinct links between the discourse of modern advertising in Germany and the Netherlands which I do not have the space here to outline but I am indebted to Schwartz's study for the theorisation of the connection between modernism and commodity sign production.

5 Kirk Varnedoe and Adam Gopnik, *High and Low: Modern Art and Popular Culture* (New York: Museum of Modern Art, 1990), p. 60.

6 Adolf Loos used precisely this strategy for his journal *Das Andere* (The Other) and in a 1903 essay argued that the illegibility of posters produced by the Secession had guaranteed it free advertising in the mainstream press which, by discussing this issue, provided much greater 'visibility' for their activities. See Janet Stewart, *Fashioning Vienna: Adolf Loos's Cultural Criticism* (London: Routledge, 2000), p. 31.

7 Spencer, *Pioneers of Modern Typography*, p. 96.

8 It is worth noting that in discussion of the *Volksuniversiteit* poster Kröller-Müller first expressed concern about Mondrian's influence on Van der Leck. She made no explicit distinction between his 'fine' and 'applied' art work.

9 For a good summary of this criticism see Alston Purvis, *Dutch Graphic Design, 1918–1945* (New York: Van Nostrand Reinhold, 1992), pp. 16–17.

10 Richard Roland Holst, 'Een slecht voorbeeld', *De Kroniek* 11 (1905), pp. 253–4.

11 Letter from Van Doesburg to J. J. P. Oud, 18 June 1919, Van Doesburg Archive, RKD.

12 'Zij maakt van den geest ook een massaproduct, zij heft de individualiteit op, zonder tot een collectieve eenheid te geraken en daar zij geen hoog geestelijk ideaal heeft, is haar werking louter nivelleerend.' Richard Roland Holst, 'Ethische factoren in de moderne schilderkunst' (1918), published in *Over Kunst en Kunstenaars: Beschouwingen en herdenkingen* (Amsterdam: Meulenhoff, 1923), p. 167.

13 See David Steel, 'Surrealism, Literature of Advertising and the Advertising of Literature in France 1910–1930', *French Studies* 41 (July 1987), pp. 283–97.

14 Theo van Doesburg, Anthony Kok, Piet Mondrian, 'Manifest II van "De Stijl". De literatuur', *De Stijl* 3: 6 (April 1920), pp. 49–54.

15 'Zou 't nog niet leuker zijn de NB in 't oog te laten springen door die zwart te maken en De Stijl rood?' (Would it not be nicer to have the NB catch the eye by making it black and De Stijl red?) Mondrian, letter to Van Doesburg, 5 August 1920, Van Doesburg Archive, RKD.

16 'De indeeling is geheel uit de praktijk ontstaan: het opvouwen en dragen in de zak' (The division came about purely for practical reasons: folding and carrying in the pocket) Letter from Van Doesburg to Oud, undated, Fonds Custodia, Paris. Van Doesburg also explained the rationale behind the redesign of the journal in his editorial in *De Stijl* 4: 2 (February 1921), pp. 17–18.

17 Machiel Wilmink, 'Jazz Effects in Dutch Printing and Some Reason for their Failure' *Advertising Display*, supplement to *Advertiser's Weekly* (5 November 1926), p. 140.

18 Friedrich Vordemberge-Gildewart, 'Fragment of an Autobiography', undated manuscript published and translated in Dietrich Helms, *Vordemberge-Gildewart: The Complete Works* (Munich: Prestel, 1990), p. 12.

19 Helms, *Vordemberge-Gildewart*, p. 256.

20 El Lissitzky, 'K. Und Pangeometrie', in Carl Einstein and Paul Westheim (eds), *Europa Almanach* (Potsdam: Gustav Kiepenhauer Verlag, 1925), pp. 103–13.

21 Mondrian's painting *Compostion in Oval with Colour Planes 2* had been in the posses-
    sion of Salomon Slijper since 1919 but was exhibited in a Mondrian retrospective at
    the Stedelijk Museum, Amsterdam in 1922.

22 For comprehensive surveys of the typographic work of Vordemberge-Gildewart and
    Schwitters, including reference to the Pelikan ink commissions, see Wiesbaden,
    Landesmuseum, *'"Typographie kann unter umstanden kunst sein": Vordemberge-
    Gildewart, Typographie und Werbegestaltung'* (1990) and Wiesbaden, Landesmuseum,
    *'"Typographie kann unter umstanden kunst sein": Kurt Schwitters, Typographie und
    Werbegestaltung'* (1990).

23 Kate Steinitz, *Kurt Schwitters: A Portrait from Life* (Berkeley: University of California
    Press, 1968), p. 41.

24 An interesting comparison might be made with Lucian Bernhard's famous *Stiller* shoe
    poster of 1908. Between this and Van Doesburg's *Fagus* advert, the emphasis has
    changed from the image of a 'type' to the representation of the production values. For
    Bernhard see Schwartz, *The Werkbund*, pp. 137–9.

25 Theo van Doesburg, 'Schilderkunst. Van kompositie tot contrakompositie' *De Stijl* 7:
    73/74 (1926/1927), pp. 17–28.

26 'Juist op de straat, juist voor het groote publiek, waarvan de meesten nooit naar een
    kunstverzamelaar of naar musea gaan, juist voor dezen moet het hoogste wat men in
    kunst bereiken kan, tentoongesteld worden . . . Wie in "Kunst voor het Volk" gelooft,
    heeft geen beter middel ter bereiking van zijn doel dan de reclamekunst' Vilmos Huszár,
    'De Reclame als Beeldende Kunst', *De Reclame* 8: 4 (1929), p. 167.

27 Vilmos Huszár, 'De Reclame als Beeldende Kunst', *i10* 1: 5 (1927), pp. 161–3; *De
    Reclame* 8: 4 (April 1929), pp. 167–79; *Bouwkundig Weekblad* 50: 20 (1929), pp. 155–60.

28 Michael Wiesser has noted this transformation in cigarette advertising from the orien-
    talism of the 1880s to the cosmopolitan branding of the 1920s in his book *Cigaretten-
    Reklame: Über die Kunst, blauen Dunst zu Verkaufen* (Munich: Edition Deutsche
    Reklame, 1985), p. 16.

29 Ex and Hoek, *Vilmos Huszár*, p. 113.

30 Piet Zwart, 'Goed Begrepen Overheidsbemoeiing?' *Bouwkundig Weekblad*, 48: 32
    (1927), pp. 286–8.

31 Ex and Hoek, *Vilmos Huszár*, p. 113.

4

Structures of interior design

One continuous theme of this book has been the way in which De Stijl reworked the tradition of *gemeenschapkunst*, the desire to create a common culture from modernism. My concentration on the public space that De Stijl contested, such as urban planning and advertising, has led me to postpone an analysis of what is often considered the archetypal product of De Stijl, namely the abstract coloured interior. As we saw in the discussion of Mondrian's text *Home – Street – City*, he envisaged his manipulation of the private dwelling as the model which could later be extended to the exterior, and eventually to the whole pattern of urban development. The individual cell as the basic unit of urban design was also crucial to Oud's conception of modern city life. By reversing the order in which these topics have been addressed, beginning with urban planning, moving to advertising and only now turning to the interior, I may be seen by some as producing a classic piece of Marxist inversion. However, I am not attempting a description of De Stijl as a mere effect of a process of modernisation. Rather, what I hope to show in each instance is the crucial role played by De Stijl in the construction of the modern Dutch subject, even if this role was often one of negation. Therefore this chapter will examine how interior space in the Netherlands, primarily that of the private house, was not an empty vessel awaiting the application of colour but already the object of a reform discourse which had highlighted issues such as hygiene, division of domestic duties and the expression of personal taste. The interior was not conceived of as separate from the exterior world, as is witnessed by the growing intervention of public bodies which aimed to regulate its appearance and use. Mondrian's desire to remake the city along the lines of the interior shows an awareness that public and private space are indelibly connected. The inhabitant of the De Stijl environment did not enjoy total mastery of it but was cajoled to behave in particular ways. If the fundamental characteristic of De Stijl interiors was the overwhelming use of colour, we shall see that this covertly introduced an excessive, almost fetishistic, attention to spatial organisation. By the later 1920s Van Doesburg positioned De Stijl against functionalism but in many ways the deconstruction of the traditional interior he and his colleagues had carried out led in this direction. However, before we can make such a judgment it is necessary to consider some interior spaces.

An obvious historical problem of describing interiors, especially those no longer extant, is how to reconstruct the manner in which they were inhabited and experienced. In order to give an introductory account of contemporary Dutch interiors, in this case domestic ones, I will begin with examples which might not necessarily have documentary value but which are highly evocative. The first is taken from a novel, the second is a painting and they each succinctly introduce ideas about the interior that will be of concern later in the chapter. To begin with, then, we have the first paragraph of Louis Couperus's 1892 novel *Extaze* (Ecstasy):

> Dolf van Attema, out for a walk after dinner, went to visit his wife's sister, Cecile van Even, who lived on the road to Scheveningen. He waited in the small front room, walking between the small pieces of rosewood furniture and the old rose moiré causeuses with the three, four large steps by which he seemed to measure over and over again the narrow width of the room. Behind the chaise-longue an onyx lamp stood burning on an onyx column, glowing under its square shade like a large hexagonal flower of light.[1]

Couperus wrote extensively about the manners and morals of the midde class in The Hague at the turn of the century. His subject in *Extase* was the life of a young widow, Cecile van Even, and her rediscovery of love. In a typical novelistic strategy, we are introduced to her by means of her house and in particular by a rather dainty reception room. The male character, her brother-in-law, feels totally out of place in this space. Couperus constantly contrast the size of Dolf to the narrowness and clutter of the room. Not only is the interior feminised by scale but also by colour: rose and rosewood. The analogy of light and flower at the end of the paragraph completes the metaphorical transformation of the interior from an artificial into a natural environment, so that Cecile's house becomes an extension of Dolf's after-dinner walk. The description of the lamp also conjures up a sense of intimacy which is born out in the items of furniture mentioned: a chaise-longue and causeuses, a type of two-seater sofa on which one might engage in *causerie* (chit-chat). In just a few sentences Couperus managed to include a complete repertoire of gendered themes for the interior connected to nature, sociability and intimacy, adding a final touch in his repetition of words (walk/walking, rosewood/rose, onyx/onyx, again/again); the feminised interior is a place of passivity and routine.

My second example is much closer in time to the De Stijl years but reveals little structural change from the first. It is a painting by Jan Sluijters, who had exhibited frequently with Mondrian before the First World War and was considered to be a leading representative of modern, fauve-inspired painting in the Netherlands. The work in question, titled *Het Gezin* (The Family) of 1925 (Figure 30), depicts his parents and two spinster sisters in the family home. As in our first example, the most noticeable aspect of the room in which the family has gathered is the lack of space. It is virtually impossible to see the carpet as every available square metre is covered by furniture. While less attention has been paid to making the items match

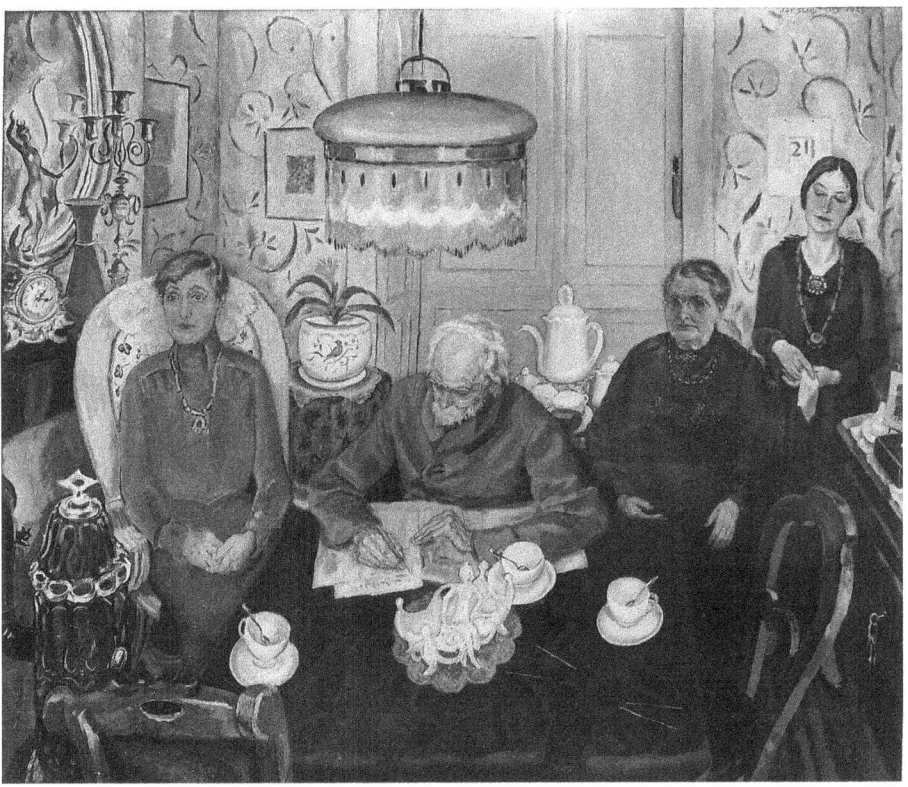

30 Jan Sluijters, *The family*, 1925

(there is in fact a completely odd assortment of chairs and tables), floral patterns predominate. Intimacy and sociability are again figured but this time through different signifiers, such as the hearth and the tea service, which indicates that the family has engaged in a collective activity. Without such signifiers the family members would look completely disengaged from one another. This is especially the case with the female figures who are posed statically and whose existence seems no different to the furniture which surrounds them. The paterfamilias occupies the central position and is, in contrast, the only figure actively engaged (notably with something intellectual). His importance is emphasised by the large ceiling lamp which hangs over him and would spotlight him when lit. Where my first example pointed firmly towards the interior as a feminised, decorative space, here we see how the family structure, with father at the head, was impressed on this space through the arrangement of objects.

The theatre of family life observable in Sluijters' painting was produced with a standard set of objects which would have featured in the majority of Dutch houses of the time. As Paul Fuhring and Rudolphine Eggink have described, this structure cut across class boundaries.[2] The defining characteristics of the middle-class sitting room was a centrally placed table and chairs with lamp above, with a good tea service providing a centre piece. Lower-class households with fewer rooms at their disposal aspired to precisely the same configuration but needed to make the space multi-functional (sitting, dining and perhaps cooking all in the same area). Sideboards became key additional items of furniture which permitted the quick transformation of a room between dining and sitting. In both cases, even when

31 Johanna van Gogh-Bonger sitting room, 1905

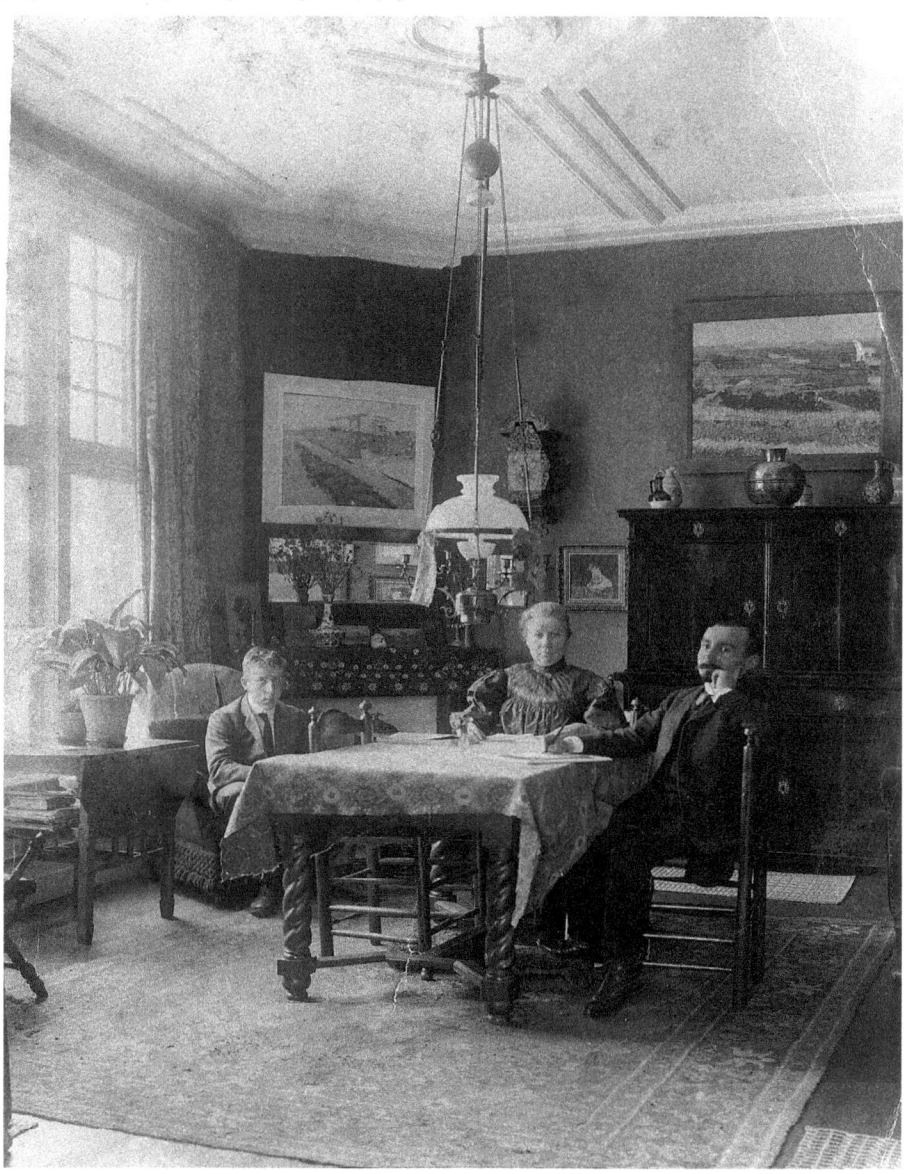

family members were absent from the home, the structure of family life was preserved through the configuration of the interior.

Even in more unconventional households, the basic structure of the interior was
preserved, as witnessed by a photograph of the sitting room of Johanna van Gogh-
Bonger taken around 1905 (Figure 31). She is seen alongside her second husband,
the artist Johan Cohen Gosschalk, and the son from her first marriage, Vincent
Willem van Gogh. Once again the format of central table with lamp above stages
the family. As in the Sluijters painting we also see the man of the house engaged in
writing. However, on this occasion the structural arrangement of objects serves to
highlight the unusual pattern of family relationships in this household; Johanna
van Gogh-Bonger, who was eleven years older than her husband, has usurped the
position at the head of the table. Her son occupies a lower seat and in his separation
from the table indicates his distance from his stepfather. The design of the interior
defined the roles that the inhabitants might play but did not necessarily predict
who would take what part.

Having established the essential characteristics of the Dutch domestic interior,
let us now turn to a very different space, one designed by Gerrit Rietveld for Truus
Schröder in 1921 (Figure 32). The room in question predated the famous Schröder
house, which I will discuss below, and was in the home that she shared with her
husband and their three children. Fritz Schröder was a successful lawyer and the
family lived in a substantial apartment above his offices on Biltstraat in Utrecht.
The marriage was troubled by constant arguments, however, particularly over the
upbringing of the children. Fritz was a practising Catholic and wanted the children
educated in a Catholic school. Truus had broken with Catholicism and was enthusiastic about progressive educational theories, in particular those of Maria

32 Gerrit Rietveld, *Interior for Truus Schröder*, 1921

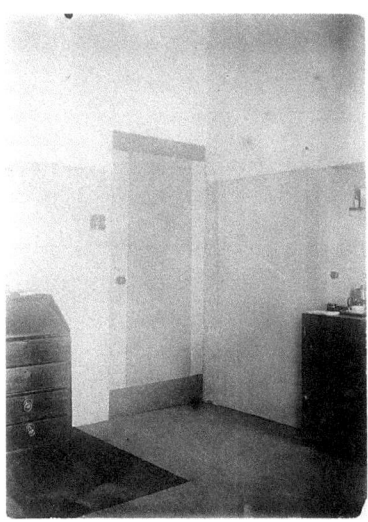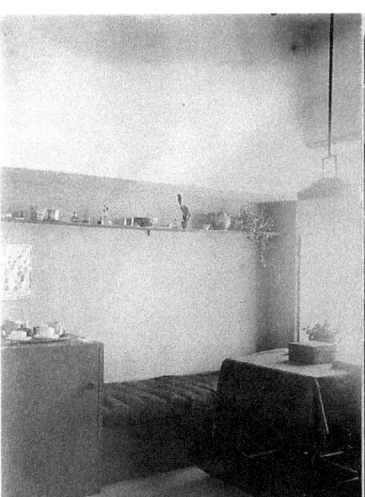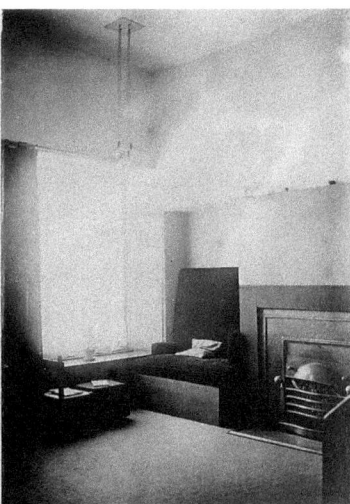

Montessori. As we shall see later, the house she designed with Rietveld in 1924 integrated some of these ideas directly into its configuration. The conflict between the conservative husband and radical wife extended to taste in interior decoration and, to appease Truus, Fritz allowed her to refit a room where she could feel more at home. Rietveld was commissioned for the job and quickly integrated features that we will see reoccurring repeatedly in De Stijl interiors.

The first thing to notice about Truus Schröder's room, in contrast to the examples we have just looked at, is the large amount of empty space it offered. Of notable absence is the centrally placed table and chairs which typified Dutch interiors of the day. The seating, comprised of a built-in bench and a low, unimposing chair, was moved to the window to take advantage of the view to the outside and natural light. The second typical feature of contemporary interiors, the hearth, also lost its focal emphasis. In fact Rietveld disguised the chimney breast by building over the niche above the bench. The effect was to make the bench appear to recede into the wall when in fact it was the fireplace which projected into the room. The walls themselves were painted in large areas of plain colour (although we can no longer be sure what the colours were). Finally, a word must be said about the lighting. We have neither the romantic glowing lamp of Cecile van Even's reception room nor the massive spotlighting ceiling lamp of Sluijter's family drama. This was the first instance that Rietveld installed an experimental light fitting that would later become a trademark item almost as recognisable as his *Red/Blue Chair*. Made up of bare flourescent tubes supported solely by the electric cables themselves, the fitting had no shade to conceal it and cast an even, diffuse light. By setting the tubes perpendicular to each other Rietveld expressed the emphasis on geometry and volumetric space that was concurrently promoted by De Stijl.

As Alice Friedman has commented, the room which Rietveld designed was not just an escape from the respectable house Truus Schröder could not longer abide, 'it was a place in which a new way of life could be discussed and experienced'.[3] For Truus Schröder that way of life involved breaking with the constructed domesticity which defined the lives of women of her background. It meant no longer being represented symbolically in the roles of wife, mother or decorative ornament. However, this did not mean that Schröder desired to be unburdened of her domestic duties. Her campaign was for the recognition of domestic tasks as work, of the same significance as any paid employment.

To show that the Biltstraat interior was typical of De Stijl concern for space we can compare it to another room designed by Vilmos Huszár and Jan Wils in the same year, 1921 (Figure 33). On this occasion the commission came from a photographer, Henri Berssenbrugge, who wished to have his studio remodelled. The studio was located on the Zeestraat in The Hague, a fashionable part of the city just to the west of the centre. Berssenbrugge had recently relocated from Rotterdam in search of a more upmarket clientele and specialised in a type of portraiture which aimed to capture something of the sitter's personality. He had also become very interested in expressionist dance, popularised in The Hague by Lili Green, and had begun photographing figures in motion. Wils constructed the new studio as a long, high-ceilinged room with windows on three sides and a roof light. Built-in benches on either side of the room left the main area clear and the space was only divided by different-sized rugs designed by Huszár in bold colours: black, blue and a raspberry red. A small fireplace was tucked away at one end of the room and, as in Truus Schröder's room, was not allowed to form a focus of attention. In fact the intrusion of the chimney breast was once again eradicated by the placement of a built-in bench next to it. Huszár accentuated the effects of recession and projection in this area by painting two colour planes above the bench and fireplace, framed by black and white respectively. Artist and architect worked closely together to their mutual advantage; Wils provided large flat surfaces for Huszár to colour while Huszár used colour to accentuate spatial features. The furniture, supplied by Huzsár, included three small tables, three chairs and a high chair, all of which were of an extremely plain design and all keyed to the height of Wils' built-in benches. The spindles of the chair legs were set at the same height as the skirting board, as were structural elements of the tables. The effect was to create a space in which everything appeared to be connected. The Berssenbrugge studio is no longer extant but a review which appeared in *Bouwkundig Weekblad* can recover for us how it looked to a visitor at the time:

> [T]his space in colour is a completely different one to that which we know. In this space-colour studio is one unity and that is the space, and the space exists out of col-ours. And these colours are *form-determining*. The feelings which this space can awake are completely new. One lives in colour, it is as if one bathes in colour, one is *in* colour.[4]

This effusive commentary draws attention to two things: space and colour. We are invited to consider the overwhelming nature of the colour of the studio. Ironically we have only black and white images of it and Berssenbrugge would only be making black and white photographs in it. However, we can see from the surviving images that the application of colour was not restricted to the four walls but with the bright carpets already mentioned and the ceiling, all six sides were treated in a similar fashion. Even the most extreme and decorative Art Nouveau interiors pro-duced in the Netherlands had only used colour sparingly, preferring to work with different types of wood to create natural effects. Thus it is not surprising that this struck the reviewer as something totally new. What is most significant though is that the colour is seen to create space rather than being simply decorative. How this might have worked is difficult to reconstruct but one example, perhaps, can be seen in a surviving photograph. The far wall of the studio, behind the high chair, was divided into three sections around the door frame. Each section was 'framed' and within the two larger sections free-floating colour planes contrasted with the background colour. The skirting board was painted in a light colour to con-trast with the adjoining wall to the right. Such effects, as I discussed earlier in connection to such projects as *De Vonk*, have often be read as destructive of the

architecture and part of the tension between architects and painters from the
beginning of De Stijl. I feel it is more helpful to think about them in the way that
the reviewer does, as articulating the space, quite literally drawing attention to
points of intersection. Finally, a very important consideration for the union of
colour and space produced here is lighting. Extremely noticeable, especially for a
photographer's studio, is the absence of spotlighting. Natural light could be controlled and admitted from four sides, but for artificial illumination only one very
discrete ceiling lamp was fitted. The Berssenbrugge studio is a clear demonstra-
tion that the emphasis given to space is hugely reliant on the even distribution of
light. This new form of lighting, diffuse rather than directed at specific objects,
produced a unified environment.

The Berssenbrugge studio was seen not merely as a solution to a practical problem
of providing a suitable environment for a modern photographer to work in but as an
object in its own right. All of the reviews discuss it in this way and it appears that the
photographer himself saw the project partly as a means of self-advertisement; clients could be drawn to the studio just to view Wils and Huszár's collaboration.
Berssenbrugge even offered it out as rentable exhibition space.[5] Intriguingly there is
a surviving photograph showing it also being used as a sitting room (Figure 34). Two
men, one seated on a built-in bench, the other on a chair next to him, are busy looking

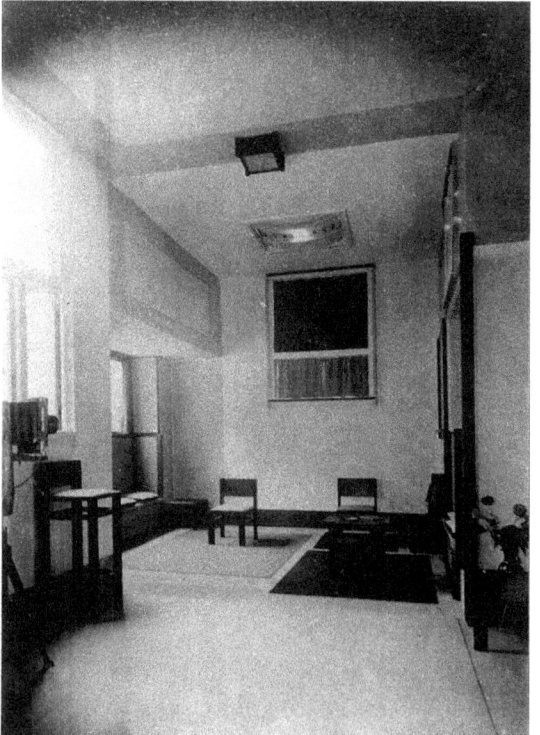
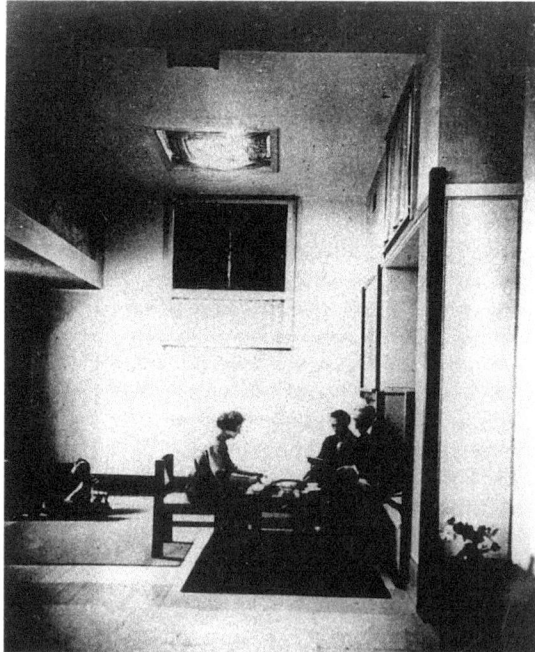

33 & 34 Vilmos Huszár and Jan Wils,
Space-Colour-Composition, Berssenbrugge Studio,
1921

at either a book or another type of printed object (a photograph perhaps). A woman sits opposite them and is pouring tea while behind her a child plays with a toy train. The activities the people engage in are virtually identical to those we discussed in relation to the Sluijters painting above. A straightforward division of labour, male/ intellectual, female/domestic, is represented. However, what has disappeared is the structure to inform us of the relationships between these people, such as offered clues to the different relationships between the occupants of the Van Gogh-Bonger household. One may guess that this is Berssenbrugge himself with his wife and child receiving a visitor. Yet it would be virtually impossible to tell which of the men is the host and which the visitor. The multifunctional nature of the studio reflects on its occupants, where little distinction is made between friend, family and customer. This is figured in the seating arrangement itself, and especially the table, which has been lowered to enhance conversation and reduce confrontation. As we will explore later in this chapter, the De Stijl interior was understood as affording atmosphere or ambiance rather than order. As such it re-orientated interior design dramatically from the direction it had taken prior to the First World War. To comprehend the change De Stijl made to the discourse on the interior it is necessary to sketch in some of this background now.

As with the other national variations on Art Nouveau, Dutch *Nieuwe Kunst* (New Art) incorporated many different factions which took the discourse on style in opposing directions. As Titus Eliëns has shown, in the Netherlands these oppositions can be broken down very roughly into a rationalist and a decorative trend.[6] These were highly influenced by such factors as the late nineteenth-century concern for the recovery of an authentic national style and the appropriation of exotic motifs, particularly from Indonesia, which had been a Dutch colony for many centuries. As with all varieties of Art Nouveau, the simultaneous pull towards parochialism and internationalism was felt in the Netherlands. Close contacts with the Belgian avant-garde fostered the appearance of a luxuriant organic style in The Hague in the 1890s, similar to that which could be found in Brussels or Antwerp. On the other hand admiration for British Arts and Crafts fed into a growing reform tendency particularly powerful in Amsterdam. All of these strands would be brought to bear on the question of the interior during the first decade of the twentieth century.

In 1898 a combined gallery and shop called *Arts and Crafts* was set up in The Hague, financed by a furniture maker, Christiaan Wegerif, with Johan Thorn Prikker as an artistic consultant. The shop did not pursue the model established by William Morris, despite its name but was set up more along the lines of Siegfried Bing's *Art Nouveau* emporium in Paris. Workshops produced high-quality furniture and metalwork for the shop, which also exhibited fine art by the likes of Jan Toorop and George Minne. The firm established an international reputation for its batik products, the fabric printing processes practised widely in Indonesia, but it also thereby attracted criticism for not being authentically Dutch.[7] The production costs of the goods dealt in by *Arts and Crafts* were also too high for it to become commercially successful and the firm folded in 1904.

Before its closure, however, reaction to *Arts and Crafts* had come in the form of an Amsterdam rival, *'t Binnenhuis* (The Interior), established in 1900 by Berlage together with the insurance company director, Carel Henny, a jeweller, Willem Hoeker, and a book dealer, H. Gerlings. Berlage had worked for Henny since 1895 when he had built the Amsterdam office of the insurance company, *De Nederlanden van 1845*, and was then commissioned to build several other offices in major Dutch cities. Berlage also built a house for Henny in The Hague in 1898 which has been described as the first *Gesamtkunstwerk* of *Nieuwe Kunst*; the architect oversaw not only the construction of the building but its entire decoration and furnishing. In fact the relationship developed by Berlage and Henny is a prototype for that formed later between Peter Behrens and AEG in Germany, whereby an architect took charge of every design aspect down to furniture and fittings.[8] Hoeker's contribution to *'t Binnenhuis* was to supply the practical production know-how, as he had already set up a factory to make ceramics, metalwork and furniture in 1897 and distributed these goods through upmarket household shops both in and outside the Netherlands. Together the men decided that the ethic of *'t Binnenhuis* should be to produce good quality, modern design available to a larger public than had previously been attempted. In distinction to *Arts and Crafts*, *'t Binnenhuis* did not flinch from the use of machine production rather than handicraft and introduced the issue of a machine aesthetic into the Dutch debate on style.

While *'t Binnenhuis* was certainly more progressive than *Arts and Crafts*, it did not totally quell concern that good design was still only in reach of the middle classes. As an example of its output we can turn to a suite of furniture designed by Berlage for the shop in 1905 incorporating a table, chairs and sideboard, the standard set of objects to furnish the contemporary domestic interior I described above. The design was very reserved to ensure ease of manufacture; decoration featured on only a few key points such as the backrest of the chairs and the tops of the table legs. The table top was designed to fold out if necessary, and in combination with the sideboard we could imagine the set destined for a room which doubled as both dining and sitting room. An example of this set preserved in the Gemeentemuseum in The Hague dates from 1911 (the model stayed in production for many years) and came from a property in Paulus Potterstraat in Amsterdam. To get a better sense of the type of household the Van Hengel family, who bought this suite, might have been, it should be mentioned that Paulus Potterstraat was one of the streets that Berlage had himself laid out in his first scheme for the expansion of Amsterdam, lying between the Museumplein and the Vondelpark and running from the back of the Rijksmuseum to Van Baerlestraat (the major boulevard of Berlage's scheme). Readers familiar with Amsterdam will know that the Stedelijk Museum is situated at the junction of Paulus Potterstraat and Van Baerlestraat. The surrounding district is precisely the area described in the second chapter, where Berlage had desired the emer-

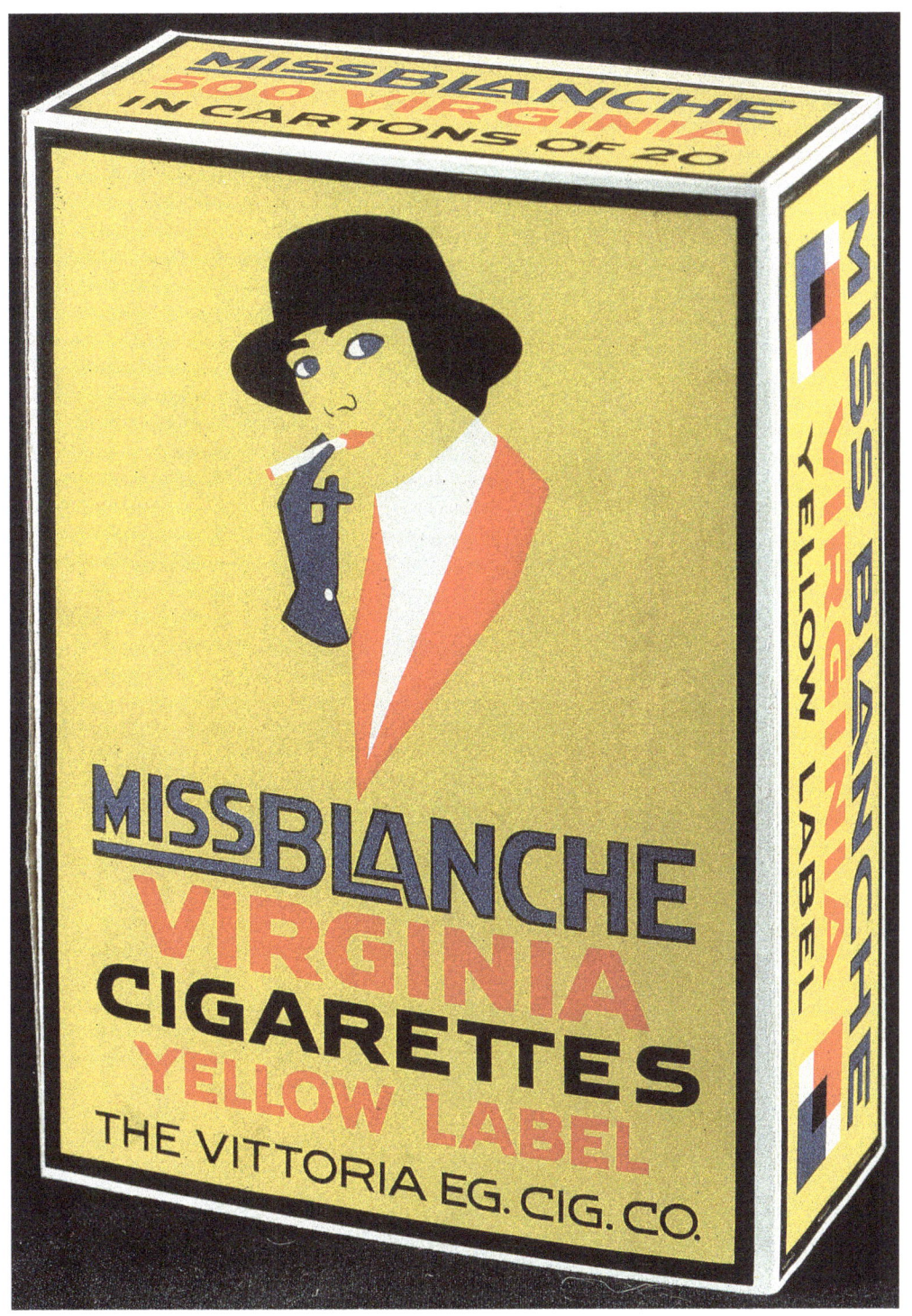

4 Vilmos Huszár, packet for Miss Blanche Virginia Cigarettes, 1927

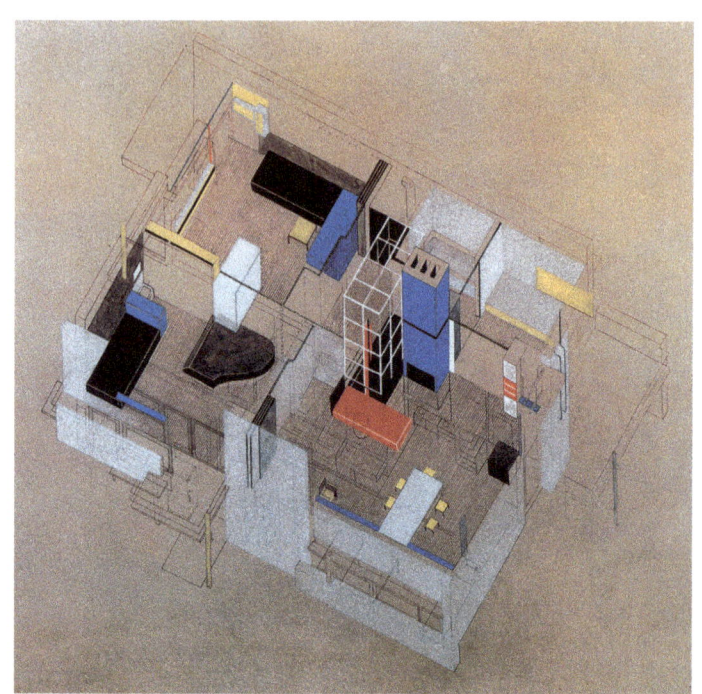

5 Gerrit Rietveld,
Axonometric Projection,
Schröder House, undated

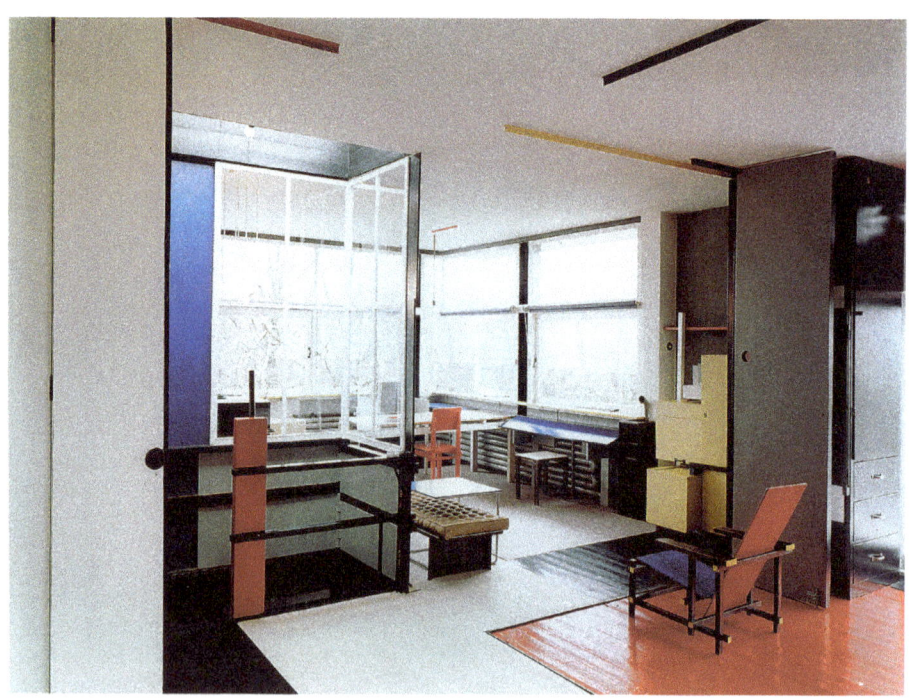

6 Gerrit Rietveld, Schröder House, 1924

gence of a new type of middle-class existence; families would relinquish single canal houses for large apartment blocks but would benefit from easy access to recreational facilities. Berlage's suite had in fact been exhibited in the Stedelijk Museum in 1905. That the families moving into the newly developing part of the city could use the local museum as a guide to furnishing their residences in an appropriate modern fashion is a fascinating synthesis of urban planning, aesthetics and product placement.

The 1905 exhibition which featured Berlage's furniture was organised by a former employee of 't Binnenhuis, Willem Penaat. His concerns that 't Binnenhuis was still producing for a very limited class of people prompted him to leave the organisation to form another cooperative, De Woning (The Dwelling). This group was far more committed to the production of cheap, mass-produced design. Penaat also co-founded an organisation in 1904 called Kunst aan het Volk (Art for the People) which staged a sequence of didactic exhibitions to explain the principles of good design to a mass audience.[9] The 1905 exhibition incorporated paired displays of 'good' and 'bad' rooms, with the onus placed on the public to decide which was which. Penaat thereby extended the debate from concern for good production to the question of good taste, and introduced a broader discussion concerning the ability of the working classes to appreciate art. As Mark Adang has suggested, the Dutch debate managed thereby to reverse the concerns of William Morris and the British Arts and Crafts movement. Where Morris had been concerned about the relation between working-class producers, now driven into factory production, and a consuming middle class, in the Netherlands the debate revolved around middle-class producers for the working-class consumer. As such, less anxiety was expressed concerning machine production, which was seen by many as a necessity for the creation of cheap, accessible goods, but more concern was paid to the perils of kitsch. According to Adang, the war effectively put a halt to the activities of organisation such as Kunst aan het Volk. The gap between rich and poor increased and fewer designers attended to the lower classes. As he states:

> We see how in the two important post war movements in the Netherlands – the Amsterdam School and De Stijl – conditions for a similar public education tendency are absent. . . . As far as design goes, the Amsterdam School is connected with the former period in terms of concern for quality of craftsmanship and the pursuit of atmospheric unity. It deviated in the lack of rational clarity of structure or sobriety in ornamentation, and in the proportions of furniture, preference for expensive materials and laborious techniques which stood in the way of wide distribution. In short, the concentration on a more elite public, lack of political will for public education and the lack of a strong, dogmatic aesthetic stood in the way of a continuation of the pre war tradition of socialist taste education. De Stijl was in the first place addressed towards fine art. . . . In design as in art theory it was too extreme to nourish a pronounced art and kitsch conception.[10]

The paradoxical nature of Adang's analysis is that the post-war period is precisely the most significant one for avant-garde involvement in social housing. The notion that it should simultaneously be a still point in thinking about kitsch in the interior is very surprising. I do not agree with Adang that the difference between pre- and post-war thinking about the interior can be therefore be devolved to such a basic class analysis. The problem with his account, and with most comparisons of pre- and post-war interior design, is that it focuses almost entirely on the production of objects. He pays no attention to the production of space, an area where De Stijl was extremely engaged, nor does he pay any attention to the use of colour in the interior, which was crucial to its transformation.

There is one building project that can help to demonstrate the different approach to colour in the interior between the pre-war reform movements and De Stijl. It was a far cry from the working-class homes *Kunst aan het Volk* was concerned for, however. In 1915 the Kröllers asked Berlage, who was company architect for Müller & Co. at the time, to build a house on their estate at Hoenderloo in the Hoge Veluwe (close to the site where the Kröller-Müller Museum now stands). Inspired by the image of the country house described in Herman Muthesius's book *Das englische Haus* (The English House), Berlage designed the property as a hunting lodge, which was named *Sint Hubertus* (St. Hubert). At the moment when construction on the house began in 1916, Bart van der Leck resigned from his position in Müller & Co., having worked with Berlage on Holland House and the refitting of the Kröller family home. The reason for his resignation was, as I related in the first chapter of this book, frustration at Berlage's continual domination of their collaborative work. However, Van der Leck returned briefly to work for the Kröllers in 1919 to complete the decoration of *Sint Hubertus* after Berlage had also resigned from his job. This house has then a unique combination of pre- and post-De Stijl colour application.

The house was named after St. Hubert and was intended to represent aspects of the saint's life in its structure. The legend of St. Hubert tells of his dramatic conversion when, out hunting, he encountered a stag with the form of a crucifix between its antlers. The plan of the house takes the form of a pair of antlers. A massive tower rising from the centre also gives the building the look of a church. *Sint Hubertus* stands next to a lake, so that the reflection of the tower against the horizontal buiding creates the form of a cross. The interior told the story of St. Hubert in a different way, principally through the use of colour. The narrative was constructed through a sequence of reception rooms and climaxed in Hélène Kröller-Müller's private sitting room.

The visitor enters the house to find himself in a large hall which, facing north, receives only a small amount of light through stained-glass windows above the doorway. From the sombre hall, one then enters a substantial dining room with large windows looking south towards the lake. The floor of the dining room was made from green glass mosaic and the coffered ceiling was covered in yellow and blue tiles. With glazed brick walls of warm ochre, the dining room is supposed to represent the saint's passion for the outdoor life: grass below and sky above. The next three rooms, a library, tea room and Kröller-Müller's sitting room, took the visitor on a spiritual journey, marking the process of the saint's conversion. Thus from the bright dining room, one enters a dim space again, the library, which has small, highly placed windows. The colours change to muted green and black floor and red and blue ceiling, apparently to indicate St. Hubert's repentance and inward turn. The library is a semicircular shape and the ceiling is again coffered but this time in a pattern of sun rays. The tea room, the next room in the sequence which is symmetrical to the library, replaced the muted colours with bright yellow, green and orange. From here a sliding door opens onto Kröller-Müller's sitting room where light and colour became brightest of all. This climactic space had walls of cream glazed brick and a bright yellow ceiling edged with light blue.[11]

When Van der Leck returned to complete the final decoration of the hunting lodge he was extremely restricted in the modifications he could make. All of the colour effects I have just described were created not from painted wall surfaces but from mosaic, glazed brick or tile. Van der Leck was left to colour only such surfaces as the iron window frames, lintels and the ceiling beams which Berlage had left exposed. In Kröller-Müller's sitting room, then, his intervention was minimal. He carried over the cream colour of the glazed brick to the framework of ceiling beams and painted yellow squares at their intersections. He painted the lintels of the window frames white with black undersides. It was only in less significant rooms, such as the guest bathroom and bedroom, that Van der Leck found opportunity for greater alterations. In these cases his treatment of colour can be clearly contrasted with that of Berlage.

The arrangement of rooms in *Sint Hubertus* and their decoration could be read as a symbolic narrative. The colours of the rooms related to St. Hubert's path to spiritual knowledge through communion with nature and the interior spaces were conceptually linked to the surroundings of the hunting lodge (one of the few forested areas of the Netherlands). As we saw at the beginning of this chapter, the production of natural effects in interiors, such as the use of particular types of wood, floral ornament or plants, was part of a long-standing tradition which made the interior comforting. Berlage's approach both extended and transformed this tradition by using colour in a naturalistic but non-descriptive fashion owing much to post-impressionist painting. Thus the contrasting blue and yellow of the ceiling of Kröller-Müller's sitting room recreates, without necessarily depicting, the sun in the sky. Given her substantial collection of Van Gogh paintings she was no doubt very responsive to this use of colour. This can be contrasted to the guest bedroom which, unlike most of the other rooms, had plastered walls rather than glazed brick or tile. Van der Leck painted this room in a stark combination of black, white and grey, using a variety of grey tints to balance the beige-tiled radiator covers Berlage had installed before his departure. After the luxuriant and multifarious colour range of the rest of the building, such a plain treatment comes as a bit of a shock. In exchange for Berlage's nature symbolism, Van der Leck treated the interior in a far more objectified manner; architectural features such as frames and lintels were accented and colour given a structural, material role to play. Colour was not subordinate to architecture, though. This is particularly evident in Van der Leck's use of black. As we saw in chapter 2, Oud refused to countenance Van Doesburg's use of black at Spangen because of its disruptive quality; on a facade it could be illusionistically mistaken for a hole. In the guest bedroom at *Sint Hubertus* Van der Leck used it, among other places, in the recesses of the coffering on the ceiling where exactly the same problem of visual deception might occur. Like Clement Greenberg's later theorisation of a non-illusionistic, painterly space, in the early years of De Stijl Van der Leck and others proposed that painting could be simultaneously flat (non-representational) and spatial (non-ornamental).

Although *Sint Hubertus* was completed after Van der Leck had disassociated himself from De Stijl, it still bears out the position he had declared in De Stijl of the antagonism between the naturalistic nature of architecture and the destruction of the naturalistic which was currently being pursued by painting. Van Doesburg, for one, adopted Van der Leck's vocabulary and spoke frequently of 'freeing' colour from architecture by means of framing it by a black or white border. Colour could be present as material rather than representation while floating free from the support onto which it was painted. What is interesting to see, however, is that it was some time before Van Doesburg settled on using solely the triad of red, yellow and blue in combination with white, black and grey. In one of his first major projects, the colour design of the De Lange house built by Jan Wils in Alkmaar in 1917, there are still traces of a symbolic use of colour similar to Berlage's decoration of *Sint Hubertus*. In a letter, Van Doesburg explained how he sought to make the colour of each room appropriate to its use:

> Hall: yellow with purple walls. Black contrasts. Bright green dado.
>
> Dining room: black dado, grey panels, freed by white; dark, deep blue dresser doors, freed by bright yellow. Picked out in green, freed by white. Outermost frame black.
>
> Drawing room: dominated by purple, framed by green panels above. All planes and panels freed by white.
>
> Living room adjoining drawing room: everything the reverse of the drawing room: green dominates framed by purple all freed by white. The most impressive room is the study: bookcase green, black and white, walls covered in green baize! All freed by white. Green stone fireplace with white tiled sides. In the middle a glass mosaic designed by myself. The doors: black panels freed by white, the rest green. By way of experiment I used red in a daughter's bedroom. Vermilion dado, white walls. Wash basin: white, red, green and blue. All free. The ceilings violet too; grey, white etc. I always bore in mind the requirements of the person using a room. For instance a girl's room: bright yellow, purple and green. A spare room for a child: yellow and blue. Attic and servants quarters white and blue. Likewise the kitchen, white and blue. The attic corridor and staircase, yellow, black and white.[12]

Unfortunately, Van Doesburg does not give a fuller explanation of why, for example, green and purple were appropriate colours for the drawing and living room. White was used in two separate ways in the De Lange house. In the major communal spaces it is applied to frame other, dominant colours. It appeared far more in its own right in the kitchen and domestic quarters, maybe as an indicator of hygiene, and perhaps through combination with blue, as a reference to the traditional colours of Delftware.[13] Yellow appeared in the hallway, which, as in *De Vonk*, was allowed greater decorative licence, but the most liberal use of primary colour in combination with white was restricted to the bedrooms of children and especially that of the daughter. This was the only place Van Doesburg felt relaxed enough to use red and the only room where he commented on colouring the ceiling as well. Throughout the house colour accentuated architectural features such as picture rails, dados and door frames but also served to demarcate service space from social space and private space.

Just as in the De Lange house, the most impressive of the early De Stijl interiors was a room for children. In 1919 Vilmos Huszár designed a bedroom for the two sons of Cornelis Bruynzeel Jr. using Van Gogh's *Bedroom in Arles* of 1889 as the basis of his design. In a 1917 article in De Stijl, Huszár quoted a section of a Van Gogh letter which described this painting, especially the calming effects of the colours.[14] The designs of the beds themselves echoed the simple shape of the one depicted in Van Gogh's painting. In other respects Huszár had difficulty in reproducing the painting. The bedroom was of awkward dimensions having two large niches at either end. In one niche Huszár placed the beds and in the other a washstand with two basins. Between the beds was a closet. Huszár's colour scheme also differed from Van Gogh's as he used yellow on the doors and walls rather than the beds. The niche where the beds were placed was painted white, blue and grey with the light and dark colours reversed symmetrically on each side. One contemporary photograph also shows the blankets on the bed tying in with this pattern, while the bed frames themselves were painted black and red. Describing the room in 1922, Huszár set his colour scheme directly in the context of post-impressionist painting: 'What the pointillists saw in nature, I have here attempted to do with planes, which are logically deduced from the plastic forms. Thus light can be plasticized in the interior.'[15]

In the photographs of the bedroom Huszár published with his article he took great care to disguise the light sources. In none of the photographs is the window visible, although it was quite substantial and Huszár had also taken care to install some stained glass in it. Similarly, it is only with a great deal of scrutiny that a ceiling light above the beds can be made out, which together with the uplighter over the washstand were the only detectible sources of artificial illumination. Yet three light switches can be seen on each side of the closet door, in reach of the boys' beds, suggesting that the room had one further light, no doubt in the centre of the ceiling. This was carefully cropped from every photograph to leave the impression that light was to be generated solely from the coloured walls.

Huszár was one of the strongest advocates in De Stijl of the colour theories of Wilhelm Ostwald, believing that the German chemist had produced the most accurate formula to date for adequating the materiality of colour pigment to the immateriality of coloured light. Ostwald had also applied numerical values to colour ranges of tone and hue which permitted artists to select ratios that would harmonise in a predictable fashion. Huszár was the first (and maybe only) of the De Stijl painters to attempt to apply Ostwald's colour chart to interior decoration and in a letter to the painter Chris Beekman recounted how he was trying to select the best colour range from Ostwald's *Harmonie der Farben* (Harmony of Colours) to use in the Bruynzeel bedroom.[16] His aim was to find a means of monumental painting that exchanged Van der Leck's theory of antagonism for balance between art and architecture.[17] For this reason, it seems, the boys' room did not find favour in the pages of De Stijl and was not illustrated in it until 1922. Even then Van Doesburg cast aspersions over the design, telling Oud that it was 'a faulty execution and faulty understanding of N.P. [Neo-plasticism]'.[18] The emphasis given by Huszár to colour harmony reduced its spatial role. In constrast Van Doesburg was more impressed by the Berssenbrugge studio, which he repeatedly illustrated in De Stijl and included in the 1923 De Stijl exhibition in Paris. The passage from colour as light to colour as material was staged most spectacularly, however, by an interior which would go on to have mythical significance in the history of modern art, to which we must now turn our attention – Mondrian's studio.

Mondrian returned to Paris in 1919 having spent the war years in the Netherlands. During his unforeseen absence he had kept up the rent on his studio, which was located at the back of the Gare Montparnasse in a purpose-built block constructed by a property developer following the extension of the rue du Départ in 1911. The road had been cut obliquely through an old block of buildings so that the new street front and the building plots were at odd angles to each other. Mondrian occupied an unusual five-sided room which was part of an infill between two buildings and, as we shall see later, this peculiar shape was to be very significant. However, this was not the space in which he first experimented with altering the interior. For reasons which still remain obscure, after only a few months Mondrian had to seek alternative accommodation, which he found in the rue de Coulmiers. It was here that he began his first major application of colour in the walls of his studio space, intimations of which we can find described in the final section of his 'trialogue', *Natural Reality and Abstract Reality*, published in De Stijl in 1920. As may be recalled, the text takes the form of a discussion between an abstract painter, a naturalistic painter and a layman as they walk from the countryside to the city, ending up in the studio of the abstract painter. While they stand in the studio, the abstract painter criticises the tendency of artists to make their workplaces into museums, filling them with antiquities or other *objets d'art*. Instead he recounts the way in which he has made the whole of his studio into an abstract composition: 'The curtains form a rectangular plane that divides the wall surrounding the window. To continue the division, I added those red, gray, and white planes on the wall. Even the white shelf with the gray box and the white cylindrical jar also contribute.'[19] The abstract painter continues to describe further combinations of furniture arrangement and wall painting, leaving only the caveat that 'there is still a lack of unity'. The ambition he expresses is to produce an interior in which all parts are set in relation to one another and combine together as a whole.

As I described in the first chapter, the development of Neo-plasticism in theory did not always exactly correspond to practice. The first experimentation with abstraction had come with Mondrian's attention to hanging arrangements in 1917 but it was not until after his return to Paris and application of colour directly to architecture that the first properly Neo-plastic paintings were made. A general consensus seems to exist that the first painting Mondrian completed in Paris was *Composition no. II*, now in Tate Modern, London, which would have been finished in early 1920. Here he abandoned the grid forms of the so-called checkerboard paintings of the previous years and returned to the sole use of red, yellow and blue in combination with black and white. The concerns he seems to have addressed all relate to controlling the surface of the painting. The checkerboard paintings, with a regular grid imposed upon them, were very flat but created a strong separation of figure and ground. Reintroducing compositional variation alleviated that problem but threatened to recreate naturalistic effects. The use of primary colour helped to banish these associations. Meanwhile, in the rue de Coulmiers studio Mondrian was experimenting with applying colour principally to the front wall, which happened to be broken by a large window glazed with matte panes and so afforded no view to the exterior. As Carel Blotkamp has reconstructed, partly using the description given in *Natural Reality and Abstract Reality* as a source, Mondrian integrated the window into a large-scale composition using coloured pieces of cardboard and furniture.[20] While literalising the modernist ambition to dispense with the idea of painting as a 'window onto the world', Mondrian also created in three-dimensional form the neo-impressionist concept of painting producing light. Considered in connection to the first Neo-plastic paintings, we can see how the attempt to counteract the grid of the window frame related to his contemporary dispensation with the checkerboard motif and how the matte surface of the glass posed the same problems of white as colour or non-colour that he was investigating on canvas.

To date the De Stijl interior has most often been considered a by-product of abstract painting. For example, according to Yve-Alain Bois, 'Mondrian alters the studio whenever he makes a discovery in his painting, and he rarely begins a new series of canvases without first pausing to repaint his studio.'[21] In my view such priority cannot be so definitely asserted. It is the case that, from the final instalment of the trialogue on, Mondrian repeatedly claimed that architecture was not yet as advanced as painting to allow an equal realisation of Neo-plastic theory. However, his first article in French, *Le Néo-Plasticisme: Principe général de l'équivalence plastique*, published by the *Galerie de l'Effort Moderne* in 1921 and excerpted in De Stijl, claimed that, 'The future of the New Plastic and its true realisation in painting lies in *chromoplastic in architecture*. It governs the interior as well as the exterior of the building and includes everything that plastically expresses relationships through colour.'[22] Furthermore, in a 1922 article, *De reali-*

seering van het Neo-Plasticisme in verre toekomst en in de huidige architectuur (The
Realisation of Neo-Plasticism in the Distant Future and in Architecture Today),
Mondrian concluded by suggesting that the principle of collaboration, which was
a key concept for De Stijl, could be rekindled only by the unification of architect,
sculptor and painter *'in a single person'*.[23] Although he did not say it, such a person
we would today call an interior designer.

In 1921 Mondrian returned to the rue du Départ studio. Before occupying it
himself, he lent the space to Georges Vantongerloo and his wife, who needed some-
where to stay while in transit to new accommodation. As a form of repayment
Vantongerloo painted the studio for Mondrian (and, according to Michel Seuphor,
even gave him a Neo-plastic tea set).[24] By the time that Theo and Nelly van
Doesburg caught up with the Vantongerloos in April 1921, they had already given
their new apartment a De Stijl make over. As with some of Huszár's interior design
projects, the dangers of De Stijl sliding into a decorative fashion were plain to see.
Mondrian did not leave Vantongerloo's paintwork untouched therefore (and kept a
solitary cup from the tea set on display in order not to hurt Vantongerloo's feel-
ings). He continued the experiments launched at the rue de Coulmiers and now
had even greater freedom to paint the furniture and walls directly. In 1926 Mondrian
had the studio photographed by Paul Delbo (Figure 35) and further photographs

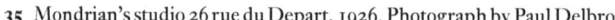

35 Mondrian's studio 26 rue du Depart, 1926. Photograph by Paul Delbro

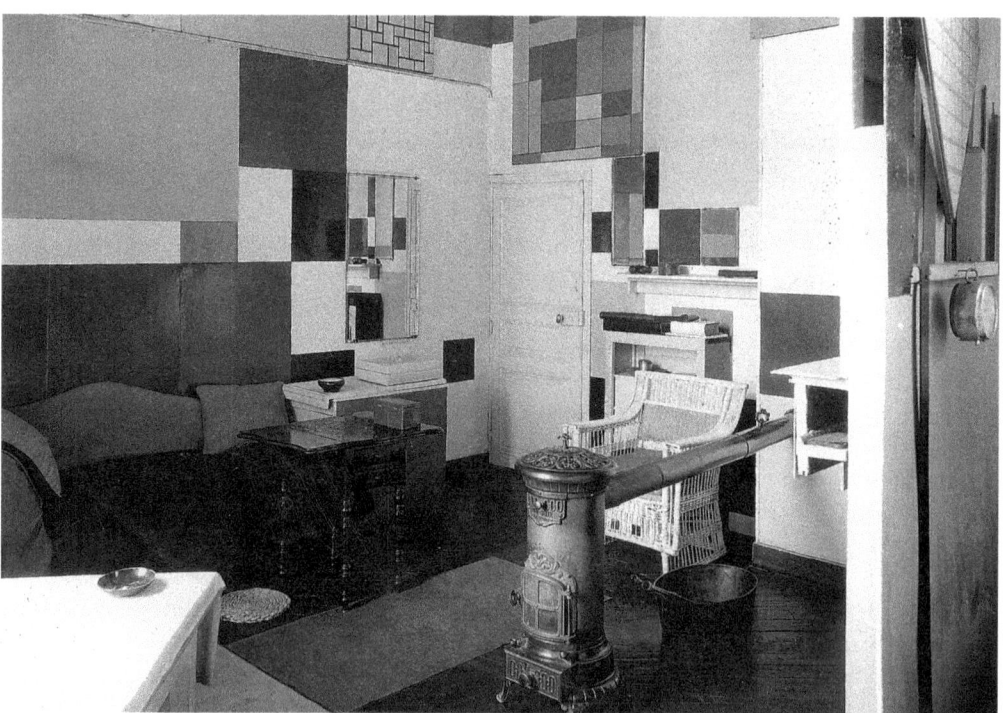

were taken by André Kertesz, perhaps at the instigation of Michel Seuphor. From this point until 1936, when Mondrian abandoned his studio shortly before the building was demolished, many visitors were drawn to see the room and further occasional photographs were taken of it. Images of the studio were published first in a Dutch national newspaper, *De Telegraaf*, and then in the journal *i10*. Prior to these carefully calculated exposures, a partial view of the studio was visible in a photograph of Mondrian which appeared in De Stijl in 1924. These documents and the reminiscences of those who saw the space allow us to see how the rue du Départ studio developed in unprecedented ways.

The experiment with the studio at the rue du Départ extended far beyond the application of colour to surface which had typified the rue de Coulmiers. As successive attempts to reconstruct the room have shown, Mondrian produced an extremely complex spatial effect which confused the memories of even those such as Seuphor who visited him frequently. It was only following the discovery of the original plans of the building that an accurate recreation could be produced (Figure 36). From these it can be seen that a sketch made by Seuphor in 1955 not only managed to add an extra wall, making a six-sided shape rather than five, but flattened out two walls to the right of the doorway into a long continuous one.[25] In her book *The De Stijl Environment*, Nancy Troy came very close to reconstructing the shape of the studio, using a range of photographs and personal reminiscences, but was still unable to get it quite correct. Why so much difficulty to imagine a room that was only a few metres across and had been repeatedly photographed? Troy answered this question by suggesting that Mondrian tried to conceal the fact that his studio was a strange irregular shape, both in the manner in which he arranged his furniture and how he permitted it to be photographed.[26] There were indeed illusionistic elements to the studio, notably the placement of two mirrors either side of the entrance which reflected each other. Similarly a large easel and cupboard projecting out into the space screened off the area by the window to the north which Mondrian seems either to have to slept in or used for storage (or both). This space was ignored by Delbo and featured on only one rather indistinct photograph by Kertesz. Troy's argument is intended to reinforce her thesis that the history of De Stijl can be read as a move from collaboration towards the total separation of art from architecture. In my view the studio demonstrates something rather different. The attention that Mondrian gave in the rue du Départ to the configuration of his studio marks a definite change from the concept of decoration as wall dressing to decoration as three-dimensional configuration. Where the rue de Coulmiers studio had concerned itself primarily with surface, the rue du Départ linked surface to space. In this Mondrian was responding directly to the models exhibited in 1923 at the De Stijl exhibition at Léonce Rosenberg's *Galerie de l'Effort Moderne*.

In February 1920, on his first visit to Paris, Van Doesburg was introduced by Mondrian to Rosenberg, one of the most important art dealers in France at the

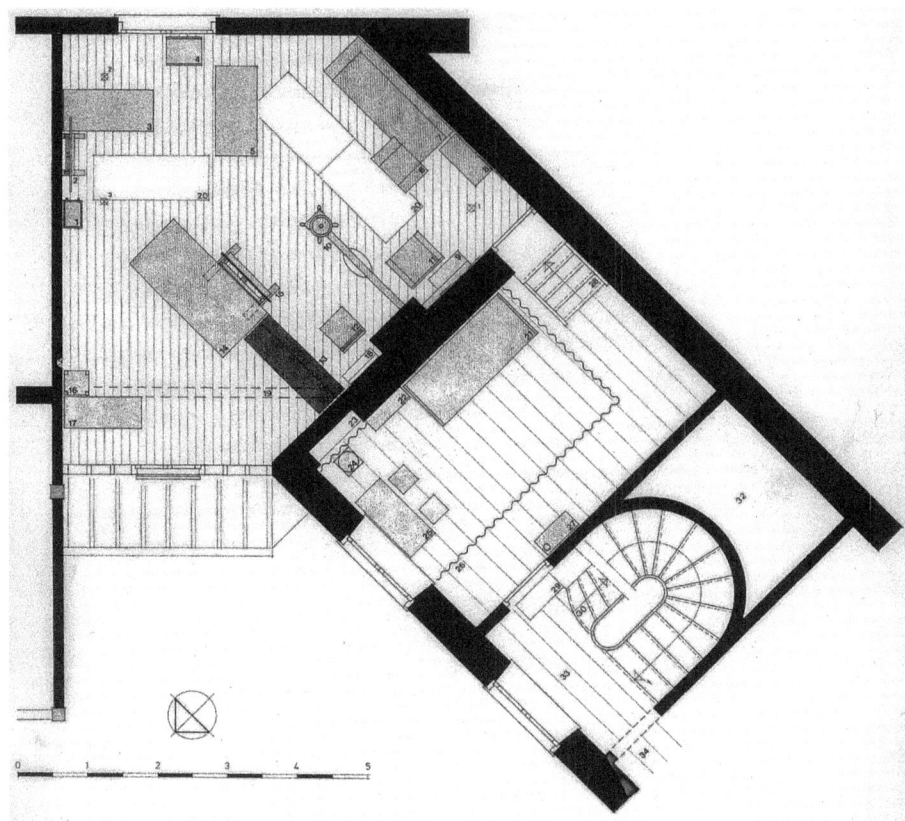

Explanation of the numbers: (1) red chest for paint-brushes; (2) black easel with wooden lath; (3) white table with box; (4) black gate-legged table; (5) white table with ashtray; (6) black gate-legged table; (7) dark brown bench with (red and grey?) cushions; (8) white chest, closed with grey cardboard; (9) white open chest, for books and personal belongings; (10) black pot-bellied stove, with oval coal scuttle; (11) white rattan arm-chair; (12) white bulrush-chair; (13) black cupboard for dinner-set and linen; (14) white bed-settee; (15) white easel with large painted cardboard; (16) little rush-stool' (17) large white chest to store paintings; (18) some unfinished paintings; (19) black construction-beam in the ceiling; (20) some rugs on the floor; (21) iron bed; (22) white open cupboard; (23) wall cupboard with (grey?) curtains. Probable earlier passage to neighbouring room (before 1911); (24) little stool; (25) table with oil-stove and two simple chairs; (26) loose hanging curtains; (27) white table with white artificial tulip next to the hat-rack; (28) wooden staircase with five steps to the atelier door; (29) door-mat; (30) staircase to loft; (31) staircase to the third floor of Mondrians apartment; and (32) light court.

36 Frans Postma, reconstruction of Mondrian's studio 26 rue du Depart, 1995

time, who represented artists such as Juan Gris and Fernand Léger. Towards the end of the year, Rosenberg appears to have offered a commission to De Stijl for the construction of a country house. In early 1921 Van Doesburg met Rosenberg again, this time in Amsterdam where the latter had brought a group of paintings to be auctioned.[27] The dealer had begun to promote Mondrian in Paris and was publishing *Le Néo-Plasticisme* as a brochure through his gallery. When Van Doesburg visited Paris again that Spring, the two men renewed their acquaintance and Rosenberg proposed that his commission for a house should form the basis of an exhibition. At this stage Van Doesburg imagined that all those associated with De Stijl, even those such as Van 't Hoff who had drifted away from the journal, would be brought together on the project. When the exhibition finally materialised in 1923 the extensive collaboration Van Doesburg had imagined was not to be seen. Instead the exhibition was centred around three models designed by himself and Van Eesteren: the *Maison Rosenberg*, *Maison Particulière* and *Maison d'Artiste* (Figure 37). To give the appearance of a group show, photographs and drawings of projects worked on by Oud, Wils, Huszár, Rietveld and Willem van Leusden were also shown but most critical attention fell on the models, particularly the two that had been brightly coloured.

While the country house for Rosenberg was aimed at realisation (although never built), the *Maison Particulière* (Private House) and the *Maison d'Artiste* (Artist's House) were not produced with any particular location in mind. They were exercises in pure fantasy and may well have been technically impossible to build in the early 1920s. Ultimately the models have won a place in the history of twentieth-century architecture for the buildings they inspired rather than pro-viding the basis of any actual construction. Their main characteristics were poly-chromatic surfaces, the interpenetration of interior and exterior space, and the eradication of clear demarcation of storeys and main facade. As images of modern houses they proposed the total destruction of the traditional order of entrance, reception rooms, service spaces and private quarters. At least that is how the

37 Theo van Doesburg, photograph of exhibition *Les architectes du groupe De Stijl*, 1923

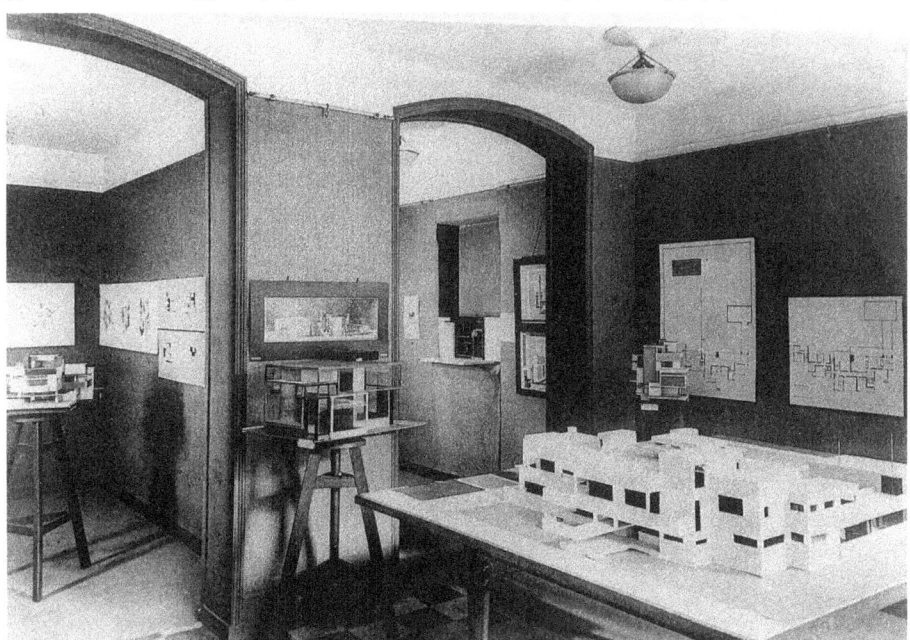

models appeared at first sight. The ground plans show rather more prosaic
consideration for distribution of functions and levels of privacy. Thus the *Maison
Particulière* still contains a back staircase connecting the kitchen with a servant's
room and both plans specifically designate which bedrooms should be considered
guest rooms, to give just two examples of how distinctions were made between
different types of space. Whether these drawings were shown when the models
were exhibited remains unclear. What is known is that the exhibition included
striking axonometric drawings coloured by Van Doesburg to give the appearance
of the structure of the buildings coming apart or turning in space.

Most of the literature concerning the *Galerie de l'Effort Moderne* models has
focused on determining the precise division of labour between Van Doesburg, Van
Eesteren and Rietveld (who constructed the model of the *Maison Rosenberg*).[28]
The question of authorship has been used as a means to discuss the status of collaborative work in De Stijl and also as a method to assess the relationship between
painting and architecture. I do not want to repeat those arguments here as they
have now completely overshadowed the wider significance of the models, especially the two polychrome ones. For what they signified to those who saw them was
not so much an ideal relationship between two practices (painting and architecture) but the disappearance of the wall as a structural element and its reinvention
as a screen. Colour was not the decorative finish to these buildings but the very
material out of which they were constructed. Here resurfaced modern architecture's most vexed question, the origin of decoration, and its most fundamental
theorisation in Gottfried Semper's principle of clothing. According to Semper,
before a wall was ever made of bricks and mortar, it would have been made from a
simple textile hanging. The pattern of a carpet or other fabric demarcated the
interior space of the house without ever having to be permanent or load-bearing.
Placing ornament at a pre-functional stage, Semper gave priority to the feminine
arts of weaving and decoration over the more masculinised rhetoric of building
technology. In Semper's eyes, architecture was the clothing of space and the means
by which it was given social meaning. The modernist predilection for the plain
white wall ignored this aspect of architecture. The use of colour exposed the white
wall to be the pretence of lack of decoration, the surface which denies itself as
such.[29] Thus the whole constructive/destructive discussion of colour in De Stijl
conceals the more important question concerning the articulation of space and in
particular the private space of the home.

As I mentioned above, Mondrian rejected the fashionable arrangement of the
artist's studio as a miniature museum. In *Natural Reality and Abstract Reality* the
abstract painter states his ambition to make the interior 'liveable', which seems
from our perspective to be the opposite effect to the careful placement of every
single object he describes. What Mondrian suggested, however, was that the artist's studio become the model for the home. Having rejected the museum,
Mondrian also dispensed with the idea of the studio as a workplace. Visitors to
the studio recalled the notable absence of any indication that this was a place of

work. According to Arthur Lehning, 'you had no idea you were in the presence of a painter. No pots of paint or brushes, nothing like that.'[30] It is quite obvious from the surviving photographs that the studio was full of paintings but visitors were not shown work in progress, and unfinished paintings were covered by a white sheet. There were two easels in the room but these were used by Mondrian only to display finished works. Mondrian did not actually paint at an easel but worked on a table which he placed next to a window. As presented to visitors, then, the studio was a place of discussion, social interaction and theorising rather than a place of manual labour. The most heavily decorated part of the room was that closest to the entrance. Here Mondrian placed a sofa and a small drop-leaf table opposite one of the easels which screened the sleeping/storage area. A larger table was positioned to divide this area from a more open space to the rear and the second easel was placed against the back wall. The three photographs Mondrian commissioned from Delbo are focused on the entrance to the studio, the sofa area and the view from the entrance to the easel at the rear. Although Mondrian painted, slept and ate in a room only a few metres square, he presented the studio as a place to exhibit, entertain and engage in discussion.[31] Not only were the later reminiscences of friends confused about the shape of the room, they were very vague about Mondrian's day to day existence and how he used the space for basic functions. This cannot be totally ascribed to Mondrian's need for privacy. Nor does it make his studio anti-functional, a proposition best expressed by looking at a practical response to the space rather than the documents we have been dealing with so far.

Mondrian received many visitors to his studio, attracted first by word of mouth and then through the publication of the photographs and journalistic reviews. One caller to the rue du Départ in 1926 was the Swiss architect Hannes Meyer (later director of the Bauhaus between 1928–30). Meyer was a committed communist and advocate of functionalist architecture. He was also developing at the time a radical mass-production aesthetic which he launched the same year in a publication entitled *Die neue Welt* (The New World). Although Meyer's vision of the new, dominated by standard, factory-produced objects, differed greatly from Mondrian's, the architect was very impressed by the artist and in particular by his studio. Looking through *Die neue Welt* it is interesting to see a photograph of Meyer's proposal for the future interior (Figure 38). White canvas 'walls' enclose a modest space in which can be found a bed, two folding chairs (one hung flat against the wall), a shelf with food products and a phonograph on a small table. This will immediately appear to most readers to be their nightmare image of modernist austerity. I will not try to defend it on this count but wish to draw attention to a few of its peculiar features. The first is the strange combination of objects Meyer has assembled which all signify activities normally kept quite separate: sleeping, eating, sitting. The second is the replacement of the solid wall with a screen (although one firm enough to take the weight of the folded chair). Finally we have the juxtaposition of the phonograph with the bed. The first item signifies noise, entertainment,

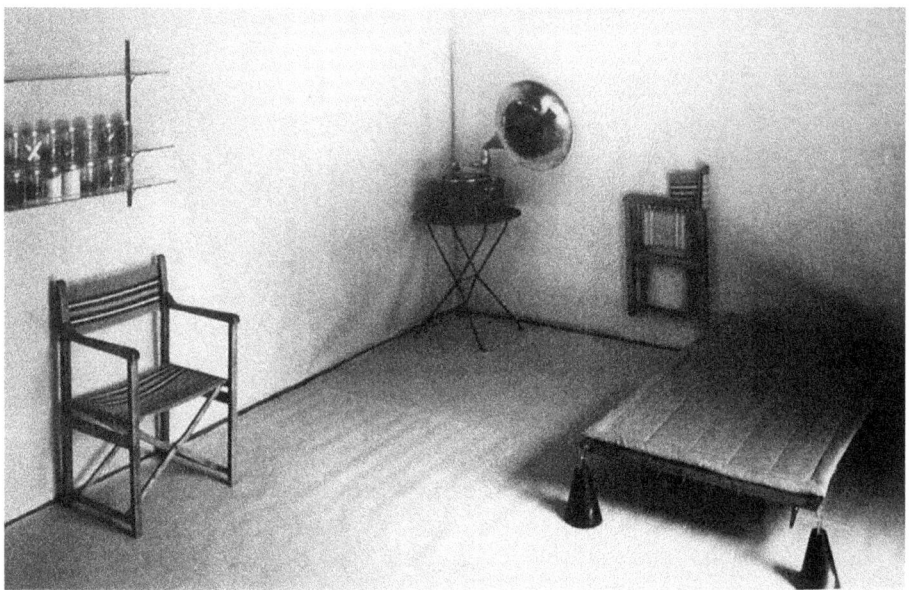

38 Hannes Meyer, Co-op interior, 1926

perhaps dancing while the second indicates rest. As I have just stated Meyer promoted a mass-production aesthetic and all the items in his interior could be replicated countless times. Standardisation, repetition and impersonality are the key
qualities expressed here. However, we can also see this interior as a reading of
Mondrian's studio; furniture is used to make formal compositions, such as the
folded chair, privacy is mixed with sociability, as expressed by the phonograph, and
the modernist cell recovers the origins of the home in the tent.

As we have seen repeatedly now, far more was at stake in the De Stijl interior
than the simple application of colour to walls. In the course of this chapter so far we
have considered the domestication of private space, the structural order of objects
placed within it, the advancement and eradication of naturalistic colour from the
interior, the connections between colour and space, the concept of the wall as a
screen and the confusion of functions (or multi-functionality) in the home. There
is one notable project which will allow us to summarise all of these ideas: the
Schröder house built in Utrecht in 1924.

One of the examples I used at the beginning of this chapter was the room designed
by Rietveld for Truus Schröder in 1921. The argument I made was that its structural arrangement differed radically from conventional interiors of the day. I drew
attention to the large amount of empty space, the displacement of the seating from
the centre to the edge of the room, the use of diffuse rather than direct lighting,
removal of focus from the fireplace and the application of simple blocks of colour
to the walls. I proposed that what we could see taking place in this room was the

removal of the symbolic order which naturalised the family hierarchy and its replacement by signifiers of relationship which were mobile and flexible. Thus the seating was lowered and was no longer dependant on a high table to confirm its purpose or predict the posture of the bodies which occupied it. Similarly the lighting treated all objects in the room equally and did not select certain positions for advantage. The use of naturalistic ornament such as floral wallpaper or archi-trave was replaced by an abstract composition which treated the wall as a flat sur-face and related it to the volumetric proportions of the room. For Schröder this room was an important part of reformulating her role within the family, which she saw in connection to the growing women's movement. However, in 1923 her cir-cumstances changed dramatically for personal rather than political reasons when her husband died, leaving her with three children, a boy and two girls aged eleven, ten and five respectively. She turned once more to Rietveld to help work out how they were now going to live together.

The apartment that the Schröder family occupied on Biltstraat was above Fritz Schröder's legal offices. Although the family was left well provided for following his death, it was necessary to find a new place to live. Truus Schröder had never felt settled in Utrecht and planned to move to Amsterdam, where her sister lived, after the children had finished their schooling. She looked first of all for a property to rent that she and Rietveld could remodel as they had previously done with her room. Unable to find anything suitable, she acquired a plot of land at the edge of town and asked Rietveld to assist in the construction of a house. As Rietveld later described, the location they stumbled upon was initially unpromising:

> No-one had ever looked at this lane before this house was built here. There was a dirty crumbling wall with weeds growing in front of it. Over there was a small farm. It was a very rural spot, and this sort of fitted in. It was a deserted place, where anyone who wanted to pee just did it against this wall. It was a real piece of no-man's land. And we said, 'Yes, this is just right, let's build here.'[32]

Although the view has now been blocked by an elevated ring road, at the time of construction the Schröder house enjoyed a broad prospect over the surrounding countryside. That this location should have been selected for the construction of one of modernism's most iconic buildings reinforces the argument I made in chapter two concerning the pattern of urban development in the interwar period. The experience of modernity was felt at its keenest at the periphery rather than the centre.

As Schröder recalled in later life, the design of the house (Figure 39) proceeded from the interior. One of the first decisions made was that the family would spend most time upstairs to take advantage of the views to open countryside. They had become accustomed to first-floor life after the years of occupying rooms above Fritz Schröder's offices. Once again we have an unusual mixture of urban and suburban forms, a *piano nobile* in a two-storey semi-detached house. Rietveld and Schröder did not invert the conventional house structure and place bedrooms downstairs; on

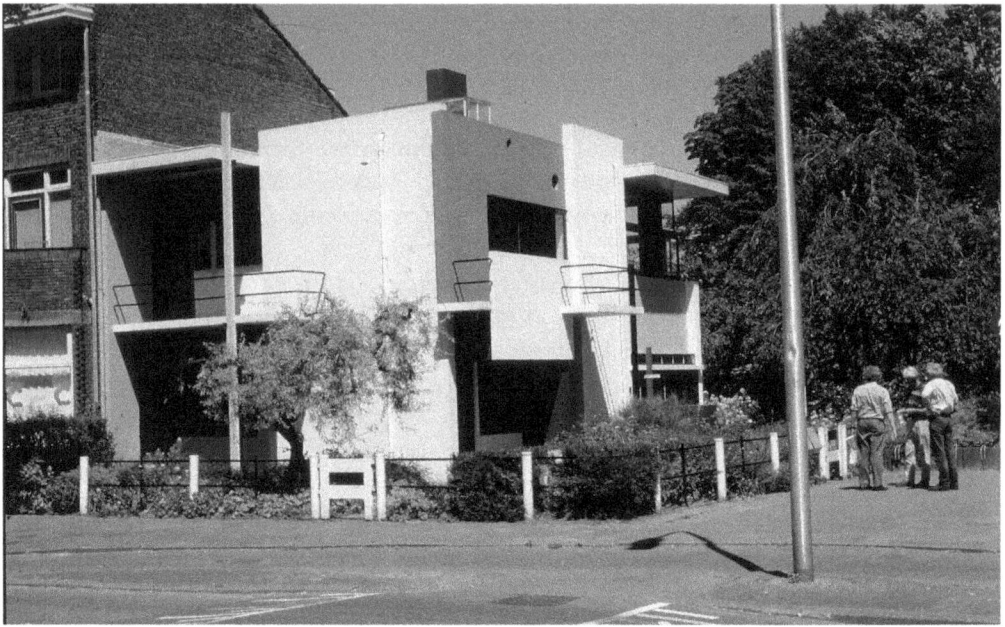

39 Gerrit Rietveld, Schröder House, Utrecht, 1924

the ground floor was the kitchen, a library, study and workroom; on the first floor was a sitting/dining area and space for the four family members to sleep and wash (Plate 5). The logic of the placement of rooms was the separation of work spaces and social/private space (as the family was accustomed to living over offices). However, as Schröder recounted, the most famous aspect of the house is the removal of boundaries between private and social spaces:

> You see, I'd left my husband on three occasions because I disagreed with him so strongly about the children's upbringing. Each time, they were looked after by a housemaid, but still I thought it was terrible for them. And after my husband died and I had full custody of the children, I thought a lot about how we should live together.
>
> So when Rietveld had made a sketch of the rooms, I asked, 'Can these walls go too?' To which he answered, 'With pleasure, away with those walls!' I can still hear myself asking, can those walls go, and that's how we ended up with one large space.[33]

The aim of this remarkable layout was that the mother could spend as much time with her children as possible. They would be part of each other's lives in a way that an existence in a house with individual rooms prevented. However, the eradication of the private bedroom directly contravened modern planning regulations designed to prevent the mixing of functions and to outlaw what was deemed to be the most unhealthy aspect of poor housing, the bed cabinet. Popular in the Netherlands from medieval times onwards, the bed cabinet was separated from the living space by a simple curtain. To get around this problem, Rietveld and Schröder described the upper storey of the house as an attic when they submitted their plans for approval.

It remains unclear at precisely what point the decision was made to include moveable screens to allow the division of the upper space in the Schröder house. As Schröder continues in her reminiscences:

> But I was still looking for the possibility of also dividing up that space [the first floor]. That could be done with sliding partitions. I think that was an idea of Rietveld's, though he found it a shame. He did it, but he thought it was a pity. Personally, I'm eternally thankful that it was done.[34]

It was possible, then to provide some privacy and close off some parts of the upper floor from view where beds were placed. The origins of this feature had sprung first from Schröder's desire to occupy the same space as her children on an equal footing and then a practical decision about affording some level of privacy. This is at odds with the customary discussion of the role of painting in architecture in De Stijl. Yve-Alain Bois reads the Schröder house directly out of the Rosenberg models. For him the screen is an invention of painting, an avant-garde gesture bequeathed to the occupant of the house.[35] Certainly Rietveld was well aware of the 1923 De Stijl exhibition in Paris, having constructed the model of the *Maison Rosenberg* for Van Doesburg and Van Eesteren. However, he does not seem to have been so interested in the screen himself, as the above quote demonstrates. When given the opportunity to design a flat for his family in the 1930s, he built it, again flouting regulations, as one large open space with bedroom niches separated by curtains in an even more anachronistic revival of the bed cabinet.

The Schröder house is a monument not only to the relationship between a mother and her children but also to that between the architect and the client. Rietveld used a room on the ground floor as an office for many years and lived there himself during the last six years of his life, after his wife's death in 1958. For over a decade after the completion of the house Schröder and Rietveld ran an interior design business together. Their first contract was given by Schröder's sister, An Harrenstein, whose living room and bedroom the pair remodelled in 1926. This was used as an illustration for an article published by Schröder in 1930 in a new journal, *De werkende vrouw* (The Working Woman), where she described the 'space-making' properties of architecture.[36] Other articles in the magazine drew attention to the home as a workplace, calling for the recognition of domestic labour as work. Schröder drew connections between interior design and 'consciousness' of spatial organisation, part of a developing argument that the home should no longer be conceived as a refuge or place for display of possessions but as a productive environment where activities such as childcare and housework make as equal a contribution to society as any paid employment. She directly rejected the role of the house as a place for relaxation after work:

If someone succeeds in creating an interior so that he is not passive in it, not deluded but stimulated to activity then he is, in my opinion, on a better path than to want to effect a so-called artistic interior or an interior which is warm, cozy, cheerful, festive etc., as people call it.[37]

Rietveld repeated these views in his own articles for *The Working Woman*, published in later editions in 1930. Again opposing an active to a passive interior, Rietveld suggested that the home was a place where 'I do things completely of my own will which have or get my full attention. The bright lit space must be open and clear. If listening to music, for example, I want to be all ears, I want to be awake and increase my activity.'[38]

The Schröder house itself seems to have acted as a giant advertisement to those interested in modernist architecture and commissions in Utrecht were soon forthcoming for Rietveld and Schröder. In addition to redesigning interiors, the pair oversaw the installation of modern amenities to existing properties. For example, in 1928 they redesigned some rooms for a certain Mrs Fraenkel at 1 Wilhelmina Park, a short distance from the Schröder house. A few months later, they completely modernised a house for the same client at 65 Prins Hendriklaan, the same street as the Schröder house itself. The surviving bill for this job shows that they not only took care of refurbishment and painting but also installed central heating, hot water, running water to bedrooms and electric lighting.[39] They also removed defunct fireplaces and transformed the property into what we would consider a modern dwelling. The total bill for Mrs Fraenkel came to 4,000 guilders, almost half of what it had cost to build the entire Schröder house, and the partners charged a 10 per cent fee for their management of the conversion. Buoyed up by such success, their next venture was to build a terrace of houses on land which had become available just opposite the Schröder house itself. Four three-storey houses were completed in 1931 which, if they did not resemble the Schröder house externally, reproduced its interior very closely. On all three levels space could be opened out or divided by screens including, once again, bedroom spaces. One of the houses was fitted out with Rietveld furniture and opened as a show house for a three-week exhibition. The largely positive reviews in the local and national press emphasised the experience of light and room offered by the houses with very little comment made concerning either the functional use of space or the propriety of open plan living.[40]

There are several ways of placing the Schröder house in a narrative of liberation, therefore. For Schröder, it enabled her to have a very different life at home and to be part of her children's lives in a way that women of her class were unaccustomed. It also opened up opportunities for her to gain employment in a new field of interior design. Finally, as the house became more and more a focus of attention, it placed her at the centre of avant-garde discussion. The means by which this was expressed architecturally included the open plan upper floor which encouraged the members of the family to share space with each other, the large windows and balcony areas which disrupted the boundaries between interior and exterior, and the moveable partitions which forced the inhabitants to continually interact with the building. There are also more subtle features which Rietveld and Schröder built in. Schröder had never liked the high ceilings of the Biltstraat apartment. Not only is the Schröder house more modestly proportioned in this regard but a whole range of adaptations were made to counter verticality. For example, the internal doors on the ground floor are slightly wider than average. Radiators used in industrial buildings were fitted because their pipes ran horizontally. Rietveld also made special shutters for the windows which could be fixed in place or completely removed when necessary, so that the hanging lines of curtains were avoided.

The apparent removal of boundaries in the Schröder house conceals very deliberate ways in which the structure was designed to be used. As much as the mother and her children negotiated a single space, it was not only the partitions that permitted a level of segregation; the manner in which Rietveld divided the floor into blocks of colour and installed his furniture contributed greatly to the fragmentation of the open plan. This works in extremely subtle ways. For example, visitors coming up the stairs from the ground floor find themselves facing the areas in which the children slept. The main seating and dining area can only be seen by turning round 180°. However, the visual reversal of privacy and sociability is controlled by the painting of the floor. A large white stripe running from the front to the back of the house separates the boy's from the girls' rooms (even when the screens are not pulled out) and leads the visitor around the stairwell to the seating area (Plate 6). Schröder later recalled her dissatisfaction with Rietveld's choice of colour, using white for a part of the floor that would receive the heaviest foot traffic.[41] The disregard for function in the use of colour must have been prompted by the need for visual clarity. Schröder's own bedroom was the smallest space on the first floor, tucked away in the darkest corner. The modesty of the room was compensated by the level of visual privacy she enjoyed. However, there was once again a reversal of visibility and accessibility; her room formed part of a circulation route around the stairwell and could be entered from two sides. The space which gave access to her room from the direction of the girls' sleeping area became the bathroom by swinging out sliding doors. These closed off the room from one end but also meant that the bathroom had to be entered from her bedroom. The boy's sleeping area was the most visible, overlooked from the stairs, the girls' sleeping area and the seating area, but it was also most clearly segregated by use of colour – Rietveld painted the floor here bright red. As a recent study has shown, the boy's room was actually the least 'permeable' space on the first floor.[42] His area mirrored the reading room on the ground floor, directly below, which was closest to the front door but paradoxically the most private space in the whole house.

The screens in the Schröder house had very little impact on the way that the space was actually used but more on the way it was seen. As Julienne Hanson has described:

The practical consequence of open planning in the Rietveld Schröder house is to restrict movement and to reinforce the discreteness of its constituent spatial domains, whilst at the same time integrating the domestic interior visually, through the transparency and completeness of its visual fields. This dominance of visual over permeable relations is indeed a new way of 'revealing reality' through space configuration.[43]

One of Hanson's conclusions from her analysis of the relation between visibility and permeability in the Schröder house is that the space is structured somewhat like an urban landscape where views are given to areas which may not necessarily be physically accessible. Rietveld and Schröder's treatment of interior design as town planning is also apparent in the way the house is zoned, both spatially and temporally; for example, at certain points of the day Schröder's bedroom has to be accessed but at others may have been out of bounds. There are striking similarities with the way that Mondrian closed down space in his studio while permitting visitors certain open views.

In conclusion, we can return to a point made in the discussion of reform tendencies in Dutch interior design before the First World War. There I contested Marc Adang's proposition that the post-war modernism lacked the attention to kitsch which was the defining characteristic of pre-war discourse on the interior. I argued that attention turns from the production of objects to the production of space and that therefore the good and bad interior are no longer determinable by the same judgments of tasteful furnishing that governed them previously. This transition has often been described as the rejection of the nineteenth-century construction of domesticity for the functional, ergonomically designed housing of modernism. In the first instance the interior is governed by emotional states which dictate patterns of behaviour distinct from the outside world. In the second, home life is viewed as a sequence of operations and tasks not dissimilar to work in a factory. The De Stijl interior will not fall neatly into either of these categories (although Oud produced some of the best functional housing of the 1920s). A term that was applied to the De Stijl interior in France at the time was *ambiance*, a quality still much sought after in interior design.[44] It implies a state of mind produced by interior space, one of ease, intimacy and sociability, but relies on opening up the home to a public life. As the next chapter will explore, this has an interesting bearing on exhibition space where crossovers between public and private space have always occurred.

Notes

1 'Dolf van Attema was op zijne wandeling na den eten aangegaan bij de zuster zijner vrouw, Cecile van Even, op den Scheveningschen weg, en hij wachtte in den kleine voorsalon, wandelend tusschen de rozenhouten meubeltjes en de vieux roze moiré cauzeuses met de drie, vier groote passen, waarmeê hij de nauwte van het vertrekje telkens en telkens scheen over te meten. Achter de chaise-longue brandde op een onyxen zuil eene lamp van onyx, onder hare kanten kap zacht gloeiend als eene groote, zeshoekige lichtbloem.' Louis Couperus, *Extase* (Amsterdam: Pandora Pockets, 1994), p. 7.

2 Peter Fuhring and Rudolphine Eggink, *Binnenhuis-architektuur in Nederland 1900–1981* (The Hague: Ulysses, 1981), p. 12.

3 Alice Friedman, *Women and the Making of the Modern House* (New York: Abrams, 1998), p. 73.

4 'Wel weet ik, dat deze ruimte-kleur atelier een heel andere is dan de ruimten die wij kennen. In dit ruimte-kleur atelier is een eenheid en dat is de ruimte, en die ruimte bestaat uit kleuren. en deze kleiren zijn *vorm-bepalend*. De gevoelens die deze ruimte kan opwekken zijn geheel nieuw. Men leeft in kleur, het is of men een bad neemt in kleur, men is *in* kleur.' J. P. Mieras, 'Het atelier van Berssenbrugge te 's-Gravenhage', *Bouwkundig Weekblad* 43: 15 (April 1922), pp. 150–2.

5 Nancy Troy, *The De Stijl Environment* (Cambridge MA and London: MIT, 1983), p. 166.

6 Titus Eliëns, *Avant-garde Design: Dutch Decorative Arts 1880–1940* (London: Philip Wilson, 1997), p. 16.

7 Eliëns, *Avant-garde Design*, p. 206.

8 For details of Behrens' work for AEG see Alan Windsor, *Peter Behrens: Architect and Designer* (London: Architectural Press, 1981), pp. 77–105. Berlage's work for Henny is also a forerunner to the role he played at Müller and Co. as company architect.

9 Mark Adang '"Breng me in uw huis, laat me uw woonkamer zien en ik zal u zeggen wie gij zijt!" Het denken over kitsch en smaakopvoeding in Nederland', *Nederlands Kunsthistorisch Jaarboek* 28 (1977), p. 217.

10 'Kijken we hoe bij tween belangrijke stromingen uit de naarorlogse kunst in Nederland – de Amsterdamse School en De Stijl – de voorwaarden tot en dergelijke volksopvoedingstendens aanwezig waren. . . . Qua vormgeving sluit de Amsterdamse School kunstnijverheid aan bij de vorige period door de zorg voor ambachtelijk kwaliteit en het streven naar eenheid in sfeer. Ze wijkt af door het ontbreken van een zelfde rationale helderheid van structuur of soberheid van ornamentering, en door de proporties der meubelen, de voorkeur voor kostbare materialen en bewerkelijke technieken, wat een grote verspreiding in de weg stond. Kortom: het zich toeleggen op een meer elitair publiek, het ontbreken van de politiek wil tot volksopvoeding en het ontbreken van een streng-dogmatische esthetiek stonden een voorzetting van de voor oorlogse traditie van socialistische smaakopvoeding in de weg. De Stijl was in de eerste plaats op beeldende kunst gericht . . . Zowel vormgeving als kunsttheorie zijn voldoende extreem om een uitgrsproken kunst-en-kitsch opvatting te voeden.' Adang, '"Breng me in uw huis"', pp. 225–7.

11 On my visit to *Sint Hubertus* in July 2001, the tour guide to the house followed exactly the path through the house I have described here and repeated the spiritual interpretation almost verbatim. It can also be found in the booklet about the house sold by the National Park, Wim Alings, *St. Hubertus Hunting Lodge* (Hoenderloo: Foundation Het Nationale Park De Hoge Veluwe, 1990).

12 'hal: geel met paarsche bespanning afgezet met zwart. Lambriseering helder groen. Eetzaal: lambriseering zwart, paneelen grijs, losgemaakt door wit; hierin buffet: deuren donker-diep-blauw, losgemaakt door hel-geel. lijstband hierom heen *groen*, losgemaakt door wit. uiterste omlijsting zwart. Salon: domineerend: *paars* daardoorheen lijstband van boven-lambriseering *groen*.

Alle vlakken en paneelen losgemaakt door wit. Huiskamer grenzend aan Salon: *alles* andersom als in Salon: domineerend goen, lijstband *paars* alles los door wit. Het geweldigste is de studeerkamer: boekenkast *groen, zwart* en *wit*, bespanning *biljard-laken*! Alles losgemaakt door wit. Schouw groene steen met witte tegels ann de zijkanten. In 't midden tegeltab een door mijn ontworpen glas mosaik. De deuren: zwarte paneelen losgemaakt door wit. Groen deurhout. Ook heb ik bij wijze van proef rood toegepast in een slaap kamer van de dochter. Vermiljoen-roode lambriseering. *Witte* bespanning. Waschtafel: wit, rood, groen en blauw. Alles los. Ook de plafonds violet; grijs, wit enz. Ik heb overal gedacht aan de behoefte van hen die het vertrek gebruikte. Zoo b.v. een meisjeskamer: helder geel; paarsch en groen. Een kinderlo-geerkamer: geel en blauw; De zolder en aangezende dienstbodenvertrekken wit en blauw. De keuken ditto wit en blauw. De zolder-corridor en trap geel, zwart en wit.' Theo van Doesburg, letter to Anthony Kok, 9 September 1917, RKD, The Hague.

13 Notably one of the purely functional rooms in *Sint Hubertus*, the linen room, was given exactly the same combination of blue and white. Kröller-Müller was also an avid collector of Delft pottery.

14 Vilmos Huszár, 'Aesthetische Beschouwingen', *De Stijl* 1: 2 (1917), p. 22.

15 Troy, *The De Stijl Environment*, p. 40.

16 Vilmos Huszár, letter to Chris Beekman, 2 August 1919, published in Sjarel Ex and Els Hoek, *Vilmos Huszár. Schilder en Ontwerper 1884–1960* (Utrecht: Relflex, 1985), p. 204.

17 Huszár stated these intentions in a letter to Chris Beekman dated 11 April 1919, published in Ex and Hoek, *Vilmos Huszár*, pp. 203–4.

18 Letter from Van Doesburg to Oud, 13 July 1922, quoted by Carel Blotkamp and Cees Hilhorst, 'De dissedenten kunstenaars: Bart van der Leck, Vilmos Huszár, Georges Vantongerloo', in Carel Blotkamp (ed.), *De vervolgjaren van De Stijl, 1922–1932* (Amsterdam and Antwerp: L. J. Veen, 1996), p. 337.

19 Piet Mondrian, 'Natural Reality and Abstract Reality', in Harry Holtzmann and Martin James (eds), *The New Art – The New Life: The Collected Writings of Piet Mondrian* (London: Thames and Hudson, 1987), p. 112.

20 Carel Blotkamp, *Mondrian: The Art of Destruction* (London: Reaktion Books, 1994), pp. 140–6.

21 Yve-Alain Bois, 'The Iconoclast', in Angelica Rudenstine (ed.), *Piet Mondrian 1872–1944* (Milan: Leonardo Arte, 1994), p. 349.

22 Piet Mondrian, 'Neo-Plasticism: The General Principle of Plastic Equivalence', in Holtzmann and James (eds), *The New Art – The New Life*, p. 137.

23 Piet Mondrian, 'The Realization of Neo-Plasticism in the Distant Future and in Architecture Today', in Holtzmann and James (eds), *The New Art – The New Life*, p. 172.

24 Frans Postma, *26, rue du Départ: Mondrian's studio 1921–1936* (Berlin: Ernst and Sohn, 1995), p. 10.

25 For Seuphor's sketch see Postma, *26, rue du Départ*, p. 33.

26 Nancy Troy, *The De Stijl Environment* (Cambridge MA and London: MIT, 1983), p. 14.

27 At this sale Mrs Kröller-Müller acquired numerous works including two Braques, seven by Juan Gris, five by August Herbin, a Léger, three by Metzinger and three by Severini.

28 A particularly significant essay in this regard is Jean Leering, 'De Architectuur en Van Doesburg', in Eindhoven, Stedelijk van Abbemuseum, *Theo van Doesburg 1883–1931* (1969), pp. 19–25.

29 The most extensive discussion to date of the significance of Semper's principle of clothing for modernist architecture can be found in Mark Wigley, *White Walls, Designer Dresses: The Fashioning of Modern Architecture* (Cambridge MA and London: MIT, 1995).

30 Postma, 26, *rue du Départ*, p. 51.

31 Mondrian also had use of an anteroom in which to cook which also contained a bed. It is unclear whether he used this bed or whether it was merely left on show.

32 Gerrit Rietveld interview with P. van Moock, 1963, quoted in Paul Overy *et al.*, *The Rietveld Schröder House* (Cambridge MA and London: MIT, 1988), p. 52.

33 Paul Overy *et al.*, *The Rietveld Schröder House*, p. 56.

34 Paul Overy *et al.*, *The Rietveld Schröder House*, p. 56.

35 Yve-Alain Bois, 'The De Stijl idea', in *Painting as Model* (Cambridge MA and London: MIT, 1990), p. 119.

36 Truus Schröder-Schräder, 'Een Inleidend Woord tot Binnen-architectuur', *De werkende vrouw* 1: 3 (March 1930), pp. 93–4.

37 'Als het iemand gelukt is een interieur zóó te maken, dat hij daarin niet passief wordt, niet wegdoezelt, maar geprikkeld wordt tot activiteit, dan is hij, meen ik, op een beteren weg dan door een z.g. artistiek interieur te willen bereiken of een, zooals men het noemt, warm, gezellig, vroolijk, feestelijk enz. interieur, en is het interessant eens na te gaan welke factoren dit hebben tot stand gebracht.' Schröder-Schräder, 'Een Inleidend Woord tot Binnen-architectuur', p. 94.

38 'Mijn huis zal dan ook niet in de eerste plaats een rustplaats zijn, maar een plaats waar ik mezelf hervind, waar de stroom van lijdelijke indrukken niet binnenkomt en waar ik eerst recht actief wordt, doordat ik er alleen die dingen doe, die geheel uit vrijen wil zijn en m'n volle aandacht hebben of krijgen kunnen. De helder verlichte ruimte moet klaar en duidelijk zijn. Bij musiek wil ik b.v. geheel oor zijn, ik wil wakker zijn en m'n activiteit opvoeren.' Gerrit Rietveld, 'Architectuur', *De werekende vrouw*, 1: 11–12 (November–December 1930), p. 317.

39 Rietveld Archive, NAI, Rotterdam, inventory number 477.

40 See for example Anon., 'Een Glorie van Licht', *Utrechtsch Provinciaale en Stedelijk Dagblad* 5 October 1931, p. 2 and Anon., 'Herrenhuizen te Utrecht. Nieuwe Bouwwijze', *De Telegraaf* 27 October 1931, p. 9.

41 Paul Overy *et al.*, *The Rietveld Schröder House*, p. 71.

42 Julienne Hanson, *Decoding Homes and Houses* (Cambridge: Cambridge University Press, 1998), p. 205.

43 Hanson, *Decoding Homes and Houses*, p. 213.

44 The special edition of the journal *Vouloir* devoted to De Stijl in 1927 was subtitled *Ambiance*.

5

Exhibiting style

The narrative I have constructed so far has taken a route from the urban scene to the private interior. At each point we have seen how issues of abstraction were closely connected to an ambition to create a public for modernism. Although gloriously unsuccessful in this aim, De Stijl contested every possible area where this could be made to happen. It is only appropriate, therefore, that the final chapter of this book should address the space in which the De Stijl concern for interior design and the appeal to a large audience collide most obviously, namely the museum. To date no consideration has been paid to the role of exhibitions, collections or galleries in the development of De Stijl. A substantial gap exists in the literature between studies of the production of the De Stijl idea and its reception. While it is certainly the case that De Stijl received virtually no institutional support during its heyday, I will discuss how it was situated in relation to the establishment of major institutions such as the Stedelijk Museum in Amsterdam, the Gemeentemuseum in The Hague and the Kröller-Müller Museum in Otterlo.

Often the focus of the discussion of the institutionalisation of De Stijl has drifted to Alfred Barr's exhibition, *Cubism and Abstract Art*, held at the Museum of Modern Art in New York in 1936, including my own discussion of this event in the introduction to this book. In the infamous chart of the development of modern art, which Barr published in the catalogue for this exhibition, De Stijl was carefully integrated with the sequence of modernist movements, and placed within the Paris–New York narrative Barr manufactured. On closer examination, it comes to light that six of the nine Mondrian paintings exhibited by Barr were taken from a public collection, that assembled by Hélène Kröller-Müller. She had accumulated the most substantial single collection of modern art in the Netherlands, which she saw as a national treasure, not just a personal one. She opened her collection to public viewing from as early as 1913. By the time her Mondrian paintings were being exhibited in New York, Kröller-Müller was negotiating the donation of her collection to the Dutch state, which resulted in the opening of the Kröller-Müller Museum in 1938. That parts of the collection soon received international attention reflected well on her judgment, and no doubt facilitated acceptance of her collection as a national institution.

This chapter is not merely about the entry of abstract art into the hallowed halls of the museum, however. It concerns the new roles being taken on by curators and

artists in the period, and their competition to control the most important exhibition spaces. De Stijl became an important locus for the discussion of new concepts
of display. The relation between art and architecture, which was constantly
addressed in its pages, also has an obvious connection to the situating of painting
within buildings. However, the tradition of monumental art from which De Stijl
emerged did not sit comfortably with the development of the so-called 'white cube'
installation which came to dominate displays of modern art by mid-century.
Responses among De Stijl associates to the growing specialisation of museums, and
the founding of museums of modern art, were manifold. As has already been mentioned in the previous chapter, Mondrian used his studio as an exhibition space. By
the end of the 1920s he was also investigating the possibility of establishing his own
museum. Huszár and Rietveld took a different route, exploring new modes of display in overtly commercial settings, such as shops and trade fairs. To focus some of
the discussion at the outset I will begin by examining a very unusual object.

For the 1939 World's Fair in New York, Vilmos Huszár collaborated with
another artist, Willem Roelofs, in the production of a maquette which was placed
in a vitrine displaying the development of Dutch culture from the 'Golden Age'
of the seventeenth century to the modern period (Figure 40). Huszár and Roelofs

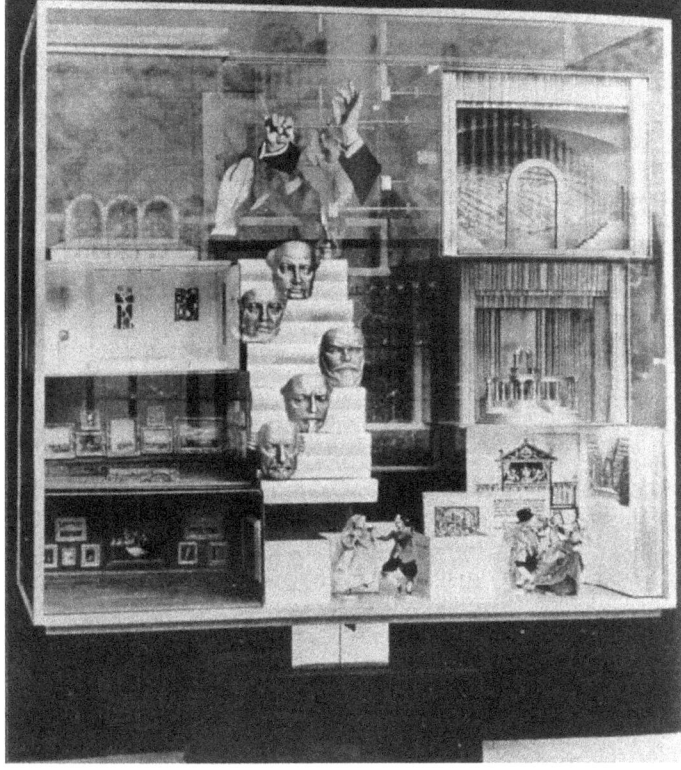

40 Vilmos Huszár
and Willem Roelofs,
Vitrine for New York
World's Fair, 1939

constructed a miniature gallery which was placed in the vitrine alongside masks of famous writers, the hands of renowned musicians and fragments of important buildings. Structured like a doll's house, the three floors of the gallery represented the high points of seventeenth-, nineteenth- and twentieth-century art. As Sjarel Ex and Els Hoek have pointed out, Roelofs, who designed the two lower storeys, was able to base his sections on actual rooms. The lower floor reproduced part of the Mauritshuis with its most famous painting, Rembrandt's *Anatomy Lesson of Dr Tulp*, hung in the centre of the main wall. The second floor skipped the eighteenth century, not seen as a culturally significant period in Dutch history, to show the work of the Hague School artists at the Puchri Studio, the gallery in The Hague with which they were most closely associated. For the top storey, however, Huszár engineered a piece of fantasy and created a De Stijl gallery. There was no such installation in any museum at the time and the only collective De Stijl exhibition to that date had been the 1923 show at the *Galerie de l'Effort Moderne* in Paris. This exhibition had focused almost entirely on architecture and Huszár had not been significantly represented in it. Unsurprisingly then, he did not use it as the source for the showcase. Of the handful of objects he included, one was currently located in a public institution; Mondrian's *Composition in Line* of 1917 was in the recently founded Kröller-Müller Museum in Otterlo. As mentioned above, for many years prior to the opening of the museum Kröller-Müller had allowed the public access to her collection, which was housed next to the offices of Müller & Co. on Lange Voorhout in The Hague. The Kröller-Müller gallery was in fact only a stone's throw from the Mauritshuis and on the same street as the Pulchri Studio. The imaginary museum presented by Huszár and Roelofs can therefore be read as a conceptual conflation of these institutions. Huszár also included a miniature version of a Van der Leck painting of a basket of apples from 1921. The first paying exhibition Kröller-Müller held at her Lange Voorhout gallery was a Van der Leck retrospective in 1927. Even if this was not, then, an authentic De Stijl exhibition, Huszár had good reason to imagine his gallery as the natural successor to the previous two.

If we compare the ways in which the rooms in Roelofs and Huszár's museum are presented, we can see that, from Rembrandt to De Stijl, the transformation in hanging is very obvious. Huszár halved the number of objects on display, dispensed with double hanging and gave each item a great deal of space. He did not frame any of the paintings he reproduced and placed a representation of a Vantongerloo sculpture on a very plain pedestal. The other notable feature of the installation is the application of colour to the right-hand wall, the ceiling and on the floor. The plain rectangles, whose colour is unfortunately indeterminable, is highly reminiscent of De Stijl interiors. Perhaps to draw attention to the architectural concerns of De Stijl, Huszár made the installation a unification of painting, sculpture and architecture. This may also explain another anomalous inclusion, that of his own painting *Danspaar* (Dance partners) of 1938/39, which in terms of a De Stijl exhibition is completely anachronistic. However, by placing a painting in the installation which revived his earlier interest in the human figure in motion, Huszár provided a sense of scale and relation to the human body that would otherwise have been difficult to imagine in such a small model. What is also striking about the constrast between Roelofs' and Huszár's rooms is the height at which Huszár placed his miniature works. As will be recalled, *Composition in Line* was the centre of the 'triptych' Mondrian created at the *Hollandsche Kunstenaarskring* exhibition in 1917. Although the paintings which flanked it are missing here, Huszár seems to have retained Mondrian's placement of it above an imaginary eye level.

By reproducing Mondrian's *Composition with Line* in his miniature gallery, Huszár marked the emergence of De Stijl in 1917. To the right of it he hung Van Doesburg's 'Composition X' of 1918, a painting which was still in the possession of Nelly van Doesburg but which was easily available in reproduction; it had appeared first in De Stijl, then in the Hungarian journal *MA* and then in Lajos Kassak and Laszlo Moholy-Nagy's *Buch Neue Künstler* (Book of the New Artist), published in 1922. As such, it was a good example of the dissemination of De Stijl imagery via the little magazines. The Van der Leck painting is even more significant in this context. The painting was owned by H. P. Bremmer, who bought it in 1921 for 3,000 guilders, equivalent to an entire year's salary for Van der Leck. Yet the collector also gave his permission for Van der Leck to issue a reproduction of the painting as part of a series of photo-lithographic prints which were sold for substantially less, three and a half guilders to be precise.[1] Bremmer then loaned the painting to the Centraal Museum Utrecht in 1923 where it went on public display. The inflated value of the original object was therefore reliant on the dissemination of the reproduction.

Having established the public life enjoyed by De Stijl art works beyond the gallery walls, Huszár was then able to play up to the position that Alfred Barr had recently accorded De Stijl in *Cubism and Abstract Art*. His vitrine guides the way for Mondrian's arrival in New York in 1940 and also for the installation produced by another previous member of De Stijl, Frederick Kiesler, at Peggy Guggenheim's *Art of this Century* gallery. This gallery divided modernist tendencies into surrealist and abstract camps, placing Mondrian and Van Doesburg favourably as the founders of a new tradition of abstract art.[2]

Although Huszár's maquette shows an exhibition space emptied of the wall covering and furniture we can see in the galleries below it, his direct painting of the wall cannot be related to any contemporary museum installation of the period. Those familiar with De Stijl would have recognised this more as a feature of interior design. Photographs of Mondrian's studio had been widely disseminated by this time, which openly conflated exhibition space and domestic space. Both Huszár and Van Doesburg had previously expressed in articles their desire that one might actually inhabit art rather than simply have a painting on the wall. This ran counter to the growing trend, represented by the white cube space, to divide the lofty sphere of aesthetic experience from the mundane world beyond. As became clear in the earlier discussion of advertising, De Stijl was a point of crossover between artistic modernism and contemporary commerce. Huszár's maquette, with its doll's house appearance, maintained a connection with domestic space while its placement in a shop window for Dutch culture, as it were, muddied the distinctions that might be drawn between looking at art and looking at any other commodity. These are all issues that can be addressed in a discussion of the emergence of museums of modern art in the Netherlands.

Although it may not immediately appear so to the thousands of tourists who visit Amsterdam every year, the Rijksmuseum is a very significant building in the history of modern Dutch architecture and development of modern Dutch culture. Completed in 1885, it was designed to house the national art collection and marked the emergence of large-scale public interest in the visual arts. The institution was also highly significant for the rediscovery of a national artistic identity and situated Amsterdam as a cultural centre of international importance. Richard Roland Holst was one of many prominent artists who grew up watching the Rijksmuseum slowly take shape. As he later reminisced:

> There was always something new to be seen on this building. Thus it won childish interest first of all and then trust later on. All at once the new sculpture was revealed, or new tiled pictures were cemented in, or curled ironwork put in place and new planting taken care of, and then suddenly the weathervanes stood sparkling on the towers. From day to day the building became more and more colourful.[3]

The architect of the Rijksmuseum, P. J. H. Cuypers, used his commission to give great prominence to a revivalist programme he had been pursuing for several years. Inspired by the French architect and theorist Eugène Viollet-le-Duc, Cuypers looked back to gothic architecture as a source for rational building methods. As Roland Holst's experience testifies to, Cuypers's building was perceived as both old and new simultaneously. Cuypers quoted liberally from the past but the rich decoration of the structure and its colourfulness were seen to be exceptionally modern. The exterior featured sgrafitto, tile painting, sculpture and ironwork. The interior had mosaic floors, tiled walls, wall paintings and much stained glass. Cuypers combined elements drawn from the Dutch gothic and renaissance with contemporary iron and glass construction. As visitors today can still see for themselves, the North facade incorporates four arches. The entrance and exit to the museum are located either side of these arches which actually bridge a road that bisects the entire building (two arches in each direction for pedestrian and wheeled traffic). For many years it was possible to drive under the gallery which held Rembrandt's *Nightwatch* (Figure 41). The Rijksmuseum stood on the boundary between the seventeenth-century city and the new urban spaces of Amsterdam South and was designed to link them together physically and conceptually. It stood at the forefront of the discourse around monumental art discussed in the first chapter; Cuypers did not merely provide a convenient house for the nation's artistic heritage, he produced an image of spiritual renewal through the union of art and architecture.

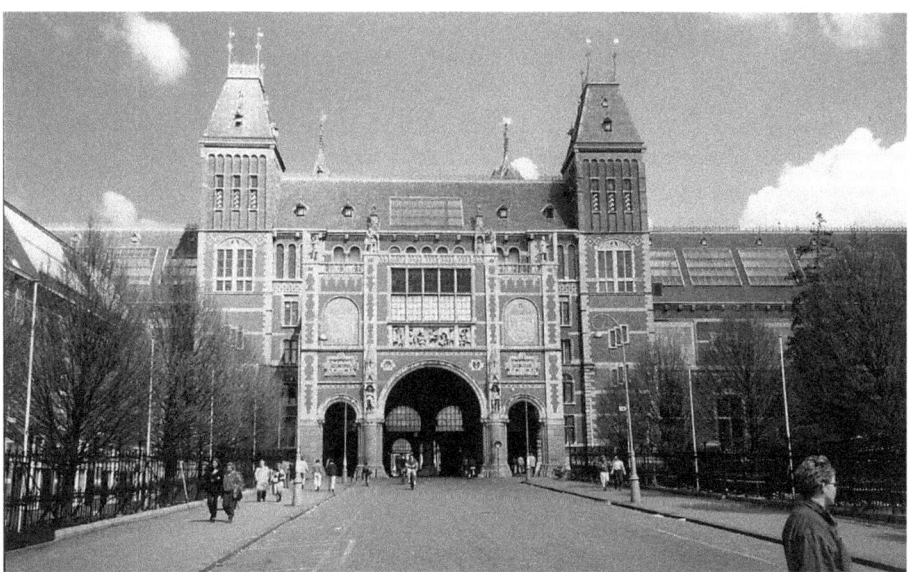

41 Rijksmuseum, Amsterdam, 1885

If the Rijkmuseum was of great significance as a building, so were its contents. A
visitor to the museum in the nineteenth century would have been presented with a
slightly different range of objects to today's tourists and art lovers though. For the
collections which comprised the museum's holdings at its inception were rather
haphazard. They included painting, sculpture and applied arts from the former
royal collection (transferred to the state by Louis Napoleon in 1808), the *Museum
van Aziatische Kunst* (Museum of Asiatic Art), the *Rijksprentkabinent* (National
Print Cabinet), the *Nederlands Museum voor Geschiedenis en Kunst* (Dutch Museum
of History and Art) and a substantial library. While the museum still houses most
of these collections, the last one hundred years or so have seen its focus narrow, so
that it is now best known internationally for a specialism in seventeenth-century
Dutch painting. A crucial factor in this transformation was the shedding of contemporary art. In the 1890s and early 1900s 'Modern Dutch Masters' such as
George Breitner, Anton Mauve, Josef Israels and H. W. Mesdag were integrated
into the museum (principally through the receipt of bequests). While these artists
are still represented in the Rijkmuseum's collections, their immediate followers are
not, after a strict division was placed between modern and historical art. The new
formulation of the national museum took a number of years to solidify and was
accompanied by the emergence of institutions specifically dedicated to the presentation and preservation of contemporary art. As I will discuss, the jettisoning of
history was, paradoxically, essential to the transformation of the Rijksmuseum into
an institution concerned only for the past. First of all I need to outline the initial
display of modern art in the museum.

In 1903 a certain Mr and Mrs Drucker made known their intentions to donate their substantial collection of late nineteenth-century painting to the Rijksmuseum. As part of the negotiations, they required suitable new rooms to be built to accommodate the modern collection (despite its recent completion, the Rijksmuseum was already short of space). By 1909 the 'Drucker Room' was completed and would be further extended by 1916. Among se`veral other donations received at this time was the collection of Cornelis Hoogendijk, which included sixteen Van Gogh paintings and thirty-two Cézannes. When the Drucker extension opened for the first time, visitors were presented with an exceptional survey of modern painting combining recent French and Dutch art, a display which drew international attention.

The curators responsible for creating this proto Museum of Modern Art in Amsterdam were B. W. F. van Riemsdijk, director of the painting department within the Rijksmuseum, and his assistant Willem Steenhof. The latter was a very interesting personality; he had originally trained as an artist, lived temporarily in a commune and was part of Amsterdam's leftist avant-garde scene. He began his post at the Rijksmuseum in 1899 but continued to paint and also wrote art criticism for *De Nieuwe Gids* (The New Guide), *De Amsterdammer* (The Amsterdammer) and later its more radical offspring *De Nieuwe Amsterdammer* (The New Amsterdammer). Through his contacts with the contemporary art world Steenhof planned to develop the Rijksmuseum's modern collection even further. When the first *Moderne Kunstkring* (Modern Art Circle) exhibition took place at the Stedelijk Museum in 1911, Steenhof organised the loan of the Hoogendijk Cézanne paintings so that they could be shown alongside the work of leading contemporary Dutch artists. In return Conrad Kikkert, chairman of the *Kunstkring*, donated a Picasso and a Braque from the exhibition to the Rijksmuseum. It may be recalled that Mondrian submitted his large *Evolution* triptych to this *Kunstkring* exhibition. Given the scale and ambition of this painting, it is worth speculating that perhaps he saw the Rijksmuseum as its ultimate destination. While this was not to be the case, Steenhof did take an active interest in Mondrian and the two men were personally acquainted. Although it appears Steenhof did not much appreciate Mondrian's more abstract paintings, he was aware of their significance. It was in fact Steenhof who proposed the salary arrangement to Bremmer that supported Mondrian from 1917 until 1921. Furthermore, in 1917 Steenhof organised the loan of part of the Bremmer collection to the Rijksmuseum, including Mondrian's *Composition in Line* of 1917 (before it became part of the Kröller-Müller collection), the central painting from the 'triptych' exhibited at the *Hollandsche Kunstkring* that year.[4] At the launch of De Stijl, therefore, Mondrian was represented in the most important art gallery in the Netherlands, at the leading edge of contemporary art.

At the launch of De Stijl, then, the presence of Mondrian's theoretical articles within the journal was a major coup for Van Doesburg. He had secured the participation of an artist generally respected as the foremost modernist painter of the day and whose status was ratified by the Rijksmuseum itself. In a complete reverse of the narrative we have come to expect, the avant-garde is not later assimilated into the institution but actually generated by it. Indeed, while Mondrian may have had good cause to see the Rijksmuseum as the ultimate destination for his paintings, the place where he had most often exhibited to this date was another new institution only a few hundred metres down the road.

The Stedelijk Museum opened in 1895 to house the municipal art collections of the city of Amsterdam along with the collection of its main benefactor, A. P. Lopez Suasso. From the start, the Stedelijk Museum latched onto the thriving art scene of Amsterdam and encouraged artists to use its galleries for temporary exhibitions. Thus, from 1897 on, the *Sint Lucas* (St. Luke) society, which represented young artists and had split from the more conservative *Arti et Amicitiae*, held its annual show there. Some years later a similar agreement would be struck with the *Moderne Kunstkring* (Modern Artists Circle) at whose exhibitions Dutch modernists such as Mondrian, Sluijters and Toorop were shown alongside their Parisian counterparts, Picasso, Braque, Vlaminck, Dufy and Le Fauconnier. It is a point that has been little stressed but from 1897 until the 1930s Mondrian exhibited in the Stedelijk Museum almost every year and in some years on more than one occasion. It was also in this location that he unveiled his most extravagant experiments, such as the *Evolution* triptych of 1911, the triptychal arrangement of three abstract paintings in 1917 (which I have repeatedly mentioned in this book) and his first diamond compositions in 1919. These very public exhibitions also generated a large amount of criticism in newly formed specialist journals and in the national press. Already, at the outset in 1917, abstract art was a museum art. When we add to this the unique connections in the Netherlands between the new museums and the discourse of monumental art, Mondrian's intense concern for the precise hanging of his paintings in relation to the interior space becomes more readily understandable.

A notable feature of both the Rijksmuseum and the Stedelijk Museum during the period I have been discussing is the influence artists had over the display of artworks. When Steenhof rehung the Drucker collection in 1918 he sought the approval of those whose work was represented in it, even if this led to a good deal of argument in some cases.[5] He also brought in a representative of the Van Wisselingh gallery in Amsterdam (which specialised in high-quality decorative arts) to coordinate the design of the interiors where the Drucker collection was located. Surviving plans show that a distinct continuity was created between the polychromatic rooms of Cuypers' original museum and the modern extension. In the main rooms of the museum, Cuypers had maintained the gothic references of the architecture with a red and green colour scheme. Although the decoration of the modern rooms had little of the elaborate mosaic and tiling to be found elsewhere in the building, red and yellow walls formed the backdrop to the paintings on display. In yet another context we see how the concept of *gemeenschapkunst*, identified by the interaction of painting and architecture, was the vehicle for expressing modernity in the visual arts.

Steenhof was keen to extend his museum further and when Bremmer's financial support for Mondrian finally ended in 1922, he launched a new initiative to secure the artist's work for the nation. In 1922 he formed a syndicate comprised of himself, Peter Alma, Salomon Slijper, Jo Steijling and Willem Stieltjes.[6] Together they drafted a plan whereby the syndicate would pay Mondrian a salary equivalent to his rent in return for one painting per year which they would then donate to a public collection.[7] The first of these paintings, *Composition in Oval* (1914), was given to the group shortly afterwards and in April 1922 Alma wrote to the Rijksmuseum offering it as a donation. To his surprise he received a curt reply from its new director, F. Schmidt-Degener, informing him that 'as the Rijksmuseum is chiefly reserved for the art from the past, whereas there is the Stedelijk Museum specially built for the art of the present, it seems to me that perhaps your offer might be better addressed to the latter institution.'[8] Schmidt-Degener had made this pronouncement without consulting his assistant, Steenhof. Shortly after this incident the latter fell prey to the new director's purge of contemporary art and was transferred out of the Rijksmuseum. Mondrian's painting was, as suggested, then offered to the Stedelijk Museum, where it was accepted on loan.

The stance of the Rijkmuseum reflected a sea change in the conception of the role of museums after the First World War, which is interesting to consider in connection to the discussion of the specificity of the arts engaged in by De Stijl. In 1918 the *Nederlandsche Oudheidkundige Bond* (Dutch Antiquarian Society) published a brochure on museum reform calling for greater specialisation and academic control over museum content. The government was prompted to set up a commission to report on the need for the reorganisation of museums across the entire country. The commission came up with three main proposals: the separation of art from other historical objects, the need for regional museums to collect objects of local significance, and thirdly that museums should be the site of art historical education.

Schmidt-Degener's refusal of Mondrian's painting and his recommendation that it go to the Stedelijk Museum is the direct outcome of the report's directives towards specialisation and art historical education. The distance the new director tried to place between the art of the past and that of the present is the direct outcome of art history entering the museum. As mentioned earlier, Steenhof was a practising artist, not an academic. From the 1920s onwards it would become virtually impossible for someone of his background to achieve the position he had of assistant director. Having lost its connection with contemporary art, the Rijksmuseum was then able to complete its transformation into an ordered, finished narrative of the past. Over the following decade the building was drained of its colour; mosaic floors were covered over in parquet, tiles painted and murals obscured.[9] At the same moment the Stedelijk Museum took on new life as a specialist modern museum, quite different from how it was imagined when built. It was then able to follow the second directive of the commission's report and collect work by leading contemporary artists who had local significance. To see this reorientation in its most blunt form, Schmidt-Degener had to go through the Rijksmuseum collection and make explicit divisions between art works seen as of exceptional artistic value, art historical value or historical value. Those falling into the last category were to be shipped out to the Amsterdam Historical Museum. The Stedelijk Museum on the other hand refashioned itself as the home of the new, the not yet historical, in a pattern that had been adopted in many Western countries.[10] It is important to note that, in 1922, the Stedelijk Museum had no provision for collecting works. Its permanent collection was fixed, although it did offer exhibition space to an independent organisation, the *Vereeniging tot het Vormen van een Openbare Verzameling van Hedendaagsche Kunst* (The Association for the Formation of a Public Collection of Contemporary Art). This is the reason why the Mondrian painting was only accepted on loan. It was only in 1923 that the local authority empowered the museum to make yearly purchases from leading contemporary artists and we can see Mondrian as something of a bridgehead in this process.

While the Rijksmuseum was being taken over by a new breed of art historian curator, the Stedelijk Museum was, as already noted, a space in which artists themselves enjoyed a good deal of freedom.[11] For example, in March of 1922 Slijper organised a Mondrian retrospective to celebrate the artist's fiftieth birthday, which formed part of the *Hollandsche Kunstenaarskring* (Dutch Artist's Circle) exhibition at the Stedelijk that year. The show was comprised of almost sixty paintings taken from Slijper's own collection and other private collections in the Netherlands, and was installed by the artist Peter Alma, whom Mondrian trusted to see that his work was correctly hung. The role played here by collector and artist is not a new one but its significance for the formation of the modern art museum is of some importance. While the art of the past was becoming ever more the preserve of the art historian, the art of the present needed its own specialists. De Stijl played a key role in the transmission of art theory in the Netherlands and Van Doesburg became its leading exponent. Before the publication of De Stijl, Van Doesburg had established his career as an art critic by writing about the exhibitions held at the Stedelijk Museum. Indeed, his contact with Mondrian was generated by a review he wrote in 1915.[12] By 1922, when Mondrian was enjoying his retrospective, Van Doesburg was busy summarising the place of De Stijl in the history of art in a lecture titled *Der Wille zum Stil* (The Will to Style) given in Jena, Weimar and Berlin, and subsequently published in De Stijl.

The Will to Style is a fascinating text which directly opposes the divisions being concurrently established between the art of the past and the present in such institutions as the Rijksmuseum. But it did so by appropriating and synthesising a variety of art historical sources. Van Doesburg argued that modernism, in the form of abstract painting, was the natural outcome of a historical trajectory which could be traced back to antiquity, a theory he expressed in a bizarre diagram (Figure 42).

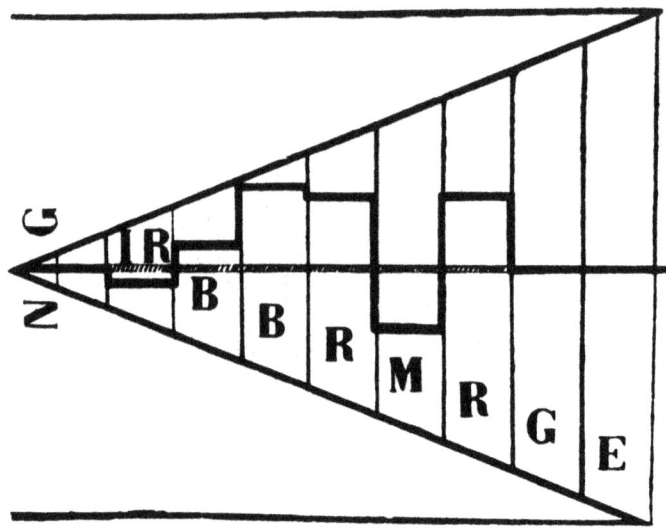

Using Alois Riegl's notion of a *Kunstwollen* (Will to Art), he rationalised the
discrepancies between the art of different periods as the outward expression of a
single motivation. Then, adopting Wölfflin's scheme of paired opposites, Van
Doesburg set out the characteristics of contemporary art in terms of definite versus
indefinite, open versus closed, clear versus vague, simple versus complex. The lecture also tackled the question of individual, national and period style found in
Wölfflin's *Kunstgeschichtliche Grundbegriffe* (Principles of Art History). Finally Van
Doesburg concluded that the stylistic elements of Neo-plastic painting could be
found throughout the products of modern life: functional objects, jazz, cinema,
cars and sky-scrapers.

The role of art theorist that Van Doesburg took on resulted in a commission in
1925 from Alexander Dorner, director of the Provinzialmuseum in Hanover, to
redesign the installation of its modern collection. Dorner was also director of the
Kestner-Gesellschaft in Hanover which held regular exhibitions of expressionist
and abstract art. On taking charge of the Provinzialmuseum Dorner instituted a
radical policy of rearranging the existing collections and began purchasing paintings by the likes of El Lissitzky, Moholy-Nagy and Mondrian.[13] Unlike the new
director of the Rijksmuseum, Dorner believed that the past and the present should
never be disconnected from each other. He rearranged the layout of the
Provinzialmuseum, which had previously been separated into the individual collections from which it had been created, and produced a linear narrative from the
medieval right through to the modern day. As a 'living' museum, he imagined this
path would continually extend into the future rather than ossify. His second
innovation was the creation of *Stimmungsraumen* (atmosphere rooms), in which
the art of any particular period was displayed in a manner appropriate to it.
Distinct from a period room, the atmosphere room did not surround art objects

with contemporary items of furniture or wallpaper but tried through lighting and
hanging to recreate the visual conditions under which the viewer had previously
encountered them.

Unfortunately little remains of Van Doesburg's scheme for the display of
modern art, which was never realised. It appears that most of his efforts went into
the design of a stained-glass window to be fitted in the modern room. Later commentators have interpreted the window as Van Doesburg's less than subtle intention to place his own abstract work at the centre of the collection.[14] Samuel Cauman
does note, however, that the theme Van Doesburg pursued was that of transparency, 'an idea that Dorner noted for later use, but on its own it lacked the strength
to create a new identity for the whole room'.[15] Ultimately the redesign of the
modern art room fell to El Lissitzky, who installed his now well known *Abstract
Cabinet*. Transparency was not made such a feature here, although other aspects –
such as the movable screens – do bear comparison to De Stijl ideas.[16] Van Doesburg's
choice of stained glass as the medium through which to express the modernity of
abstraction made more sense in the context of the Dutch obsession with monumental art. If it had been realised, Van Doesburg's modern art room would have
also affirmed the interrelation of painting and architecture that Mondrian was
demonstrating to visitors to his studio. One thing is absolutely clear, though. While
De Stijl theory proposed that painting express its specificity, the presentation of
modernism advocated by De Stijl associates emphasised synthesis with other arts
rather than the separation suggested by the 'white cube'.

The institutionalisation of *gemeenschapkunst* which had been thwarted by the reorientation of the Rijksmuseum had another chance for realisation in the proposals for
a museum to house the Kröller-Müller collection. Hélène Kröller-Müller had
begun purchasing the work of leading Dutch artists around 1906. By the end of the
First World War she had the largest private collection of modern art in the
Netherlands, which now included significant works of French art and a substantial
number of Van Gogh paintings. She transformed her role of collector to patron
(such as in the case of Van der Leck), and also sought the employ of leading architects such as Peter Behrens, Ludwig Mies van der Rohe and H. P. Berlage. Her
biographer, Sam van Deventer, recalled that as early as 1911 she had an epiphanic
vision of housing her collection in a specially commissioned building which would
then be bequeathed to the state.[17]

The proposal for a museum was first publicised at a celebratory dinner for Anton
Kröller in 1914, who was completing his twenty-fifth year as director of Müller &
Co. After the meal, which was attended by several distinguished figures including
government ministers, Bremmer gave a slide lecture about the Kröller-Müller collection and announced the plans that Berlage was to build a museum to be available
to the whole nation. Previously the Kröllers had conceived of commissioning a
museum house where residential and exhibition uses were combined in one. Both
Peter Behrens and Ludwig Mies van der Rohe had produced designs for such a

building, and even made full-scale mock ups out of sailcloth, but without success. During the negotiations with the German architects, Kröller-Müller travelled on more than one occasion to Berlin. Amongst the many buildings she visited was Schinkel's *Altes Museum*, which is an interesting model to consider for her plans.[18]

From the very outset the Kröller-Müller Museum was intended to be as much an important piece of architecture as the house for an important art collection. By using Schinkel as a touchstone, Kröller-Müller reawakened the critical furore which had surrounded the construction of the *Altes Museum*. Although it is now seen as the paradigmatic nineteenth-century art museum, it was not wholly well received. Critics noted that the architecture was not merely the frame for the collection but actually dominated the objects it housed.[19] The concept of Schinkel's museum was to display solely fine arts, which had been separated from the musical instruments, fossils and scientific paraphernalia which previously accompanied them in *kunstkammern*, as well as from the applied arts and crafts. This separation was signified by the use of neo-classical architecture, which associated the museum with intellectual and spiritual elevation. However, the narrative generated by the architecture and that produced by the distribution of objects in the museum were at odds with each other. As Douglas Crimp has described, the tension made physically manifest a paradox of idealist aesthetics, 'the conflict between normative beauty and the forward march of history'.[20] The museum was intended to educate the spectator with a linear narrative projecting the past into the present. Simultaneously the architectural framework served to freeze the history of art in time or perhaps as a better analogy, bury it in a mausoleum. Van Doesburg's involvement with Dorner's 'living museum' and his lecture *The Will to Style* are both attempts to overcome the very same paradox.

Where the story of the origins of the Kröller-Müller Museum and the early history of De Stijl cross most notably is in the failed collaboration between Berlage and Van der Leck on the Art Room at the Kröller family residence, Groot Haesbroek. This room was intended for education and aesthetic stimulation. Around 1906 Kröller-Müller began to take classes in art appreciation from Bremmer, an accomplished artist in his own right who worked in a neo-impressionist mode. Not only was Bremmer well connected in artistic circles, he also wrote criticism, published his own journal called *Beeldende Kunst* (Fine Art), was the author of several books and owned a substantial art collection. So impressed was Kröller-Müller by this man that she began inviting him to the family house. For a number of years Bremmer would arrive on Friday evenings to impart his knowledge to the family and guests. All of her purchases were guided by Bremmer's tastes and by 1912, when she advanced from buying from local galleries and Dutch auction houses, he accompanied her on trips to Paris, where he was able to take her directly into artists' studios.[21] Together they made an irresistible team which she imagined in such inflated terms as, 'he was my prime minister and next to him I felt like the Queen'.[22]

The esteem in which Kröller-Müller held herself was reflected in Van der Leck's colour scheme for the Art Room, the walls of which he planned to paint white with red and blue horizontal bands echoing the Dutch flag. He designed a carpet for the centre of the room on which was to be placed a table and chairs made by Berlage, around which the family gathered for instruction by Bremmer. The art critic adopted a simple method of formal comparison for his 'lessons'; two reproductions were stood side by side and their differences discussed.[23] Huszár, who took painting lessons from Bremmer in 1906, used precisely the same method of formal comparison in his series of articles titled *Aesthetische Beschouwingen* (Aesthetic Observations), which were published in the early editions of De Stijl.[24] Along two walls of the Art Room Berlage installed three large showcases, to store the folios Bremmer used and to display Kröller-Müller's ceramic collection. As the other two walls were broken by large windows, Van der Leck found his portion of the collaboration severely diminished. He expressed his dissatisfaction in a letter to Kröller-Müller in December 1916 in which he castigated Berlage's lack of cooperation and gave voice to the aspiration that would soon bring about the publication of De Stijl:

> Not until a more modern view has developed, in which all the arts have equal value, can the consequence of this principle have an influence on the position of the arts in architecture. Only then will a unity come about, not through subordination of one art to another, but through equal independence.[25]

Van der Leck withdrew his participation in the Art Room project and the attempt to integrate his abstract monumental wall painting with Berlage's interior design was abandoned. However, the concept of the Art Room as the coalescence of art, architecture and education continued to exercise an influence over Kröller-Müller's plans for many years and the first installation of the Kröller-Müller Museum, which opened in 1938, contained a partial reconstruction of the room.

As discussed in the previous chapter, Berlage abandoned his contract with Müller & Co. in 1919 and never realised the plans he had drawn up in the previous five years for a magnificent museum to be located in the large expanse of woodland the Kröllers had acquired between Apeldoorn and Ede (where the hunting lodge *Sint Hubertus* was built). His role was quickly taken over by Henri van der Velde, some of whose buildings Kröller-Müller had visited on her trips to Germany before the First World War.[26] He continued the plans for a grand museum and between 1921 and 1926 created extraordinary designs for a monumental building with brightly coloured interiors. He drew the museum as a cross-shaped two-storey construction. On the ground floor were to be placed the majority of the nineteenth-century paintings in the collection, both French and Dutch, distributed around a central hall with a fountain. Upstairs pride of place was reserved for the Van Gogh room at the very centre, with rooms dedicated to Toorop, Thorn Prikker, Mendes da Costa and Van der Leck occupying the surrounding spaces. Van Gogh was 'framed' then by four artists who all had reputations in the field of monumental art

(Toorop and Mendes da Costa were notably two of the collaborators on the Amsterdam Stock Exchange). The centrifugal concept of the installation was to be reinforced by visual sensation; colour contrast was to become more intense at the heart of the building. A colour sketch of the Van Gogh room shows how Van de Velde planned to use bright yellow and green ceramic tiles in stripes on the walls, floor and ceiling. The paintings themselves are represented in his drawing hanging unframed against plastered inserts in this dazzling arena. A dramatic downturn in the fortunes of Müller & Co. meant that the museum was not built in this form (although some of the foundations Van de Velde had begun to put in place still remain). By the end of the 1920s Kröller-Müller had begun the protracted process of donating her collection to the state, a requirement of which was the construction of a museum. Van der Velde returned to build a rather more modest 'transitional museum', which opened in 1938 and did not feature the polychromatic extravagance he had earlier desired.

Although Van der Leck was to be prominently featured in the Kröller-Müller Museum as devised by Van de Velde, there seems to have been little discussion of it amongst De Stijl associates. An exception to the silence is the intriguing correspondence between Mondrian and Slijper in the late 1920s. When Mondrian returned to Paris in 1919, Slijper took responsibility for his career in the Netherlands. Mondrian also sent him the entire contents of his Paris studio, all the pre-war naturalistic works that he was no longer interested in. Slijper's role as patron was very different from a simple admirer and benefactor. He acted as Mondrian's agent, found potential buyers and distributed paintings to them, arranged exhibitions and even attempted criticism on his behalf. The letters Mondrian sent to his friend therefore contain extensive details about both Mondrian's financial situation and the handling of his paintings.

Discussion between Mondrian and Slijper of installation issues began early on in their relationship, after Slijper took possession of the *Evolution* triptych in 1916. Mondrian sent him a drawing indicating precisely how it should be hung. Over the next decade this painting featured frequently in their correspondence as Slijper explored the possibilities of selling it on. I have already discussed Slijper's role in the syndicate which donated Mondrian paintings to the Stedelijk Museum in 1922 and 1923 but what has not yet been mentioned in any of the literature on De Stijl are the plans the two devised to offload Slijper's collection en masse to a museum as early as 1928. Once again this followed a reappraisal of *Evolution*, which it seems Slijper had chance to sell in late 1927.[27] What became of this potential sale is unknown as the painting would remain with him for another twenty-eight years. However, by this stage Mondrian was keen that his oeuvre should not be too greatly fragmented. As Slijper held by far the greatest number of his paintings (around sixty works), he began looking for a large institution to pass them on to.

In a letter from Mondrian to Slijper dated 6 January 1928, he speculated about the chances the latter would have to find an institution willing to take on such a large body of work. As an alternative he suggested they might be able to buy a property and establish their own museum. Although ambitious for its time, this was not an unprecedented idea. As early as 1905 the Mesdag Museum, based on the work and collection of the painter H. W. Mesdag, had opened in The Hague. Mondrian pressed Slijper to enlist critical support for such a project and the first name he mentioned in this regard was that of Bremmer. In his letter Mondrian continued to bemoan the end of his financial relationship with Bremmer, and therefore ultimately with Kröller-Müller, and mentioned her museum in this context. The letter concludes with Mondrian encouraging Slijper to contact Bremmer as soon as possible.

As I pointed out in the discussion of Mondrian's studio in the previous chapter, he presented his personal space as a private gallery where he could completely control the perception of his paintings in connection to the architectural environment. The concept of a private museum discussed with Slijper in 1928 is a perfectly logical extension of the course that he had taken since his return to Paris. It would also avoid the curatorial interference that was emerging in national institutions. Alternatively, Mondrian hoped to become part of the Kröller-Müller Museum project which emerged as the closest heir in the post-war period to the *gemeenschapkust* tradition initiated by Cuypers' polychromatic Rijksmuseum. That business rather than the state should be the source of finance for such an initiative did not seem to trouble Mondrian. In fact other De Stijl collaborators avoided museums altogether, judging the new commercial spaces of shops and trade fairs as the best place to find a public sympathetic to a modernist aesthetic, a situation I shall now briefly outline.

In 1927 Huszár wrote a letter of protest to Felix del Marle, editor of the journal *Vouloir*, who had just dedicated a special issue to De Stijl. He complained that Del Marle had falsely credited Mondrian with the first environmental works, namely the studio experiments initiated on his return to Paris in 1919. Huszár pointed out to Del Marle that he had designed his first abstract interior well before, in fact as early as 1917. This date precedes the interiors I mentioned in the previous chapter such as the boy's room in the Bruynzeel house. Indeed Huszár could have been referring to only one project, the trade stand he produced for *Bruynzeel en Zonen* (Bruynzeel and Sons), which he began designing in 1917 and was installed in February 1918 at the *Jaarbeurs* (National Trade Exhibition) in Utrecht (Figure 43). Huszár was, as we have already seen in his advertising work, the figure in De Stijl most enthusiastic about the combination of abstraction and mass culture. His ambition was to produce an 'art for the people' by applying modernist aesthetics to commercial forms, the consequence of which can be seen in the Bruynzeel stand. The product being exhibited was parquet flooring and Huszár used the patterns of the wood to create a rhythmic design across the entire wall surface. By doing so he aimed to provide a visual equivalent to the new rationalised means of production and distribution the Bruynzeel company was pursuing; thus the anomaly of looking

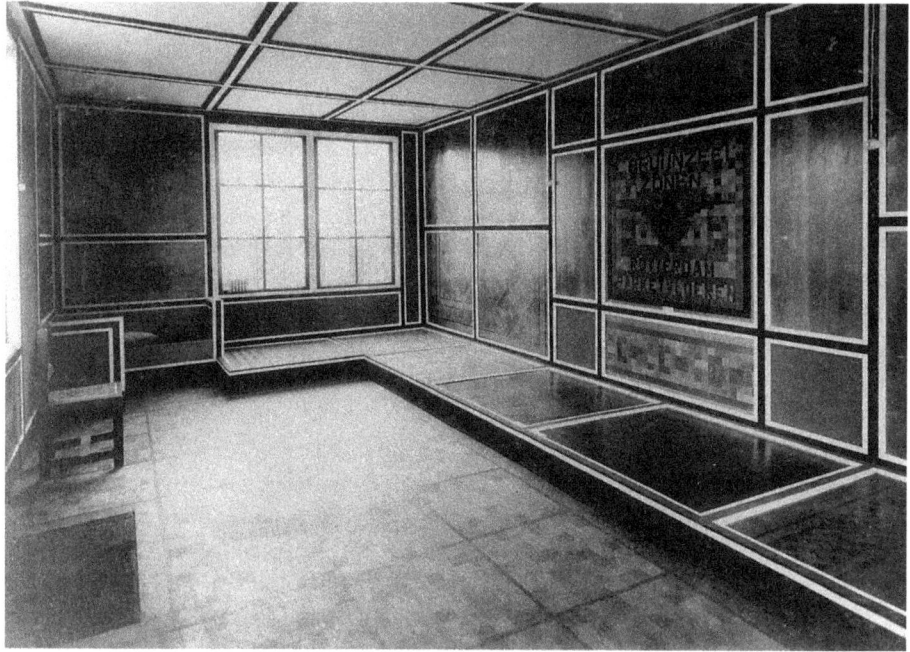

43 Vilmos Huszár, trade stand for Bruynzeel, 1918

at flooring hung on the wall. Huszár did not, as might be expected, include any place where samples could be handled and materials felt. What was being sold was an image which was also conveyed in perhaps the cleverest aspect of the design, the integration of the Bruynzeel name and logo into one of the wooden panels and its construction from parquet itself.

The reasons why Cornelis Bruynzeel Jr. might have commissioned Huszár for the job relate not only to his personal tastes but to the aspirations he had for his business. Bruynzeel had opened his first wood finishing factory in 1897 in Rotterdam with twelve employees. He travelled frequently to America and aimed to transfer the commercial practices he had seen there to the Netherlands. By the 1920s he had transformed his company from its modest beginnings and made *Bruynzeel en Zonen* into the most mechanised wood-producing business in Europe. He expanded the range of products from flooring to doors ('one door a minute' was his Ford-like motto) and eventually to modular kitchen cabinets. In the interwar period the company expanded to employ several hundred workers, moved to a large new factory designed by Jan Wils at Zaandam and became an international concern. Bruynzeel's sons, Cornelis III and Willem, whose bedroom Huszár redesigned in 1919, went on to manage different parts of the company as it expanded. The stand at the *Jaarbeurs* is witness to these ambitions and in it can be found the basis of the company ethic of machine production, modularity and brand identity.

To fully imagine what makes the Bruynzeel stand exceptional one has to imagine how it would have contrasted with its neighbours. As Penny Ramakers recounts, the first exhibitors at the *Jaarbeurs*, which had only been held for the first time in 1917, had little experience or idea of how to show off their wares:

> Some manufacturers stuffed their areas as full as possible with goods and piled their commodities next to and on top of each other. Others came with richly furnished 'show rooms' for the day or conjured their stand into a cosy domestic space. Magazijn Smit displayed its bicycles at the first Jaarbeurs on a persian carpet, paintings hung on the walls and the room further graced by plants, plates and a decorative border along the wall. The 'comfy' chair for 'doing business' stood as usual prominently in the middle.[28]

Huszár's Bruynzeel stand did offer clients some opportunity to linger, featuring a built-in bench at the far end. The only other item of furniture was a very simple chair which did nothing to distract from the severity of the display. While clients may have been trying imagine Bruynzeel flooring in their homes, no concession was made to the cosiness described above.

For the following year Bruynzeel commissioned Bart van der Leck and Pieter Klaarhamer to design the stand. They mollified the geometry while maintaining the same panelling effect. It no longer covered every inch of the wall and the space was humanised by the inclusion of a modest vase of flowers. Most significantly a table and two chairs were returned to the centre, where client and manufacturer could 'do business'. This design would come in for some very public criticism, however, in a review of the *Jaarbeurs* written by Piet Zwart.[29] At the time Zwart was in the process of being converted to the principles of De Stijl following a series of debates held at the *Haagsche Kunstkring* (Hague Artists Circle) in early 1919. In these discussions Huszár had put forward the De Stijl position and Zwart had responded on behalf of traditional craft values. Shortly afterwards Zwart radically changed his outlook. He went to work for Wils as a draughtsman and then collaborated on a series of interior design projects with Huszár (including work for Bruynzeel). His main criticism of Klaarhamer and Van der Leck's stand was that it was too formulaic (rather than formalist). Although he did not mention Huszár's effort of the previous year, Zwart suggested that Klaarhamer and Van der Leck had taken a backward step. He then presented a new set of guidelines for temporary exhibitions:

> 1. the fact of its temporality must be clearly be preserved.
>
> 2. it must be the background to the articles exhibited and play no pretentious part in and of itself.
>
> 3. it must comply with the requirements of the elements of the interior architecture for its assembly.
>
> 4. its design must originate from modern consciousness (where all old, obsolete, exotic and dead stylistic reminiscences are forbidden).[30]

Examples of exoticism had been rife in previous fairs. For example, at the first *Jaarbeurs* in 1917, the architect Jan Gratama had built a pavilion for a manufacturer of reinforced concrete in the form of a Javanese pagoda. Zwart's guidelines dismissed these fantasies on a number of counts. First was the need to declare the temporality of the display, second that it should not overwhelm the product and third that it should work with the architectural environment in which was placed. If we consider these criteria in connection to Huszár's stand of 1918 we can find nearly all of them met, especially in the way Huszár worked with the space available and did not try to convert it into something more homely. The only aspect missing was that of temporality. It was this quality that Zwart himself attempted to integrate when designing his first trade stand in 1921 for a celluloid manufacturer.

In his first drawing of the stand for the celluloid manufacturer, Zwart repeated many of the features we have seen already, including the table and chairs for 'doing business'. He also included cabinets with drawers, no doubt for storing product samples. In the second design all of this traditional furniture was eradicated in favour of simple open shelves which jutted out in to the room (Figure 44). Coloured black with white edging, the shelves were supported by struts of red, yellow and blue, which set up sculptural compositions in space. As Nancy Troy has noted this produced 'an experience of space made active, fused in a dynamic, abstract whole'.[31] However, did this not contravene his second guideline and no longer merely act as a background? His obvious problem was how to produce a background for celluloid. With a transparent material to sell, Zwart made his

44 Piet Zwart, Jaarbeurs trade stand, 1921

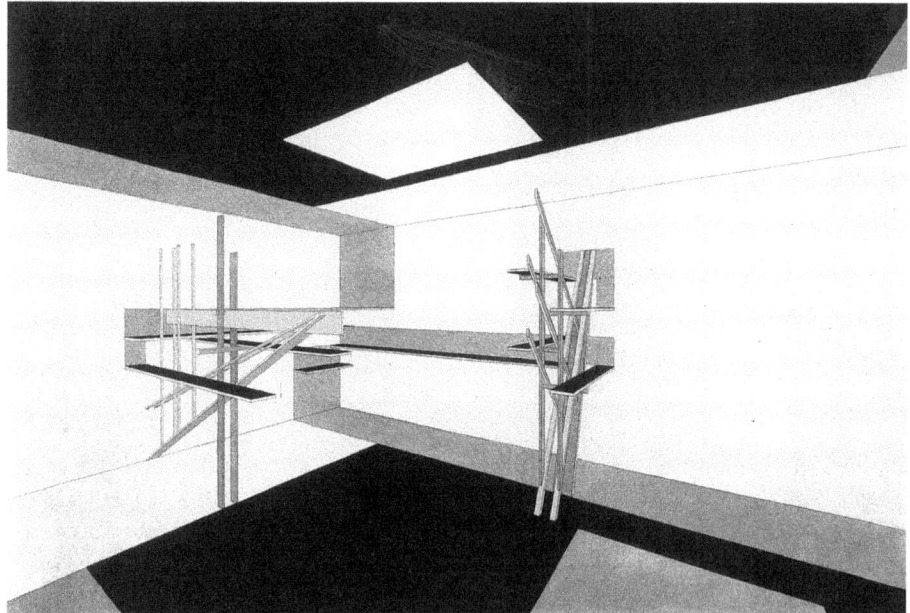

stand into an exercise in transparency. There was almost no need to place the product on the shelves, as the stand was in itself representing the product. Along with the consideration for product identity, the other factor of the exhibition theory in development here was the importance of the stand as a visual experience. While we have considered the stripping away of domestic cosiness as a necessary part of the production of a modern trade form, we should also have noted the sparsity of text. What was being sold here was a look, particularly the look of modernity.

Throughout the rest of the 1920s Zwart took the trade stand and industrial exhibition to new levels. His most high-profile commissions came from the *PTT* (Post Office) and from the *Nederlandsche Kabelfabriek* (Netherlands Cable Company). He constructed a stand for the latter in 1924 almost entirely out of cables and tubular shapes, using Rietveld's hanging flourescent lamp design to carry the theme even through to the light fitting. He composed the tubular forms to create an image of an urban landscape through which the cables carried power. Without having to provide any written information beyond the name of the company, Zwart created an explicit image to put across what the product meant for modern life. He even used cross-sections of large cables to mimic the form of records and film reels, all the benefits of an electrified society.

The parallel to Zwart's efforts in the commercial field was the installation designed by Huszár and Rietveld for a 1923 exhibition in Berlin. Troy has outlined the circumstances in which the design was possibly commissioned as well as the reasons for it not having been realised.[32] It was created following the success of El Lissitzky's 'Proun Room' at the *Grosse Berliner Kunstaustellung* (Great Berlin Art Exhibition) in the autumn of that year and like the former was intended to provide the spectator with an arresting perceptual and spatial experience. A ground plan drawing by Huszár demonstrates that the two artists intended the spectator to follow an explicit path around the space in an anticlockwise direction 'reading' the room from right to left. As the route was followed, the spectator was presented with an ever greater complexity of colour compositions applied to the walls which overlap one another and traverse the corners. At the climax of the installation were to be found examples of Rietveld's multicoloured furniture suggesting, in Troy's view, 'the joining of the arts to form a total, abstract environment'.[33]

Such an interpretation befits the design if imagined in a fine art setting but I have often been perplexed by the inclusion of Rietveld's furniture at an art exhibition (although it is true that within De Stijl his chairs were often discussed in the same terms as sculpture). It is rather paradoxical that, given the development of the modern exhibition space is dependent on the removal of the aura of domesticity, in this example furniture returns as something to look at but not something to sit on. We might also imagine this as a trade stand for De Stijl interiors, considering that both Rietveld and Huszár were seeking clients who wished to have their homes redesigned. In the same year, 1923, Rietveld put together a model interior combining his furniture with Van der Leck paintings on the wall. Where this was displayed is unknown as the only document to have survived is a solitary photograph. Rietveld lived and worked in Utrecht and that he might have taken out a stand at the *Jaarbeurs* is not beyond possibility. He was also selling his furniture through the department store *Vroom en Dreesman* at the time. During this period Rietveld repeatedly conflated exhibition design, interior decoration and new opportunities for consumption, a tendency typified by the shop designs and vitrines that he produced during the 1920s.

In the previous chapter I discussed Rietveld's role in the 1923 De Stijl exhibition in Paris, for which he produced the model of the Van Doesburg and Van Eesteren's *Maison Rosenberg*. I did not make any mention at the time of the contribution he made to the exhibition in his own name. Van Doesburg included photographs and drawings of projects carried out by other De Stijl collaborators and Rietveld was represented by one of his first architectural projects, the refitting of the *Goud-en Zilversmids Compagnie* (Gold and Silversmiths Company) shop in Amsterdam, completed in 1921 (Figures 45 and 46). While Rietveld himself was never totally satisfied with the outcome of this design, it received acclaim in the architectural magazine *Bouwkundig Weekblad* and was highly thought of by Van Doesburg.[34] The project involved rebuilding the storefront, located on the Kalverstraat, one of the main shopping streets in the city, and rearranging the salesroom inside. Given that it was a jeweller's shop, glass cases were a dominant feature. As Rietveld wrote to Van Doesburg, he wanted the shop to be seen as 'a large etui, or rather a showcase with etui'.[35] The surviving photograph of the interior shows how Rietveld attempted to divide up the long narrow space, breaking up the walls and ceiling with colour planes and distributing vitrines in alignment with these divisions. In advance of his famous flourescent lamp, he hung clusters of naked light bulbs from the ceiling and also fitted them to the inside of the vitrines to produce as much light as possible. How the customers coped with the amount of reflected light this must have produced is unrecorded but it all contributed to the conception of the shop as one large showcase. On the exterior Rietveld produced a truly ingenious design which extended the theme and helped to draw customers in. He set the door back to create a porch which he then divided into a series of stacked blocks. The lower of these, edged in white, appeared to thrust out into the street and brought the trader's wares directly in front of the passing shopper.[36] The block behind carried the company logo and the final plane featured the shop name. Rietveld visually reversed the order in which a trader was traditionally recognised, presenting the object before the name and between them a logo. The concept of the vitrine, to display the product in a magical fashion, is here given its explicit logic in the production of modern commodities.

Over the rest of the 1920s, Rietveld received numerous commissions for the redesign of shopfronts, which became ever more daring. These included *Wessels en Zonen* in Utrecht, which sold a large variety of bags and suitcases. Here Rietveld repeated the concept of the jeweller's shop and once more created a vitrine which seems disconnected from the facade. On this occasion the width of the frontage

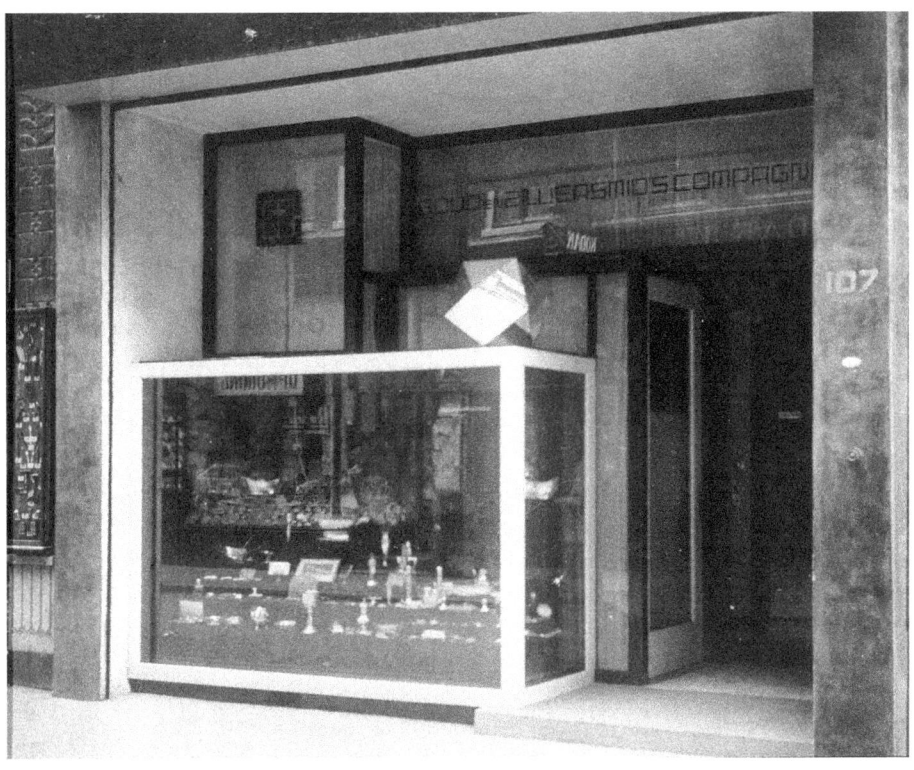

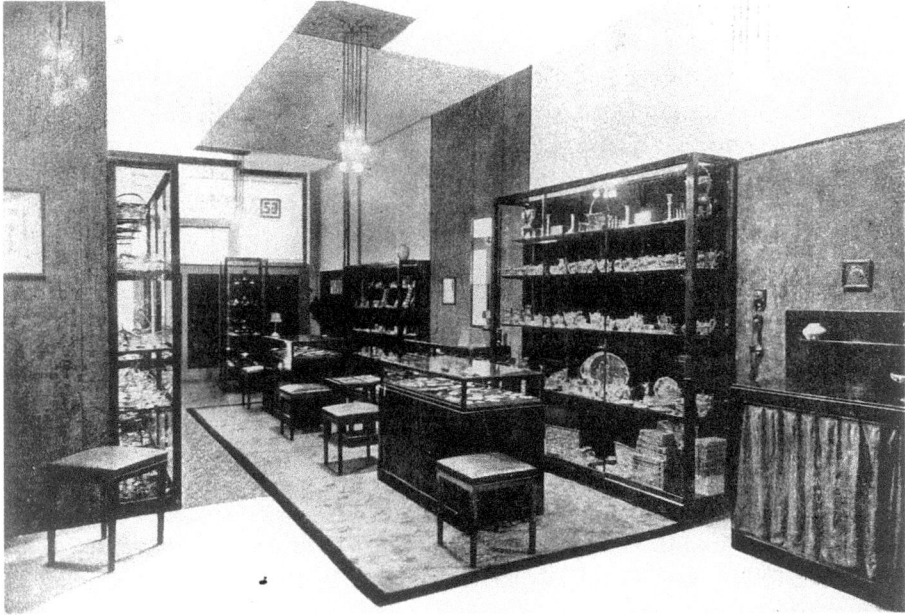

45, 46 Gerrit Rietveld, Gold and Silversmiths' Company, Amsterdam, 1921

discouraged him from following precisely the same stacking in-depth effect as
before but another innovation here was the inclusion of top lighting which
enhanced the distance of the vitrine from the rest of the building. His two most
remarkable refittings were both installed in 1928: the *Record* shop in Utrecht (a
retailer of leather goods) and the *Zaudy* store in Wesel in Germany, which sold
home furnishings. In both of these designs Rietveld set the window display at an
oblique angle to the facade. In the first example, the shop was located on a street
corner and Rietveld made use of the previously blank facade on the side of the
building by cutting across it diagonally while also incorporating the street into the
storefront. The second project was even more daring as the angle of the shop
window seemed to break the plane of the facade (without actually doing so) and
once again thrust the shop into the street. The shop window was again disconnected from the main structure of the building and could be viewed from either
side creating what a contemporary review called 'an arcade-like entrance'.[37] In each
instance the concept of the vitrine was reimagined. The use of greater expanses of
glass broke down the distance between the consumer and the object, placing the
shop in the same space as the passer-by. Simultaneously, though, the attention to
the arrangement of goods and the use of artificial lighting distanced the objects and
placed them in their own mysterious world.

During the same years Rietveld was working with Schröder on domestic interior design projects into which they actively incorporated display cases. The
Schröder house itself had a vitrine placed next to the front door, as well as two display cases in the girls' sleeping area upstairs. Schröder also used the projecting
window of the downstairs study to exhibit paintings for sale by friends such as Van
der Leck.[38] In the Amsterdam flat of Schröder's sister, An Harrenstein, a display
case was hung high on the wall in the sitting room. It ran almost the entire length of
the wall and was positioned at such a height that it prevented the residents placing
any pictures above or below it. Contemporary photographs indicate that it mainly
held glassware which could have served practical as well as aesthetic ends. A visitor
to the Harrenstein flat, Louise van Leer, was impressed enough to commission
Rietveld and Schröder to refit her new marital home in Hilversum along similar
lines. Again a large display cabinet was fitted in the sitting room and surviving photographs show that it also held mainly glass objects. These were lit from the side by
a typical Rietveld motif of an unshaded flourescent tube. Just as in the *Goud- en
Zilversmids Compagnie* shop, the entire Van Leer interior was conceived as one large
display case. The dining area, for example, featured the first use in the Netherlands
of a false glass ceiling with concealed lighting above.

Huszár, Rietveld, Schröder and Zwart were all prepared to integrate fine art
abstraction and modernist architecture with the world of commerce. The trade
stands, shop fronts and model interiors all point to the directive of the *Manifesto of
De Stijl* that its aesthetic be realised in everyday life. The fusion of exhibition design
with interior decoration and consumerism was the alternative to the growing specialisation of the museum. Ultimately this aspect of De Stijl disappeared from view

as it came to be seen more and more as a fine art phenomenon. The final stage of this process was completed in the early 1930s (again prior to Alfred Barr's *Cubism and Abstract Art*) with the opening of the Gemeentemuseum in The Hague. By this point Van Doesburg was dead and De Stijl defunct. Little opposition could be voiced, therefore, to the presentation of abstract art in the cool white spaces of this exemplary building, as I shall now discuss in conclusion.

Although Berlage relinquished his plans for the Kröller-Müller Museum, he would have the opportunity to realise his ideas concerning modern museum design shortly afterwards when commissioned by the municipality of The Hague to rehouse its collections. In 1918 a decision was made to clearly separate modern works from historical, and the latter were moved into rented space at the Panorama Mesdag.[39] Between 1919 and 1924 Berlage produced his first plan, which Pieter Singelberg has compared to contemporary buildings by Frank Lloyd Wright in respect to its accentuation of horizontal planes.[40] However, it was not until the second plan was drafted in 1927 that the most innovative features of the interior of the museum were resolved. These included the provision for large amounts of natural lighting from above, whose regulation through opaque glass screens could be carefully controlled. Berlage also provided routes for the visitors which would allow galleries to be accessed without the need for them to retrace their steps.[41] Freedom of movement was encouraged by the absence of any built in furniture and weary visitors could rest only by carrying around specially designed stools.

The municipal collections of The Hague included a large amount of ceramics, furniture and musical instruments which Berlage placed in the more dimly lit ground-floor galleries. The fine art collections, the majority comprised of paintings from the Hague School, took pride of place on the first floor where they might fulfil the order of the inscription in the main hall to 'honour divine light in the revelations of art'. The impressionist tradition of late nineteenth-century Dutch art was swathed in natural light pouring in from the ceiling. Unlike Van de Velde's Kröller-Müller Museum, Berlage concentrated more on the technology of display than an overwhelming symbolic architecture. He used colour and light far more subtlely and gave greater consideration to circulation patterns than had ever been attempted in a Dutch museum before. In these circumstances it is interesting to consider an early donation made to the collection in 1933 by a group of architects represented by the journal *De 8 en Opbouw* (The 8 and Construction), who clubbed together to purchase Mondrian's *Lozange Composition with Four Yellow Lines*. Unlike the earlier donations to the Stedelijk, which were rather cautious in their selection, this syndicate had chosen an extremely radical work, one of the most minimal Mondrian would ever paint.

The architect who initiated the Mondrian donation was Charles Karsten. He had visited the artist's studio several times since 1929 and purchased paintings for himself. He was also responsible for taking an often-reproduced photograph of Mondrian standing in his studio next to *Lozange Composition with Four Yellow Lines*

(Figure 47). The photograph was first published in an edition of *De 8 en Opbouw* in October 1933. Karsten placed the image of Mondrian next to a self portrait by the Hague School artist Josef Israels to suggest the continuity Mondrian would make with the previous representatives of Dutch modernism in the context of the museum. Both images were then captioned with the following quote from Le Corbusier: 'In the confusion of this chaotic period, many are accustomed to think against a black background. However, the work of the epoch, so bold, so dangerous, so bellicose, so conquering, seems to await us who will think against a white background.'[42]

As I have described on more than one occasion in this book, Mondrian used his studio to demonstrate the manner in which he thought that his painting should be viewed. The placement of *Lozange Composition with Four Yellow Lines* above an orthogonally oriented canvas in Karsten's photograph has been widely used as a guideline for the installation of Mondrian's diamond shaped canvases, which are often placed above eye level. However, what Karsten suggested by captioning his photograph in such a manner, before the painting entered the Gemeentemuseum, was that Mondrian's studio was some kind of Corbusian white space. The photographs Mondrian commissioned himself in 1926, discussed in the previous

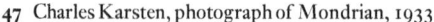

47 Charles Karsten, photograph of Mondrian, 1933

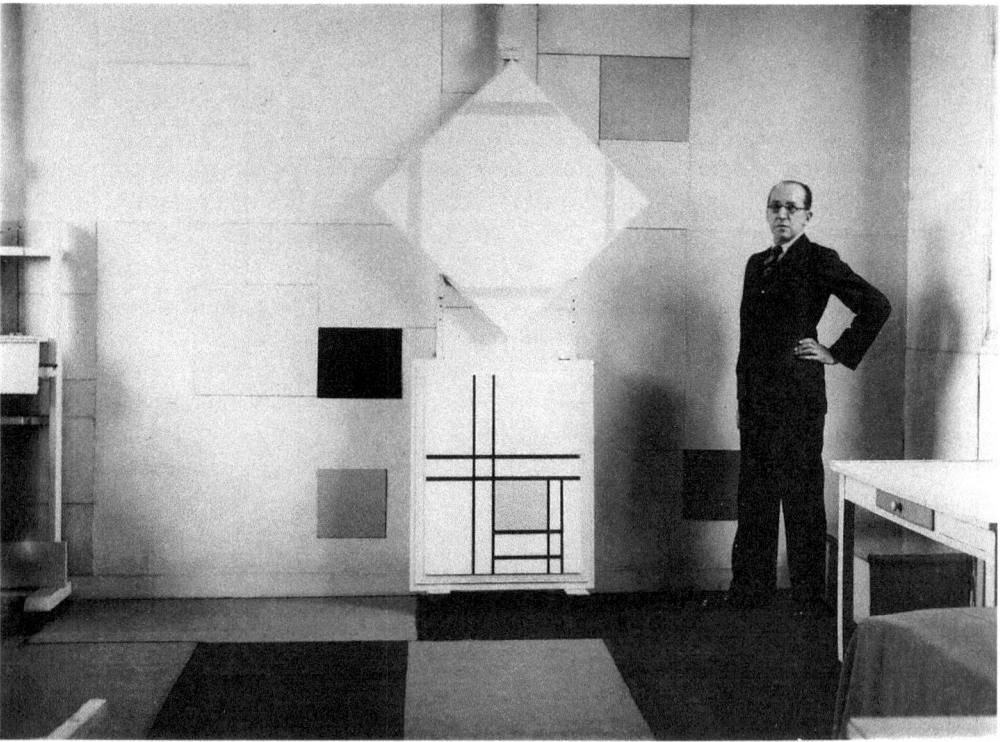

chapter, all showed the studio in its polychromatic splendour (although the photographs were obviously black and white), complete with furniture. Karsten chose
to ignore most of this to justify the contemporary removal from the museum of
anything which detracted from the object itself. From here begins the narrative
that this book has tried to counteract, the enshrining of De Stijl in a historical
framework that has sought to exclude its inheritance from *gemeenschapskunst* and
its very real attempts to unite abstraction with a common culture.

Notes

1 For details of the financial arrangements between Van der Leck and Bremmer, and the
   series of photo-lithographic reproductions, see Cees Hilhorst (ed.), *Vriendschap op
   afstand. De correspondentie tussen Bart van der Leck en H. P. Bremmer* (Bussum: Thoth,
   1999), pp. 112 and 121.

2 There is a complex and fascinating history beginning to emerge of Nelly van Doesburg's
   role as a curator and art dealer during the 1930s and 1940s. She was particularly close to
   Peggy Guggenheim and guided her taste significantly. See Wies van Moorsel, *Nelly
   van Doesburg 1899–1975* (Nijmegen: SUN, 2000), pp. 162–72.

3 'Aan dit bouwerk was telkens iets nieuws te zien, daardoor won het de kinderlijke
   belangstelling eerst en het vertrouwen daarna. Nu eens was het nieuw beeldhouwwerk
   dat vrijkwam, of het nieuw tegeltableaux die ingemetseld werden, of krullend ijz-
   erwerk dat geplaatst en nieuwe beplantingen die verzorgd werden, dan weer waren het
   windwijzers die plotseling op de torens te fonkelen stonden. Met den dag werd het
   bouwerk kleuriger.' Richard Roland Holst, *Over kunst en kunstenaars. Beschouwingen
   en herdenkingen* (Amsterdam: Meulenhoff, 1928), pp. 226–7.

4 Carel Blotkamp, *Mondrian: The Art of Destruction* (London: Reaktion, 1995), p. 47.

5 J. F. Heijbroek, 'Het Rijksmuseum voor Moderne kunst van Willem Steenhof.
   Werkelijkheid of utopie?', *Bulletin van het Rijkmuseum* 39: 2 (1991), p. 207.

6 Alma was a contemporary artist who painted in a modern representational mode.
   Slijper was, as described in the first chapter, a close friend of Mondrian as well as the
   major collector of his pre-abstract painting. Steijling was also an old friend of Mondrian
   who regularly helped him transport and distribute his work, and Stieltjes was a Parisian
   acquaintance who had bought several paintings himself.

7 Joosten details this arrangment as one quarter of Mondrian's rent (1,500 francs a year)
   paid every three months for two years. Joop Joosten and Robert Welsh, *Piet Mondrian:
   Catalogue Raisonné* (New York: Abrams, 1998), vol. II, p. 123.

8 'Het komt mij voor, waar het Rijks Museum in hoofdzaak bestemd is voor de kunst van
   het verleden, terwijl er voor de kunst van het heden, het Stedelijk Museum speciaal is
   gebouwd, dat wellicht Uw aanbod zich beter richt tot deze laatste instelling.' Schmidt-
   Degener to Alma, 21 April 1922, quoted in Joosten and Welsh, *Piet Mondrian: Catalogue
   Raisonné*, vol. II, p. 233.

9 A later history of the Rijksmuseum contains fulsome praise for Schmidt-Degener's
   eradication of Cuypers' decoration. It explicitly states that the covering of mosaic
   floors reduced noise (silence is more appropriate to a museum than the sound of many
   feet on hard surfaces, according to the author) and the walls were given an even sponge-
   effect paint covering: 'We worden niet meer geïmponeerd door valschen schijn, we

verlaten, na onzen ommegang, het Rijksmuseum, rijker aan echte waarden. Onze aandacht wordt gericht naar die zaken, ter wille waarvan het Rijksmuseum werd gebouwd.' (We are no longer oppressed by a false glow. We leave the Rijksmuseum after our tour enriched with real values. Our attention is directed to those things for which the Rijksmuseum was built.) A. Muermans, *Het Huis aan de Kade: De roemvolle histoire van het Rijksmuseum te Amsterdam en val al die zaken, waarin een klein volk groot kan zijn* (Amsterdam: Keurboekerij, 1941), p. 40.

10   The relationship between the Rijksmuseum and the Stedelijk Museum that Schmidt-Degener had in mind was that which became established in the early twentieth century between national galleries and modern collections in other major cities; such as between the Louvre and the Luxembourg in Paris, the Metropolitan Museum and the Museum of Modern Art in New York and the National Gallery and the Tate Gallery in London.

11   The relationship between artists, curators and academics at the Stedelijk Museum is of great pertinence to the historiography of De Stijl. The post-war recovery of De Stijl by the Stedelijk Museum occurred under the directorship of Willem Sandberg, who wished to maintain the direct involvement of artists; Rietveld designed the 1951 De Stijl exhibition there. Hans Jaffé was also a curator at the museum at the time but his academic, art historical, approach to Dutch modernism led to conflict between him and Sandberg, ending with his departure from the institution to the University of Amsterdam in the early 1960s. See Carel Blotkamp, 'Kunstgescheidenis en moderne kunst: een lange aanloop', in Peter Hecht, Chris Stolwijk and Annemieke Hoogenboom (eds), *Kunstgescheidenis in Nederland* (Amsterdam: Prometheus, 1998), p. 100.

12   Theo van Doesburg, 'Moderne Kunst: Stedelijk Museum. Amsterdam. Expositie Mondrian, Leo Gestel, Sluijters, Schelfhout, Le Fauconnier', *Eenheid* 283, 6 November 1915. From 1912, when he began writing criticism, until the publication of De Stijl in 1917, nearly all of Van Doesburg's reviews were of exhibitions held in the Stedelijk Museum, such as the annual shows of the organisations *St. Lucas, De Onafhankelijken* and *Moderne Kunstkring*.

13   Dorner maintained a close friendship with Sophie Küppers, the widow of the previous director of the Kestner-Gesellschaft and future wife of El Lissitzky, who was acting as an agent for these artists at the time.

14   Evert van Straaten, *Theo van Doesburg: Painter and Architect* (The Hague: SDU Publishers, 1988), p. 182.

15   Samuel Cauman, *The Living Museum* (New York: New York University Press, 1958), p. 107.

16   El Lissitzky visited the Schröder house in 1926, from which he could have taken the idea of movable screens, which he used in his exhibition designs of the time.

17   Sam van Deventer, *Kröller-Müller: De Geschiedenis van een Cultureel Levenswerk* (Arnhem: Roos and Roos, third edn., 1998), p. 47.

18   In the notes that Kröller-Müller made on her trip she inadvertently referred to the *Altes Museum* as the *Neues Museum*, an interesting slip of the pen as it were. See Johannes van der Wolk, *De Kröllers en hun architecten* (Otterlo: Rijkmuseum Kröller-Müller, 1992), p. 105 n. 48.

19   The main voice of opposition came from Alois Hirt, an academic who taught the history of architecture at the University of Berlin. The polemic he engaged in with

Schinkel is comprehensively summarised in Douglas Crimp, *On the Museums Ruins* (Cambridge MA and London: MIT, 1993), pp. 291–304.

20 Crimp, *On the Museums Ruins*, p. 301.

21 An example of Bremmer's contacts was the purchases Kröller-Müller made directly from Paul Signac in 1912 and 1913 after visits to his studio.

22 'Hij was mijn eerste minister en naast hem voelde ik mij koningin: trots was ik alleen daarop, dat ik mij op kunstgebied gaarne ondergeschikt aan hem voelde.' Hélène Kröller-Müller, letter to Bob Kröller, 18 June 1921, quoted by Van der Wolk, *De Kröllers en hun architecten*, p. 12.

23 The structure of Bremmer's teaching can be found exactly reproduced in his publications, such as *Een inleiding tot het zien van Beeldende Kunst* (Amsterdam: Versluys, 1914), which was made up of a sequence of short chapters each discussing a pair of images depicting the same subject matter, though often of chronologically disparate objects. Kröller-Müller used exactly the same method in her publication *Beschouwingen over Problemen in de Ontwikkeling der Moderne Schilderkunst* (The Hague: Volksuniveristeit, 1925).

24 For the relation between Huszár and Bremmer see Sjarel Ex and Els Hoek, *Vilmos Huszár. Schilder en Ontwerper* (Utrecht: Reflex, 1985), pp. 16–21.

25 Bart van der Leck, letter to Hélène Kröller-Müller, 18 December 1916, quoted in Nancy Troy, *The De Stijl Environment* (Cambridge MA and London, 1983), p. 15.

26 When Kröller-Müller was interested in employing Behrens in 1911 she paid a visit to Karl Ernst Osthaus in Hagen, who was a major patron of the architect. Osthaus had also recently had a house built by Van de Velde which Kröller-Müller could see first hand.

27 Letter from Mondrian to Slijper, 30 December 1927, in Slijper Archief, RKD, The Hague.

28 'Sommige fabrikanten propten hun domen zo vol mogelijk met handelswaar en stapelden al hun artikelen naast en op elkaar, anderen kwamen met rijk gestofferde "pronkkamers" voor de dag of toverden hun stand om tot een knusse, huiselijke ruimte. Zo had Magazijn Smit uit Amsterdam zijn rijwielen op de eerste Jaarbeurs op een "pers" uitgestald, schilderijen aan de muur gehangen en de kamer verder opgeluisterd met wandborden, planten en een sierband langs de muur. Het "gezellige" zitje voor het "zaken doen" stond echter doorgaans prominent in het midden.' Penny Ramakers, 'De Jaarbeurs', in Ellinoor Bergevelt and Petra Dupuits (eds), *Industrie en Vormgeving in Nederland 1850–1950* (Amsterdam: Stedelijk Museum, 1985), p. 61.

29 Piet Zwart, 'Kunst op de Jaarbeurs', *Elseviers Geillustreed Maandscrift* 29 (1919), pp. 316–20.

30 '1e het feit van zijn tijdelikheid moet duidelijk bewaard blijven. 2e hij moet achtergrond zijn voor de te exposeren artikelen en mag geen pretentieus doel in- en opzichzelf hebben. 3e hij moet voldoen aan de elementaire, aan binnen-architectuur te stellen eisen. 4e zijn vormgeving moet uit het moderne tijdbewustzijn geboren zijn (waarmee alle oude, verouderde en exotische, ondoorleefde stijlreminiscenties gebannen zijn).' Zwart, 'Kunst op de Jaarbeurs', p. 318.

31 Nancy Troy, 'The Abstract Environment of De Stijl', in Mildred Friedman (ed.), *De Stijl: 1917–1931, Visions of Utopia* (Oxford, Phaidon, 1982), p. 173.

32 Troy, *The De Stijl Environment*, p. 129–31.

33 Troy, *The De Stijl Environment*, p. 132.

34 See Marijke Küper, 'Gerrit Rietveld', in Carel Blotkamp (ed.), *De Stijl: The Formative Years, 1917–1922* (Cambridge MA and London, 1986), p. 274.

35 Gerrit Rietveld, letter to Theo van Doesburg, 28 March 1922, quoted by Küper, 'Gerrit Rietveld', p. 269.

36 Although many shops had highly developed window displays by this time, Rietveld's placement of such valuable objects in the front of the store was quite bold. Even Truus Schröder expressed her reservations about this feature, saying later that: 'I did think that the jewels – valuable objects – were too low down, too close to the pavement. It shouldn't be done like that, but otherwise I thought it was a good design.' Paul Overy *et al.*, *The Rietveld Schröder House* (Cambridge MA and London: MIT, 1988), p. 44.

37 Anonymous review in *Werbekunst: Blätter für Schaufenster, Geschäftsaustellung, Reklame* 5: 12 (March 1929), n.p.

38 Overy *et al.*, *The Rietveld Schröder House*, p. 121.

39 The reader may recall that this was in the same building complex as the Berssenbrugge Studio rebuilt by Wils and Huszár in 1921, part of which was also made available for temporary exhibitions.

40 Pieter Singelberg, 'Het Haags Gemeentemuseum', *Nederlands Kunsthistorisch Jaarboek* 25 (1974), pp. 1–89. Jan Wils reponded favourably to this feature of the building in a review, 'De plannen voor de stedelijke museum-gebouwen te 's-Gravenhage', in the national newspaper *Het Vaderland*, 8 January 1921.

41 Circulation problems was one of Berlage's main criticisms of the Rijksmuseum. As a guide book from 1910 clearly demonstrates, visitors to Cuypers' building were expected to double back on themselves frequently and the recommended tour involved passing through the entrance hall no fewer than three times in different directions. Anon., *Guide Through the Rijksmuseum at Amsterdam* (Amsterdam: J. Vlieger, 1910).

42 'Dans la confusion de cette période bouleversée, beaucoup se sont accoutumés à penser sur fond noir. Mais l'œuvre de l'époque, si hardie, si périlleuse, si belliquese, si conquérante, semble attendre de nous que nous pensions sur fond blanc.' Le Corbusier, quoted by Charles Karsten, 'Cavalcade', *De 8 en Opbouw* 4: 22 (1933), p. 197.

Select bibliography

Archives consulted

Centraal Museum Utrecht

Rietveld-Schröder Archive

Netherlands Architecture Institute

Oud Archive
Rietveld Archive
Van Eesteren Archive
Van 't Hoff Archive
Wils Archive

Rijksbureau voor Kunsthistorische Documentatie

Huszár Archive
Slijper Archive
Van Doesburg Archive

Selected secondary sources

Adang, Mark, ' "Breng me in uw huis, laat me uw woonkamer zien en ik zal u zeggen wie gij zijt!" Het denken over kitsch en smaakopvoeding in Nederland', *Nederlands Kunsthistorisch Jaarboek* 28 (1977), pp. 209–59.

Amsterdam, Stedelijk Museum, *Industrie en Vormgeving in Nederland 1850–1950* (1985).

Anscombe, Isabelle, *A Woman's Touch: Women in design from 1860 to the present day* (New York: Viking, 1984).

Baljeu, Joost, *Theo van Doesburg* (New York: Viking Press, 1974).

Baudrillard, Jean, *The System of Objects* (London: Verso, 1996).

Beckett, Jane, ' "De Vonk", Noordwijk: An Example of Early De Stijl Co-operation', *Art History*, 3: 2 (1980), pp. 202–217.

Beckett, Jane, 'Discoursing on Dutch Modernism', *Oxford Art Journal* 6: 2 (1983), pp. 67–79.

Beckett, Jane, 'Colour Theory and Formations of the Dutch Avant-Garde 1900–1926" (Ph.D. dissertation, Courtauld Institute, 1998).

Benevolo, Leonardo, *The European City* (Oxford: Blackwell, 1983).

Berlage, H. P., *Studies over Bouwkunst, Stijl en Samenleving* (Rotterdam: W. L. & J. Brusse, 1910).

Berlage, H. P., *Over Stijl in Bouw- en Meubelkunst* (Rotterdam: W. L. & J. Brusse, fourth edition, 1921).

Bernini, Beatrice and Rijk, Timo de, *Het Nieuwe Wonen in Nederland 1924–1936* (Rotterdam: 010 Publishers, 1990).

Blotkamp, Carel, *Mondrian in Detail* (Utrecht: Reflex, 1987).

Blotkamp, Carel, *Mondrian: The Art of Destruction* (London: Reaktion Books, 1994).

Blotkamp, Carel (ed.), *De Stijl: The Formative Years, 1917–1922* (Cambridge MA and London: MIT, 1986).

Blotkamp, Carel (ed.), *De vervolgjaren van De Stijl 1922–1931* (Amsterdam and Antwerp: L. J. Veen, 1996).

Bock, Manfred (ed.), *Cornelis van Eesteren. Architect Urbanist* (Rotterdam: NAI Publishers, 1993).

Bois, Yve-Alain, *Arthur Lehning en Mondrian: Hun vriendschap en correspondentie* (Amsterdam: Van Gennep, 1984).

Bois, Yve-Alain, *Painting as Model* (Cambridge MA and London: MIT, 1990).

Bremmer, H. P., *Een inleiding tot het zien van Beeldende Kunst* (Amsterdam: Versluys, 1914).

Broos, Kees, *Piet Zwart, 1885–1977* (Amsterdam: Van Gennep, 1982).

Broos, Kees and Hefting, Paul, *Dutch Graphic Design* (Laren: V+K Publishing, 1993).

Brugmans, H., *Nederland in der Oorlogstijd* (Amsterdam: Elseviers, 1920).

Bulhof, Francis (ed.), *Nijhoff, van Ostaijen, "De Stijl": Modernism in the Netherlands and Belgium in the first quarter of the 20th Century* (The Hague: Martinus Nijhoff, 1976).

Bürger, Peter, *Theory of the Avant-Garde* (Minneapolis: University of Minnesota Press, 1984).

Casciato, Maristella, *The Amsterdam School* (Rotterdam: 010 Publishers, 1996).

Cheetham, Mark, *The Rhetoric of Purity: Essentialist Theory and the Advent of Abstract Painting* (Cambridge: Cambridge University Press, 1991).

Colenbrander, Bernard (ed.), *Style: Standard and Signature in Dutch Architecture* (Rotterdam: NAI Publishers, 1993).

Crimp, Douglas, *On the Museum's Ruins* (Cambridge MA and London: MIT, 1993).

Cusveller, Sjoerd, *De Kiefhoek: een woonwijk in Rotterdam* (Laren, V+K Publishing, 1990).

Deventer, Sam van, *Kröller-Müller: De geschiedenis van een cultureel levenswerk* (Arnhem: Roos & Roos, third edition, 1998).

Doesburg, Theo van, *On European Architecture: Complete Essays from Het Bouwbedrijf 1924–1931* (Basle, Berlin, Boston: Birkhäuser Verlag, 1990).

Doesburg, Theo van and Schwitters, Kurt, *Die Scheuche* (Hanover: Aposs Verlag, 1925).

Doig, Allan, *Theo van Doesburg: Painting into Architecture, Theory into Practice* (Cambridge: Cambridge University Press, 1986).

Drucker, Johanna, *The Visible World: Experimental Typography and Modern Art* (Chicago: University of Chicago Press, 1994).

Eliëns, Titus, *Avant-garde Design: Dutch Decorative Arts 1880–1940* (London: Philip Wilson, 1997).

Eliëns, Titus, *H. P. Berlage (1856–1934): ontwerpen voor het interieur* (Zwolle: Waanders Uitgevers, 1998).

Evans, Robin, *Translations from Drawing to Building and Other Essays* (London: Architectural Association, 1997).

Ex, Sjarel and Hoek, Els, *Vilmos Huszár. Schilder en ontwerper* (Utrecht: Reflex, 1985).

Fanelli, Giovanni, *Stijl – Architektuur* (Stuttgart: Deutsche Verlags-Anstalt, 1985).

Freijser, Victor, *De Stijl van Jan Wils: Restauratie van de Papaverhof* (The Hague: Gemeente 's-Gravenhage, 1989).

Friedman, Alice, *Women and the Making of the Modern House* (New York: Abrams, 1998).

Friedman, Mildred (ed.), *De Stijl: 1917–1931: Visions of Utopia* (Oxford: Phaidon, 1982).

Haarlem, Frans Halsmuseum, *Nederland 1913: Een reconstructie van het culturele leven* (1988).

The Hague, Gemeentemuseum, *Kunstenaren der Idee: Symbolistische Tendenzen in Nederland, 1880–1930* (1978).

The Hague, Gemeentemuseum, *Het Nieuwe Bouwen: Neo-plasticism in Architecture: De Stijl* (1985).

Hanson, Julienne, *Decoding Homes and Houses* (Cambridge: Cambridge University Press, 1998).

Heijbroek, J. F., 'Het Rijksmuseum voor Moderne kunst van Willem Steenhof. Werkelijkheid of utopie?', *Bulletin van het Rijkmuseum* 39: 2 (1991), pp. 163–231.

Hilhorst, Cees (ed.), *Vriendschap op afstand. De correspondentie tussen Bart van der Leck en H. P. Bremmer* (Bussum: Thoth, 1999).

Hoek, Els (ed.), *Theo van Doesburg. Oeuvre Catalogus* (Bussum: Uitgeverij Thoth, 2000).

Hoeven, Ernst van der, *J. J. P. Oud en Bruno Taut: Ontwerpen voor een nieuwe stad. Rotterdam – Berlijn* (Rotterdam: NAI Publishers, 1994).

Holst, Richard Roland, *Over kunst en kunstenaars. Beschouwingen en herdenkingen* (Amsterdam: Meulenhoff, 1923).

Holtzmann, Harry and Martin James, Martin (eds), *The New Art – The New Life: The Collected Writings of Piet Mondrian* (London: Thames and Hudson, 1987).

Jaffé, Hans, *De Stijl, 1917–1931: The Dutch Contribution to Modern Art* (London: Alec Tiranti, 1956).

Jaffé, Hans, *De Stijl* (London: Thames and Hudson, 1970).

Jansen, Tony and Rogier, Jan, *Kunstbeleid in Amsterdam 1920–1940* (Nijmegen: SUN Uitgevers, 1983).

Joosten, Joop, 'De sporen van het penseel: Textuur in het werk van Mondriaan', *Jong Holland*, 9: 4 (1993), pp. 44–9.

Joosten, Joop and Robert Welsh, Robert, *Piet Mondrian: Catalogue Raisonné* (New York: Abrams, 1998).

Kooten, Toos van (ed.), *Bart van der Leck* (Otterlo: Kröller-Müller Museum, 1994).

Kossmann, E. H., *The Low Countries* (Oxford: Clarendon Press, 1978).

Kröller-Müller, Hélenè, *Beschouwingen over Problemen in de Ontwikkeling der Moderne Schilderkunst* (The Hague: Volksuniveristeit, 1925).

Küper, Marijke and Zijl, Ida van, *Gerrit Th. Rietveld, 1888–1964: Het volledige werk* (Utrecht: Centraal Museum, 1992).

Langmead, Donald, *J. J. P. Oud and the International Style: A Bio-bibliography* (Westport CN and London: Greenwood Press, 1999).
Langmead, Donald, *The Artists of De Stijl: A Guide to the Literature* (Westport CN and London: Greenwood Press, 2000)
Lijphart, Arend, *The Politics of Accommodation: Pluralism and Democracy in the Netherlands* (Berkeley and Los Angeles: University of California Press, 1968).
Loosjes-Terpstra, A. B., *Moderne Kunst in Nederland 1900–1914* (Utrecht: Veen/Reflex, 1987).

Mallgrave, Harry, *Hendrik Petrus Berlage: Thoughts on Style* (Santa Monica: Getty Center, 1996).
Mannheim, Karl, *Ideology and Utopia. An Introduction to the Sociology of Knowledge* (San Diego, New York and London: Harcourt Brace, 1985).
Meijers, Deborah, 'De democratiseering van schoonheid: Plannen voor museumvernieuwingen in Nederland 1918–1921',' *Nederlands Kunsthistorische Jaarboek* 28 (1977), pp. 55–104.
Mooij, Charles de and Trappeniers, Maureen, *Piet Mondriaan: Een Jaar in Brabant 1904/1905* (Zwolle: Waanders Uitgeverij, 1989).

Overy, Paul, Lenneke Büller, Frank den Oudsten and Bertus Mulder, *The Rietveld Schröder House* (Cambridge MA and London: MIT, 1988).
Overy, Paul *De Stijl* (London: Thames and Hudson, 1991).
Oxenaar, Rudolf, 'Bart van der Leck tot 1920: een primitief van de nieuwe tijd' (Ph.D. dissertation, Rijksuniversiteit Utrecht, 1976).

Polak, Bettina, *Het Fin-de-Siècle in de Nederlandse Schilderkunst: De symbolistische beweging 1890–1900* (The Hague: Martinus Nijhoff, 1955).
Polano, Sergio (ed.), *Hendrik Petrus Berlage: Complete Works* (New York: Rizzoli, 1988).
Postma, Frans, *26, rue du Départ: Mondrian's studio 1921–1936* (Berlin: Ernst and Sohn, 1995).
Purvis, Alston, *Dutch Graphic Design, 1918–1945* (New York: Van Nostrand Reinhold, 1992).

Rebel, Ben, 'De Volkswoningbouw van J. J. P.Oud', *Nederlands Kunsthistorische Jaarboek* 28 (1977), pp. 127–68.
Rossem, Vincent van, *Randstad Holland* (Rotterdam: NAI Publishers, 1994).
Rossem, Vincent van, *C. van Eesteren, The Idea of the Functional City: A Lecture with Slides 1928* (Rotterdam: NAI Publishers, 1997).
Rothschild, Deborah, Ellen Lupton and Darra Goldstein, *Graphic Design in the Mechanical Age: Selections from the Merrill C. Berman Collection* (New Haven and London: Yale University Press, 1998).
Rotterdam, Boymans-van Beuningen Museum, *Het Nieuwe Bouwen in Rotterdam 1920–1960* (1982).

Rowe, Peter G., *Modernity and Housing* (Cambridge MA and London: MIT, 1995).
Rudenstine, Angelica (ed.), *Piet Mondrian 1872–1944* (Milan: Leonardo Arte, 1994).

Schoenmakers, M. H. J., *Beginselen der Beeldende Wiskunde* (Bussum: Dishoek Uitgeverij, 1916).
Schwartz, Frederic, *The Werkbund: Design Theory and Mass Culture before the First World War* (New Haven and London: Yale, 1996).
Semper, Gottfried, *Der Stil in der technische und tektonische Künsten oder Praktische Aesthetik. Erster Band: Textile Kunst* (Frankfurt: Verlag für Kunst und Wissenschaft, 1860).
Singelberg, Pieter, 'Het Haags Gemeentemuseum', *Nederlands Kunsthistorisch Jaarboek* 25 (1974), pp. 1–89.
Spencer, Herbert, *Pioneers of Modern Typography* (London: Lund Humphries, 1969).
Stoelinga, Thomas, *Russische Revolutie en vredesverwachtingen in de Nederlandse pers, maart 1917–maart 1918* (Bussum: Fibula-van Dishoek, 1967).
Straaten, Evert van, *Theo van Doesburg 1883–1931* (The Hague: Staatsuitgeverij, 1983).
Straaten, Evert van, *Theo van Doesburg: Painter and Architect* (The Hague: SDU Publishers, 1988).
Straaten, Evert van, *Theo van Doesburg: Constructeur van het nieuwe leven* (Otterlo: Kröller-Müller Museum, 1994).

Tafuri, Manfredo, *Architecture and Utopia: Design and Capitalist Development* (Cambridge MA and London: MIT, 1976).
Tibbe, Lieske, *R. N. Roland Holst 1868–1938: Arbeid en schoonheid vereend, Opvattingen over Gemeenschapkunst* (Amsterdam: Architectura & Natura, 1994).,
Troy, Nancy, *The De Stijl Environment* (Cambridge MA and London: MIT, 1983).

Vanstiphout, Wouter, Cassandra Wilkins, Michael Speaks and Gerard Hadders, *Mart Stam's Trousers: Stories from Behind the Scenes of Dutch Moral Modernism* (Rotterdam: 010 Publishers, 1999).
Varnedoe, Kirk and Gopnik, Adam, *High & Low: Modern Art and Popular Culture* (New York: Museum of Modern Art, 1990).

Welsh, Robert, Bakker, Boudewijn and Bax, Marty, *Piet Mondriaan: The Amsterdam Years, 1892–1912* (Bussum: Thoth, 1994).
Wigley, Mark, *White Walls, Designer Dresses: The Fashioning of Modern Architecture* (Cambridge MA and London: MIT, 1996).
Wolk, Johannes van der, *De Kröllers en hun architecten* (Otterlo: Rijkmuseum Kröller-Müller, 1992).

Index

Note: page references in *italics* refer to an illustration; 'n.' after a page reference indicates a note number on that page.

EU authorised representative for GPSR:
Easy Access System Europe, Mustamäe tee 50,
10621 Tallinn, Estonia
gpsr.requests@easproject.com

www.ingramcontent.com/pod-product-compliance
Lightning Source LLC
Chambersburg PA
CBHW052141170526
45159CB00017B/3133